Ladies,

Women, &

Wenches

Gender & American Culture

Ladies, Women, & Wenches

Choice & Constraint
in Antebellum
Charleston & Boston

Jane H. Pease &
William H. Pease

The University
of North Carolina Press
Chapel Hill & London

Library of Congress
Cataloging-in-Publication Data
Pease, Jane H.
   Ladies, women, and wenches : choice and constraint
in antebellum Charleston and Boston / Jane H. Pease and
William H. Pease.
      p.   cm.—(Gender & American culture)
   Includes bibliographical references (p.).
   ISBN 0-8078-1924-7 (alk. paper).—
   ISBN 0-8078-4289-3 (pbk. : alk. paper)
   1. Women—United States—Social conditions—Cross-
cultural studies.   2. United States—Social conditions—
To 1865—Case studies.   3. Women—Massachusetts—
Boston—Social conditions.   4. Women—South Carolina—
Charleston—Social conditions.   I. Pease, William Henry,
1924–   .   II. Title.   III. Series.
HQ1419.P43   1990   89-21450
305.42′0973—dc20   CIP

Manufactured in the United States of America
94 93 92 91 90   5 4 3 2 1

In tribute to three women who,

long before and well after we

were born, made choices that

shaped their lives and ours.

Eva Coleman Saunders Annal Edgerly

1888–

Olive Coleman Hanna

1886–1977

Arline Brooks Pease

1888–1973

Contents

Illustrations

Preface

This book embodies three strands of our professional lives: our continuing interest in nineteenth-century American social realities and aspirations; our more recent exploration of sources and methods that extract private experience from public records; and our long-standing curiosity about the imperatives that gender has imposed on both past and present.

In this context we have examined the lives of women living in Charleston and Boston between 1820 and 1850. While this was the gestation period of American feminism, it was more importantly a time when political life and economic activity were so reoriented that fundamental social changes followed—and with them popular demands that they be halted or redirected or extended. Much of this activity was urban. Thus, when we turned our attention specifically to women, we not unnaturally chose two cities that we had already studied and written about in some detail and that exhibited the distinctive regional and racial characteristics in which we were especially interested.

This study, then, reflects historians' largely new dedication to exploring women's past, their somewhat more fleeting resurrection of urban history, and their widely proclaimed but less practiced application of a comparative approach. It is also informed, however, by our more distinctly personal belief that individual choice and personal preference create significant variations within social structures bounded by gender and class, race and region. And, finally, because we have always tried to understand the atypical as well as the typical,

Ladies, Women, and Wenches is one more effort to plumb those two most—and least—American of cities: Boston, the lodestone of our youths; and Charleston, where we now live.

Our general research on Boston and Charleston was aided by grants from the American Philosophical Society, the National Endowment for the Humanities (RS-1454-80), the National Science Foundation (SES-8023796), and the University of Maine Faculty Research Fund. To complete our work on ladies, women, and wenches, we were additionally aided by a grant from the University of Maine's Women in the Curriculum program. Since our recent retirement from teaching, we have been given access to the resources of the University of South Carolina as fellows of the Institute for Southern Studies and to those of the College of Charleston as associates in history.

We are also indebted to the libraries, archives, and historical societies that for almost twenty years have provided us the books, journals, government documents, and manuscripts on which this study is based. These repositories are so numerous and their staffs have been so helpful that to thank them individually and appropriately here is impossible. Nonetheless, it is incumbent on us to acknowledge the interlibrary loan staffs of the Fogler Library of the University of Maine and the Robert Smalls Library of the College of Charleston for their invaluable assistance.

The following institutions have given us generous permission to quote from manuscripts in their collections: the Amelia Gayle Gorgas Library of the University of Alabama; the Arthur and Elizabeth Schlesinger Library of Radcliffe College; the Baker and Houghton libraries of Harvard University; the Trustees of the Boston Public Library; the Historical Society of Pennsylvania; the Library of Congress; the Longfellow National Historic Site of the National Park Service; the Massachusetts Historical Society; the New York Public Library; the South Carolina Historical Society; the South Caroliniana Library of the University of South Carolina; the William R. Perkins Library of Duke University; and the Southern Historical Collection of the University of North Carolina. And for permission to quote from copyrighted material we thank the University of Georgia Press and Little, Brown and

Company. Our illustrations and permission to reproduce them here come from the Arthur and Elizabeth Schlesinger Library of Radcliffe College, the Longfellow National Historic Site of the National Park Service, the Massachusetts Historical Society, and the South Caroliniana Library.

Finally, to many friends, male and female, whose views about women's roles are either more traditional or more radical than ours, we owe a substantial debt. They have forced us to reassess our assumptions in ways that might otherwise have escaped us.

JHP
WHP

Charleston, S.C.
April 1989

Ladies,

Women, &

Wenches

1
Choice and Constraint

Traditionally the history of women has been the history of the daughters, sisters, wives, and mothers of men. Women's history, like woman's place, was in the home. The families and homes that shaped their lives were the creations of men—men who were the heads of households, the sources of income, the wielders of power, and thereby the determinants of the class, status, occupation, and life-style of their women. Within the last twenty years, however, historians have set a new course, exploring women's history as a female experience separate and distinct from that of males. Some have explored how and why society imposed new gender rules on women at particular times and places and how women responded to them; others have examined the special bonds that women created among themselves.[1]

But when women's history has ventured out of the home or beyond the close circle of sisterhood into economic and political realms, it, like the women it chronicles, has entered a public world, one admittedly dominated by men. Not surprisingly, therefore, it has assumed a class structure common to both genders and has applied to women the same divisions that have traditionally separated gentleman from yeoman, bourgeois from proletarian. Thus, whether rooted in class or in gender, women's history has been largely written within a conceptual framework of conflicting dualities.[2]

As a result, this new history, which has clarified much about early- and mid-nineteenth-century womanhood, has also restricted our understanding of its complexity. Except in biographies, the rigidity of its conceptual models has often obscured women's options and the various trade-offs that shaped the contours of their lives. Thus, the polarities of the gender and the class models obscure how the choices that women made, like the economic and social forces that restricted those choices, were affected by their interaction with other factors.

By exploring how, in two notably different urban cultures, American women of the Jacksonian era shaped their lives, we can weigh how region as well as urbanization molded the possibilities and limitations governing all women's lives. In addition, by assessing both the interactions of marriage and work, the influence of each on women's religious, philanthropic, and reform activity, and distinctively female uses of education and property, we can illuminate the considerable variation in women's lives. And, finally, by considering women's choice of life-style—ranging from conformity to defiance of the new social prescriptions for women's behavior—we can better understand the ever more insistent imperative for self-control that an expanding commercial and industrial economy imposed.

Each of these realms may usefully be analyzed on a scale marked at one end by extreme dependence, at the other by full autonomy. It is true that few women could choose from the full spectrum under any circumstances. But few had no choices at all. However bound they were by society's prescriptions defining their role, however limited they were by the class structure of their society, women did select among options as they chose spinsterhood or marriage, domesticity or paid work, charitable activity or the social whirl, the solace of religion or the escape of drink. And the choices women made in any one sphere of their lives either expanded or contracted the choices they made in others as, consciously or unconsciously, they balanced secure dependence against chancier independence, compliance against rebellion, emotional comfort against intellectual fulfillment.

Because nineteenth-century society prescribed marriage as women's proper course, marital status was a major framework within which autonomy and independence were played out. Marrying almost always meant losing present or sacrificing future autonomy, for common law decreed that husband and wife were one, and that one was the husband. Unless a wife was protected by a marriage settlement or trust sheltering the property she had earned or inherited, control of it passed to her spouse. On the other hand, law and social usage both required that the husband support his wife and children. Thus promised a measure of financial security, at least while her husband lived and earned an income, the woman who chose marriage might gain personal satisfaction from rearing children as well as social approval for filling her proper role. Yet to see all women as either wives or spinsters is to settle for an incomplete picture of most women's life course. All were, of course, single for some part of their lives; many who married became single again when death or desertion left them without a spouse. Most women probably moved through the full spectrum from spinster to wife to widow. Some repeated part of the cycle in remarriage. Others never married at all.

Nonetheless, even in the nineteenth century, marital status was but one measure of a woman's relative autonomy or dependence. Interacting with it was a second spectrum, whose poles marked either a woman's actual or potential economic self-sufficiency or her absolute economic reliance on male family members. Yet regardless of their household's standard of living or level of financial well-being, dependent wives, daughters, unmarried sisters, and widowed mothers generally performed some domestic labor within the home in return for the support offered by husbands, fathers, brothers, or sons. On the other hand, those who worked for wages in shops, factories, or the homes of strangers were, while less dependent on male kin, generally less well-off. Those most nearly independent were the few women of whatever marital status who had sufficient education to be professionals, sufficient resources to run their own businesses, or sufficient inheritance to live on its income.

A third spectrum embraced those noneconomic activities outside the home that, at minimum, offered moral support for accepting life as it was and, at maximum, provided opportunities to assume complex responsibilities, to find psychological independence, to enhance self-confidence. For a very few, activity and office holding in voluntary associations gave real power in the public sphere. For many more urban women, philanthropic and reform activity provided a

4 Ladies, Women, and Wenches

choice of roles well beyond that which their predecessors or rural contemporaries enjoyed.

At the same time, however, these urban women were burdened more heavily than either their predecessors or rural contemporaries by an increasingly rigid definition of the behavior appropriate to all women and of the special codes that set off ladies at one end of the social spectrum and wenches at the other. Admittedly, within a republican context, the term lady should have been anachronistic, an outmoded remnant of feudalism. Yet the word continued in use, more often than not either indicating class determined by birth, wealth, or marriage or denominating ladylike decorum even when a woman was poor or very recently risen in position. Lady thus marks one pole of a social spectrum of relative respectability as wench does the other. Americans most frequently used wench to denominate blacks, thus the term appears frequently in Charleston advertisements for fugitive slaves or servants offered for sale. But it also appears sufficiently often in Boston newspapers reporting the arrests of prostitutes to make it a useful label for the opposite pole of female behavior. Together they define a system of relative respectability imposed by a class hierarchy peculiar to females that was associated with but was also a distinctive variation on the class structure usually determined by male family members' social and economic standing.[3]

If, then, it is true that the lives of women were indeed shaped by the men who were their kin, it is equally true that their lives were enormously different from those of men. In the end, it is only by evaluating all the spectra of their lives that we can begin to weave the woof of women's options on the warp of gender roles to create a women's history whose varied design displays both the patterns unique to women and the shadings contributed by the specific time, place, and society in which they lived.

Those women who, in 1820, lived in Boston or Charleston, then America's fourth and fifth largest urban centers, lived in cities buffeted by political and economic change. Once provincial outposts made rich by trade within the protective system of the British empire, then regional centers as the early Republic took shape, and most recently economic hostages to the War of 1812 and the deep depression that followed, each now looked in anguished fascination as New York threatened to engulf their traditional trade and put them on the periphery of an emerging national economy with which neither city was prepared to deal.[4]

Yet deal they did in remarkably similar ways. When the Erie Canal promised to channel all western produce through the New York port, Charleston and Boston pioneered in building railroads to the West and developing new coastal and transatlantic shipping lines. Pressed by mercantile demands for credit, they expanded their banking systems. And confronted with populations grown too unwieldy for traditional governmental systems, they modified the old and created new urban services.

On the other hand, their responses and subsequent patterns of growth also differed markedly. Charleston's first railroads faltered, penetrating only into South Carolina's already-languishing agricultural interior and thus falling far short of their proclaimed goal of reaching the Ohio or the Mississippi rivers. Boston, opting for spoke-like lines radiating from the city, built roads that first flourished as a transportation network among Massachusetts' smaller manufacturing and commercial towns and then stretched into rural New England and across the Hudson. When Andrew Jackson's hostility destroyed the Second Bank of the United States, Charleston created a single new bank whose initial million-dollar capital guaranteed its survival in the subsequent panic and depression, while Massachusetts, in the 1830s, first chartered seventeen new city banks, all with minimal capital, and then saw seven of them fail.

Patterns of urban government differed no less markedly. Replacing traditional town-meeting and selectman government with a mayor and two-house city council in 1821, Boston thereby created the means to reorganize and professionalize the city's penal and welfare systems as well as its public health and safety departments and to expand its free public school system. Charleston, when it attempted to centralize power and responsibility for its governance fifteen years later, achieved only the most limited results. Although a salaried mayor replaced an unpaid intendant, no changes were made in the city's legislative body, and a fundamental reorganization of the fire department was completely thwarted in a way to curtail similar efforts in other spheres. Finally, the city's sole action to extend public—though not free—education was to charter the nation's first municipal college and establish a high school primarily to prepare students for that college.

To look at the lives that women lived in each city is, therefore, both to look for similarities shaped by a common urbanity and to observe the differences created by the particular social and economic milieu in which they lived. These urban women were excluded, as were virtually all American women, from the political process—whether reorganizing city government, pressing Congress for the passage or repeal of protective tariffs, opposing or promoting a national banking system. They were minimally, if at all, visible in corporate efforts to charter steamboat lines, railroads, or banks.

Yet women were directly affected by all ventures that either promoted or subverted their city's prosperity. In the thirty years from 1820 to 1850, Boston's population grew from 43,000 to 136,000. Charleston's remained virtually static, ranging between 25,000 and 30,000. Pursued beyond mere numbers, this meant that far more Boston women experienced life as rural in-migrants or European immigrants than did Charlestonians, that employment opportunities for the poor like investment opportunities for the propertied were shaped by different demographies. And in Charleston, slavery was a distinctive determinant in all lives. The more than half who were slaves were altogether excluded from the republican ideology that white Americans enjoyed regardless of gender. And for the others, slavery's meaning ranged from the leisure associated with readily available domestic servants to greater managerial roles in handling their property. But no matter what its individual implications, the presence of slaves both preserved an older republicanism and restricted democratization, when, from 1835 at least, Charleston, fearing an abolitionism spawned in Boston, not only forbade direct challenges to slavery but resisted any change that might erode white solidarity.

Thus Charleston women experienced few of the reform enthusiasms that ran through Boston. While, like other urban women, they organized religious and charitable associations, they did not move as far into the public political sphere as did those female Yankees who sought to alter the basic structure of their society. And their city's reluctance to embrace any social engineering also limited the options that expanded the free public secondary as well as the primary schooling offered their Boston sisters. Moreover, the resultingly different levels of literacy significantly affected the informational and cultural resources available to the women of each city.

Finally, the fact that half of Charleston's inhabitants were set apart by their race as well as their slave status from the behavioral expectations imposed on white women promoted a toleration of lifestyles that in Boston commonly resulted in public condemnation and institutional punishment. Conversely Boston's laws and public institutions proved repressive not only for its small black minority but for its white majority, which, by 1850, was almost evenly divided between native-born women on the one hand and immigrants on the other.[5]

Nonetheless, when mid-nineteenth-century Americans defined proper female behavior, they enunciated a single formula for true womanhood in the belief that the ideal woman so differed from the ideal man that all women had more in common by virtue of their sex than did all residents of a single city, all communicants of one church, all members of a particular class. These polar absolutes of gender, widely portrayed in learned sermons and popular ditties, were wonderfully spelled out in a much-copied piece probably first published in the *North American Review*. Read in both Boston and Charleston, it announced that "Man is great in action—Woman in suffering. Man shines abroad—Woman at home. Man talks to convince—Woman to persuade and please. Man has a rugged heart—Woman a soft and tender one. Man prevents misery—Woman relieves it. Man has science—Woman taste. Man has judgement—Woman sensibility. Man is a being of justice—Woman an angel of mercy."[6] Passive, domestic, emotional, nurturing, Everywoman was set on a course that would complement—but never challenge—Everyman. Veiled in physical weakness, her moral strength influenced adult male kin as her teaching gave her children their lofty values. But should she ever leave her pedestal for an intellectual, active, or public life, she would ruin her health, damage her family's well-being, and tarnish the image of womanhood.

So it was that women in both cities shaped their lives within guidelines for proper behavior that supposedly transcended regional differences yet permitted in one city what was forbidden in the other. Race and class, for instance, were determinants in both cities, but slavery in Charleston and its absence in Boston gave those factors markedly different meanings that, on the one hand, extended the options available to southern white women while it clearly straitened those of slaves even more than it did those of free blacks in either city. Nonetheless, in both, most Afro-American women like most working-class white women might echo Sojourner Truth's "Ar'n't I a woman too?" as their only proper response to the *North American Review*'s female stereotype.

And if they had to temper their styles to externally ordained socioeconomic realities as well as to cultural prescriptions, so too did women have to deal with the constraints that their own prior choices, like unanticipated changes in their immediate families, imposed on their lives. The either-or choices of marriage or spinsterhood, like the necessity for doing paid work when a father failed in business or a husband died or deserted, inevitably shaped the time a woman could give to religious observance or philanthropic activity. Likewise the girl who stayed in school as long as she could might not only increase her occupational options but also enhance her marriage options in ways that wealth or beauty might do for others. And the simple passage of time within a woman's life cycle necessarily altered her family obligations and thus her freedom to take on other roles as nursing infants became toddlers, toddlers went to school, and finally grown children left home altogether.

But in making the choices that were visibly available to them at any one time, women also made trade-offs that had long-range implications. Quite unaware of how their immediate choices would affect them later on, they nonetheless initiated trains of events over which they frequently had no control. In short, even choice and constraint were not inherently polar opposites but instead marked the extremes of yet another spectrum. Therefore, to assess how much either factor shaped the lives of antebellum urban women we must ask a series of interrelated questions. What could they, either individually or in groups, achieve given the social, economic, political, and ideological realities within which they lived their lives? How, in fact, did they navigate among those limitations and potentials to create—or just take advantage of—the alternatives available to them? And, finally, how did constraints and choices governing one sphere of their lives shape the rest?

2

Spinsters,
Wives, and
Widows

The cult of domesticity, like republican motherhood, presupposed marriage and family as the focus of female existence. Accordingly its proponents assumed that virtually all women were wives and mothers. Yet this perspective overlooked two factors. The first is that every woman's life involved a childhood and girlhood before she married and that even her roles as wife and mother changed during her adult years of marriage. The second is that sizable numbers of adult women were at any one moment neither wives nor mothers.

To understand, therefore, what living in mid-nineteenth-century Boston or Charleston meant to women of all sorts, we must look at the entire female population of each city. Here we are especially fortunate because in 1845 Boston's city council commissioned statistician Lemuel Shattuck to compile an extensive city census. Three years later, when the Charleston city council undertook a similar census, it was consciously modeled on the Boston pattern. Thus we have unusually full and reasonably comparable data for a demographic examination of the spinsters, wives, and widows of both cities.

As we might expect, most women in Boston and Charleston were married. But Shattuck's statistical snapshot of all female Bostonians over twenty reveals that "most" was barely more than half, that over a third of all women in the city were single, and that 11 percent were widows. Even of those in their early thirties—the age when they were most likely to be married—a quarter were still single. And by the time women were in their late forties, 20 percent of them were already widows. Half of all women over sixty were widows. Thus if we combine widows and spinsters, almost 70 percent of Boston's elderly women lived without husbands. Consequently a history of women that concerns itself primarily with wives not only overlooks the third of all Boston women who had never been married but also blurs significant differences inherent in the adult life cycle—ignoring half of all women in their twenties and more than half of those over fifty-five.[1]

Patterns of marital status in Charleston were, on the whole, similar to those of Boston—provided one recognizes that official statistics about that status omit the black population altogether. In 1848 exactly half of all adult white female Charlestonians were married, almost a third were single, and a fifth were widowed. The principal difference, therefore, between the two cities was the greater proportion of widows in Charleston. But that reflects a second difference. Charleston women married earlier than their Boston counterparts. They were, in fact, half again as likely as Bostonians to be married by the time they were twenty-five. Therefore, because Charleston men married later than their Yankee brothers—and were thus even more likely to die before their wives did—Charleston women even in their early thirties were 20 percent more likely to be widows than were their Boston sisters. And those additional years that separated husband and wife while both lived doubtless reinforced the image of husband as patriarch, which, in turn, cast the wife in a relatively childlike role with obvious implications for marital politics.[2]

If the differences created by regional variations in age at marriage that generated so large a pool of white widows were consequential, the gender imbalance that shaped marriage patterns among Charleston's black population was even more significant. Because the law neither recognized nor recorded slave marriages and because even church discipline devalued slaves' wedding vows, we can only guess at black marriage rates. Nonetheless it is clear that the likelihood of marriage between blacks was severely limited by demographic realities. In every age group over five years of age there were more females than males. And the older the age group, the greater the imbalance, as more male slaves than female either were drafted out of the city for plantation labor or succumbed to a greater risk of youthful death. By the time they were in their thirties, there were five slave women for every four men. By the time they were in their forties, there were six women for every four men. And among free people of color the gender gap was even more pronounced. In every age group from the twenties to the fifties, females outnumbered males nearly two to one. It is, therefore, logical to surmise that even if black women, unlike white, married men their own age or younger, they were still decidedly less likely than white women to live in households with husbands. Not surprisingly, fewer than half of all the households in Charleston in 1830 that were headed by free blacks contained both a free adult male and a free adult female—whether married to each other or not.[3]

Furthermore, the cult of domesticity was neither expected to nor did it in reality shape the lives of those black women who did marry. No slave husband could hope to provide his wife and children with economic security; no slave wife could expect to devote herself exclusively to the care of her own children in her own home. Unlike free white women, slave women who married did not, even theoretically, trade economic autonomy for the security of dependence. And free women of color who married free men of color could seldom anticipate that their husbands would support them in life or bequeath sufficient property to sustain them as widows.

While such restrictions on a husband's power might promise greater equality between spouses, it also created other sharp variations between white and black family structures; for just as race and servile condition surely diminished the economic rewards of wifehood for black women, it also had a complex effect on their motherhood. Since the lot of slave children derived from their mother's—not their father's—status, it was in the slaveowner's economic interest that slave mothers bear offspring. Nonetheless, slavery appears to have had a negative effect on childbearing—or at least on the number of children a slave mother was likely to rear. If, for example, we measure fertility by the ratio of the number of children under five to the number of women of childbearing age, we find that, more than race or region, status influenced childbearing. In Charleston for every hundred free women, black or white, between the ages of twenty and forty, there were sixty-nine children under five; but among the slave population there were only fifty-five such children for every hundred fertile women. In Boston, on the other hand, there were sixty children under five for every hundred fertile women. That proportion, ironically, is closer to Charleston's slave than to its free ratio, but it is closest of all to the number of children for all Charleston women regardless of status or race—sixty-three.[4]

It seems reasonable to infer that these figures reflect the influence of class distinctions on the nature of motherhood; that poverty in Boston, like slave status in Charleston, reduced the number of children a mother would rear. In that case mortality rates for slave and poor infants may be more significant than differential fertility. We cannot, to be sure, group Boston mothers by economic and social standing to parallel Charleston's count by race and slave status, nevertheless we can make comparisons by looking at child death rates. In the enlightened capital of Massachusetts in the early decades of the nineteenth century, half of all infants born alive died before they were five. And, though the loss of at least one child was a haunting fear for all married women and a grim reality for most, that reality pressed hardest on Boston's Catholic families—largely Irish immigrants—whose children were least likely to survive. The infant mortality rate was somewhat lower in smaller and less crowded Charleston, but it hardly consoled white mothers, who, on average, lost one of every four children born to them, or black mothers, who lost two of every five.[5]

Charlestonians' fear of the endemic and epidemic diseases that regularly ravaged their city during its semitropical summers may well have created a contrary perception. No woman in either city, however, knew the unrecorded fertility rates and few were cognizant of their city's mortality statistics, which reported that from 33 to 47 percent of all deaths were of children under five,[6] yet their own observations doubtless warned most of them that death struck among the very young more than among any other age group. And girls charting their futures saw that the women in their own families and social circles who married were likely to lose at least one child, would probably care for children until they were well over fifty, and would spend their old age as widows. Small wonder, then, that many feared pregnancy, delayed marriage into their late twenties, or remained single. These were logical responses even for women who valued family, who had been reared to be the mothers of the Republic, and who lived their adult lives when the cult of true womanhood was inseparable from the cult of domesticity.

Individual women's lives, however, are not summaries of statistical data in which only faceless averages appear. One by one, girls grew up, got married—or did not—and then went through the rest of their lives maintaining or trying to change the roles that their own choices as well as external circumstances had imposed on them. Their diaries and letters, their published memoirs and stories, and the public records of their experience provide the threads that, woven together, tell what it was like to live as women in Charleston or Boston in the early to mid-nineteenth century.

Unfortunately, slaves and the daughters of other humble families left few personal records of their teens and early twenties, years that, for both groups, were more defined by the work they did than the social rounds that, for more privileged young women, preceded marriage. Employed primarily as domestic workers in the homes of others or laboring as miserably paid seamstresses, they had little time for intricate patterns of courtship, lacked funds for long vacations and elaborate recreation, and, in the case of Charleston's slaves, experienced only a short interval between their own childhood and motherhood.

Yet court they did. Employers regularly lamented the men who visited their kitchens and occasionally stayed long hours into the night. Urban churches were almost as conducive to socializing as were country ones—so much so that a sizable portion of Charleston's Bethel Methodist white congregation formed a new institution to avoid the joviality and confusion that black parishioners created as they seized the hours before and after services for social interchange. For others, family and neighborhood circles provided the milieu in which the young of both sexes mingled freely. And moralistic warnings against their dangers assure us that young women—singly and in groups—did attend the public amusements and outdoor festivities where men looking for a good time might also find a wife.[7]

Equally determined by class and but minimally differentiated by city was the world of privileged young women. Daughters of prosperous parents, they enjoyed an extended girlhood, often remaining in school until their mid- to late teens, then embarking on a round of visits, parties, and outings that allowed them a freedom that many were reluctant to surrender for early marriage. After a childhood in which dancing school, games, and afternoon or evening parties supplemented school and family life came evening parties, dances, and formal visiting at the homes of family friends. For belles, balls furnished the most exciting times.[8] Generally in private homes but occasionally at public halls, they practiced the graces and displayed the attitudes they had learned to attract suitable unmarried men. They strove to be physically attractive but not overtly sexual. Clad in dresses formfitting above the waist but ample below,[9] they chatted, danced, and flirted "well enough" to intrigue but not overwhelm potential beaux. Some followed rules set by old-fashioned mothers who permitted their "pretty looking" daughters only the chaste cotillion or quadrille; others were allowed to waltz—so long as they did not "permit the cavalier to approach nearer than a certain distance." And some, poor souls, danced not at all. As Charles Francis Adams, age twenty-one, wrote his mother, these "fine ones" left to sit "in a corner" were also "generally the ugly ones."[10] But young men flocked around the belles—or even those "young married ladies" for whom Frank Lee confessed a "failing." And Anna Dwight was no more than typical when she reminded Henry Lee of the forty parties he had attended in Boston one spring and then went on to report Mary Lyman's engagement to Amory Appleton and Susan Dana's marriage to William Lawrence.[11]

Form-fitting above the waist, but ample below, these styles were recommended by Godey's Lady's Book *in July 1841. (Courtesy of the Massachusetts Historical Society)*

There were other amusements as well. In Charleston privileged youth went in winter to the races and the theater and in summer to nearby Sullivan's Island, where "young ladies and gentlemen" spent long days and dallied "on the beach at sunset." Upper-class Boston girls reveled during the summer at nearby Nahant, only a two-hour sail from home, or made expeditions to more distant Berkshire towns, often with the same friends with whom they attended winter concerts and cotillions. Even for the daughters of more middling families, charades, amateur theatricals, and dances were commonplace. And for all the girls who wrote about it, horseback riding was the most invigorating of sports—far better than archery or swimming.[12]

It was away from such pastimes, in which schoolmates, sisters, and sometimes intensely loved female friends participated, that suitors wooed and parents pressed young women toward marriage—wifehood and motherhood. But for some girls at least the present was more appealing than the future. Possibly influenced by a recently published short story, a group of Carolina schoolmates planned a five-year reunion from which those who had married would not only be barred, but be compelled to submit written descriptions of what their lives had become "as wives or widows" and to lay bare "the secrets of [their] prison-house[s]." Perhaps it was the prevalence of such attitudes that inspired a Charleston newspaper to proclaim that when a woman married, "she should give up her heart, feelings, fancies and opinions to her husband, and never allow a sister's influence to be superior to his."[13]

Indeed, the pressures to marry—and marry early—were as much economic and social as familial and personal. In Boston, where settled sobriety was believed essential to business success, the pressure was largely on men. Favorable R. G. Dun credit ratings depended in part on whether or not a man was married and had children—or whether his wife had brought him money and a family connection of good repute. Young tradesmen were advised not just to be prompt, hard-working, and shrewd, but to marry prudent wives and spend their evenings at home. A bachelor mechanic over thirty was allegedly as rare in Boston "as a phenix among birds." Even wealthy merchants urged their sons to court and marry early. Nothing would benefit Amos Lawrence's oldest son more, so his father observed, than to latch on to "an interesting and sensible woman" and "get well soused in love."[14]

Such pressures on men in a city whose population was some-what—but only somewhat—more female than male created indirect pressures on women as well. Nonetheless, Boston women married, on average, somewhat later than their white equivalents in Charleston, where the gender balance among whites was the reverse of Boston's.[15] The difference between the two cities in this case defies statistical explanation. It may have been that Boston women enjoyed the greater autonomy that a period of employment or urban diversions offered them. It may also have been that Charleston women were under more direct pressure to marry. Sarah Grimké, recalling her youth in the southern city's fashionable world, lamented that girls were "taught to regard marriage as the one thing needful, the only avenue to distinction." Certainly there was no southern equivalent of those northern advice manuals that commended spinsterhood as superior to a bad marriage. In any case, Boston's statistics tell us that many of its young women delayed marriage, agreeing perhaps with Georgina Amory that "tho two years were a long courtship, it was not too long to be courted." And there were doubtless others who, like Miss Amory, married earlier than they wished after engagement had cast the die, leaving them "nothing but death to separate" them from their betrothed, and who therefore struggled to "look upon the bright side of the question."[16]

In any case, courtship was a critical as well as a pleasurable period by virtue of the choices it offered. Yet the prerogative in courting almost always lay with the male, however much mothers, aunts, sisters, and friends might try to manipulate the outcome. "I believe," the popular author Lydia Maria Child wrote, that "men more frequently marry for love, than women; because they have a freer choice." Very rare was that "*very fine* woman" who used a male intermediary to propose marriage to Harrison Gray Otis, a widower over seventy. Indeed, Otis's indignation at the "decent looking pimp," his temptation "to damn the fellow & show him out," only demonstrated how rare it was for a female to court a male.[17]

More typical was the procedure of young planter Frederick Porcher, who spent a year in Charleston courting the well-chaperoned Emma Gough at her mother's home, where they were married the next year. Conversely, there was the unsuccessful suit of William Middleton, indignant that the young Elliott girl rejected a man considerably her senior for his "coldness & formality of manner." But why not? He had never once inquired about her when she was out of town. And surely neither she nor her mother put much stock in his excuse that he did not do so because he "always felt for the gentler sex a species of respect almost amounting to awe" that had kept him mute.[18]

As indicative of courtship's pangs and Charleston parents' supervisory role in a daughter's romantic life were the tribulations of Anna Hayes Johnson. Enamoured of a North Carolina congressman twice her age to whom she had become secretly engaged on a visit to Washington, she returned to Charleston and heard nothing more

from him. For several months, until he finally renewed his suit, young
Anna suffered anger, disappointment, and depression as well as guilt
that she had pledged not to confide in her father, a Supreme Court
justice.[19]

In neither Johnson's nor Elliott's case, however, was age difference the factor it would have been in Boston. Charlotte Everett could
scarcely restrain her indignation when pretty, young Euphemia Fenno
married Frederic Tudor, "a horribly old & ugly man—not worth the
having with all his money." And the twenty-two-year gap between
Congressman Nathan Appleton and his second wife prompted crusty
old Harrison Gray Otis to comment that while she was "a very nice
woman if he must marry . . . I should think he had better burn, as the
flame could not be all-consuming." Notably more unthinkable were
even small discrepancies in the other direction. A woman's being little
more than three years older than a would-be suitor could quite dis-
courage him, threatening, perhaps, his own male power base.[20]

Once courtship had proceeded to engagement, however, scandal
lay in a failure to proceed to marriage. At one end of the social scale,
Meredith Sullivan was roundly condemned by Boston elite for break-
ing his engagement to a western girl who had spent the winter with
his family and then faced disgrace "without a relation, & scarcely a
friend, hundreds of miles from her home." At the other end, great
public "excitement" was generated by a jury's decision to award only a
financial settlement to the pregnant Rebecca Davis, who had sued
Samuel James for breach of promise. More tragically, when Samuel
Bradlee refused his daughter permission to marry her fiancé, a former
employee who had failed at business, the young couple hanged themselves in her father's store.[21]

The circumstances of Mary Bradlee's suicide remind us that
factors other than emotional attractions determined the choice of
spouse. Because a married woman was legally and financially dependent on her husband, fond parents necessarily considered a suitor's
ability to support their daughter and her potential offspring. Whether
he was the fortune-seeking roué who eloped with young Hannah
Heyward after having gone through two other fortunes or the hard-

working mariner whose maximum income of $500 could not support the daughter of Episcopal bishop Nathaniel Bowen in suitable style, Charleston families and friends equally expressed their concern.[22] Sometimes more than money was at stake. Differing value systems and unknown social affiliations seemed to threaten girls who married outside homogeneous and familiar groups. Harriott Kinloch Middleton, herself the mother of two teen-age daughters, lamented that the daughter of another staunchly unionist Charleston family planned to marry a man not only too young and too poor but from a family with markedly different political opinions. And when "old Boston" Elizabeth Lyman became engaged to a Henshaw who not only was "without a sous and in no business" but the offspring of an upstart Democratic family, Lyman friends lined up with Elizabeth's "father and mother and all of her kin" in opposing the match.[23] Choosing a man whose values and whose past were known, like choosing a man known to be prudent and able to support a wife, was thus critical in gaining parental consent to a decision that would irrevocably shape a daughter's future.

Whether by positive choice to remain single or failure to find a suitable mate, many women did not marry. Ann Reid, one of the latter, at first lamented her fate—always the bridesmaid, never the bride. But by the time she was thirty, her own experience and perhaps that of her married friends gradually convinced her to bless her good fortune. She was free from household duties and could dedicate herself to religion. Anna Lesesne, for her part, found solace in more secular amusements—visiting, playing the piano, and reading. Without the financial resources of either of these Charleston women, Lydia Maria Child, who married only after being convinced she never would, argued both before and after her marriage that "a woman of well-regulated feelings and an active mind, [might] be very happy in single life"—"far happier," she added, "than she could be made by a marriage of expediency." Cultivating inner resources, pursuing a sound education, and finding things to "occupy their thoughts" all equipped single women with "abundant resources for employment and amusement." And Mary McGee, apparently possessed of such resources and, like many who did marry, intimidated by impending marriage, broke her engagement to wealthy Jonathan Phillips only three days before their scheduled wedding because she feared the social burdens that so fortunate a match would thrust upon her. Having made their choices, spinsters arranged their lives accordingly. Some lived alone. Others had the company of workmates or fellow inmates in boardinghouses. But probably more of them lived with family members, as did Ann Reid, who lived with her mother, and Sophia Child, who both managed her father's Boston house and minded her brother's children.[24]

Those who, instead, made the choice to marry embarked on a new existence, however familiar the wifely tasks and position that they had observed in their mothers. Being the wife and becoming the mother was certainly quite different from observing household affairs as a daughter. For some, a honeymoon of travel delayed the full transition, although few enjoyed anything like Edward and Eliza Brooks's two years in Europe or even the series of day trips that Hannah Burgess and her sea captain husband made from Boston to nearby Medford and Cape Cod.[25] Some young couples, given houses and furniture by fond parents, entered at once on housekeeping, but many others boarded in their first year or two of marriage. And only the most fortunate were those like Susan Boott and her new husband, Francis Jackson, who roughed it in a stylish little house in Pemberton Square, where they invited friends to four-course potluck suppers served on silver and washed down with claret, Madeira, and ale—the latter very new and very daring.[26]

Whatever her circumstances, it was generally sooner than later that the bride settled in to being the wife. But in an era that expected even demanded—wifely submission, a bride faced the sharp transition from being the courted center of attraction to reshaping her life to the expectations of her spouse. Caroline Gilman, the Massachusetts-born wife of Charleston's Unitarian minister, explored the experience in the novels she wrote about the two cities. Her New England housekeeper and the southern matron both resented their new husbands' preoccupation with business and public affairs once the honeymoon was over. The one in a new house fully furnished as a wedding gift, the other in a ramshackle farmhouse filled with "whatever was too old or dilapidated for the city," each experienced anger and depression at a newfound loneliness amid the trials and boredom of housekeeping. Finally both learned that only submission could make their marriages work. Exhorting the "young and lovely bride" to "watch well the first moments when your will conflicts with his to whom God and society have given the control," Gilman urged her to "reverence his *wishes* even when you do not his *opinions*." The key element of happiness, she admonished, was "self-control almost to hypocrisy." The "good wife" must smile through adversity and illness "or else languish alone," whereas the husband was entitled to his wife's "ear and heart" as he poured out his trials and to "her soft hand" when he was sick.[27] Other writers, male and female, gave the same advice. Charleston-born Susan Petigru King warned prospective brides that the first months of marriage were the ones in which they must "be guarded" and dwell on their own faults rather than those of their husbands. To "bear and forbear" was their role. Dr. William Alcott, whose advice in *The Young Wife* sold widely both North and South, laid it down as the first rule: "Do everything for your husband which your strength and a due regard to your health will admit."[28]

No less a subjection to new demands was the transition to motherhood. Generally women had even less choice in timing their pregnancies than they did in setting their wedding dates. Although the first child was almost invariably welcome, bringing with it maternal fulfillment and sometimes renewing the attention a new father gave his wife, subsequent childbearing was more likely to be viewed equivocally. While a woman who yearned for a child was "not as she wishes to be," a mother of many, "oh, strange perversity of fate," was "as she does not wish to be."[29] Moreover, public statistics like private confessions make it clear that many women preferred to limit or at least to space childbearing. We know that fertility rates declined in the early nineteenth century faster in urban than in rural areas and more in wealthy towns than in poor ones—a development that suggests, at least, that prosperous urban women who could would deliberately limit the number of their children.[30]

*Caroline Howard Gilman adjusted her career as author and editor to her do-
mestic roles as wife of Charleston's Unitarian minister and mother of seven
children, three of whom died in infancy. (Courtesy of the South Caroliniana
Library)*

Obviously many factors shaped women's responses to mother-hood. Slave women apparently became mothers at an earlier age than did free white women. If records of slave women sold with their children in Charleston are any indication, over half had borne their first child by age twenty and more than two-fifths had produced offspring between the ages of seventeen and nineteen. Yet we know also that in Charleston the proportion of slave children under five to all slave women of childbearing age was less than for any other group—an observation that may suggest not only high infant mortality but deliberate curtailment of childbearing in a slave woman's mature years.[31]

Whether a similar phenomenon occurred among Boston's poorest women is an open question. Surely many regularly became mothers or suffered miscarriages until they could no longer conceive. Boston reformer Henry C. Wright was appalled by the Broad Street tenements he visited, "all full of children" crowded together in dirty, smoky rooms. A single old house facing an inner court was alleged to contain between 100 and 120 persons, the members of some twenty prolific Irish families.[32] It is, however, principally from the letters and diaries of the elite that we learn the anxiety with which individual women faced extended years of bearing and rearing children. Caroline Gilman, who reported herself "happy, & thoughtful, & fearful, & hopeful" before the birth of her first child, faced confinement some seven years and three pregnancies later with the "chastened feeling which tells me this *may* be the time to prepare & be ready for God[']s providence." Mary Crowninshield Mifflin exemplified the many Massachusetts women whose diaries carefully chronicled menses—and, when missed, the miscarriages and childbirths that followed. And Charlestonian Caroline Laurens's diary recorded an eighteen-month period in which she bore two children and had one miscarriage.[33]

Not least of women's anxieties were the danger and pain of childbirth when pregnancy-related causes accounted for more than 5 percent of all adult female deaths in both cities.[34] Doctors were shocked by "the frightful effects which have been produced upon the fairer portion of our race from ignorance and maltreatment." Yet, while they attributed much of the problem to births unattended by physicians, Boston's medical association continued to set the fees for delivering a child higher than for any other service except for major amputations and operations. In fact the doctor might be clearly unsympathetic. A professor of obstetrics in Charleston's medical school defined his speciality as mitigating the pangs inflicted on women in punishment for Eve's transgression.[35]

In any event, with or without the services of a trained male physician expert in using forceps in difficult births, delivery generally occurred at home and in the company of other women. Boston's Lying-In Hospital, founded in 1832, accommodated no more than twenty-five patients annually in its early years. Charleston had no such facility—its almshouse hospital the only refuge for poor women lacking a home appropriate to giving birth. When lawyer's wife Sarah Dana bore her first child her mother, a nurse, a physician, and, most unusually, her husband attended her in her Boston bedroom. Mary Child, wife of a rising young clerk, was aided by a doctor and nurse but substituted an older family friend for her mother. But a doctor's or a trained midwife's attendance was not universal, even among the privileged. In South Carolina, Meta Grimball, wife of a wealthy planter, recorded "12 confinements," only four of them involving a white midwife and none a physician.[36] In the other eight we must assume she was served only by friends and servants.

Life changed less with pregnancy, however, than with the children who followed. Until the last weeks before their deliveries, most women were not only active as usual in their homes but, wearing loose gowns, pursued their customary routines, going out in public for errands and visiting—even attending parties. After childbirth those who could afford a nurse or had kinswomen available to help most likely restricted their activities for a month, the first week or two keeping to their rooms and then to the house, then finally going out for their first ride or walk, resuming church attendance, and taking up again all their regular household as well as their new maternal responsibilities. For much of this interval the infant might go unnamed, referred to simply as "the baby" until it had survived its first weeks or even its first months. Women who could breast-feed their infants for a year or more, both for the child's health and because common belief maintained, however erroneously, that a nursing woman could not conceive. While even their diaries do not discuss their sexual lives, we have enough hints beyond declining birth rates to know that women used their limited knowledge to control their fertility. The letters of southern women who could afford them chronicle expeditions from home and husband intended primarily to avoid or postpone yet another pregnancy.[37]

Few women, however, could or would arrange prolonged absences from the marriage bed and so sought alternatives. Abstinence and coitus interruptus—both depending as much on husbands as on wives—are generally believed to have been the major means of birth control practiced by nineteenth-century Americans. But women clearly sought as much information as they could obtain about their own physiology and the reproductive processes to exert additional control over their lives. They flocked to health reformer Sylvester Graham's lectures for "ladies only," designed to be of "great benefit to all females, who feel their responsibility as mothers, be their station in life what it may." But no sooner had his Boston series begun than a crowd of angry men gathered outside Amory Hall to protest their "grossly indecent character." Successful in frightening Graham away, they also shouted down the women who attempted to speak, making "discordant imitations of animals . . . barking, mewing, howlings, yellings, crowing, hissing and groaning."[38] Nor was the mob alone in expressing male indignation. Dr. John Bartlett, an obstetrician, publicly condemned Graham for defiling the purity of better Boston with his scabrous, ribald, revolting, and obscene "*secret lectures* to Married Females." Graham's language was alleged to be such as no doctor would use to a midwife in "the sanctity of the sick chamber." In response, some ninety-three married and twenty-six single women of respectable station and family, equally indignant that they could not get the information they sought from their physicians, dared come to Graham's defense in a public letter to the press.[39] Here was an openness about female sexuality, though less blunt than that of the late twentieth century, that would have startled these women's late-Victorian grandchildren.

It is only fair to note that when similar lectures were delivered in Boston by a woman, there were no riots. But in the same year that Mrs. Mary Gove gave her lectures in physiology, a Boston court sent freethinker Abner Kneeland to prison for the alleged blasphemy of "recommending to pregnant women under certain circumstances to procure abortion & instructing them in the means." Nevertheless, procuring an abortion was not a crime in South Carolina and was illegal in Massachusetts only after the fetus had "stirred." Taboos notwithstanding, newspapers in both places carried advertisements for abortifacients, pills to cure "blocked menses," which were quite specifically not recommended for married ladies.[40]

Even though the ideal of republican motherhood imposed on American women a burden of political obligation—making them responsible for rearing the civic-minded citizens on whom the survival of the new nation depended—the records of domesticity show less preoccupation with patriotism than with nurture, education, and discipline. Mothers early devised amusements and instruction for the very young—toy boats to sail in tiny ponds or tops whose sides were marked with letters to lure a toddler toward literacy. When children were sick, mother was their chief nurse. In wealthy southern households, however, a talented slave nurse was often a permanent resident whose exclusive ministrations to one child ceased only when another was born. Thus in Charleston it was primarily humbler families who shared the nearly universal Boston pattern in which aunts and grandmothers commonly supplemented the constant attention demanded of mothers, while fathers too took young children on walks or pulled them about in small wagons.[41]

Harmonious domesticity was celebrated in family portraits and public discourse. Advice on child-rearing abounded. Still in all, there was little consensus about just how children should best be disciplined; and, in Boston at least, the merits of physical punishment were actively disputed. Writing in the same spirit soon to raise civic debate over schoolmasters who chastened pupils with ruler and switch, Lydia Maria Child—once a teacher but never a mother— advocated self-control as the key element of proper discipline. A mother should govern her children with calm and quieting words, diverting mischievous ones from destructive to constructive activity without recourse either to whipping or to scolding. Admittedly, answering all their children's questions and giving them undivided attention was, like "all good things," demanding of "a great many sacrifices, and a great deal of self-denial." But some Boston mothers tried to hew the line—though whether they were following Child's advice or simply the family practice they had themselves experienced as children is uncertain. In any case, the results were not always those anticipated. Mary Lee, wife of a prominent but not very successful merchant, had started raising the five children she had borne in a twelve-year period with greater regard for their "*inclinations*" than her "*will.*" But as the oldest boy grew up to misbehave at Harvard and the oldest daughter did nothing but party, Mary Lee resolved "to establish a more fixed discipline toward the younger children" and entreated the older ones to help at least by not questioning "*aloud* the wisdom of my decisions." And while Maria Chapman, wife of another Boston merchant, never changed her belief that all physical force was immoral and that any assertion of a parent's will over a child's was both brutal and shameful, her unmarried schoolteacher sisters, who often shared the care of the Chapman children, found them variously "worthless," aggressive, and of "evil spirit."[42]

Writing from a different perspective, Caroline Gilman defended the "virtue" of a "rational, well-managed rod" and found it an acceptable means to a "well-regulated" family. More sensitive than Child to the differing demands that class imposed on a mother's time, she argued that total abstention from physical punishment, even when it did work, was the prerogative of the comfortably well-off. A laundress or a seamstress coping constantly with the insistent demands of paid work to support her children had no time for shaming mechanisms, verbal diversions, or keeping the careful watch needed to insure that a child punished by being put on a bench or in a dark closet actually

This romantic picture of Lydia Maria Francis Child, from Seth Beach's
Daughters of the Puritans *(1907), portrays her at the beginning of her long
career as teacher, novelist, essayist, and editor of both a children's magazine
and an antislavery newspaper. (Courtesy of the Massachusetts Historical
Society)*

stayed there. Indeed, Gilman, a displaced Yankee in a southern town,
fretted more about children's premature exercise of power over slaves
than about a parent's assertion of authority over a child.[43] Perhaps this
was so because slave children were often both companions and servants to young masters and mistresses of the same age as they, but

perhaps also because greater southern tolerance for physical punishment, whether for free white children or for slaves, inhered in a
culture that touted patriarchy and understood family to encompass
servants as well as blood kin.

Whatever their discipline of young children, mothers in both
cities ceded to fathers the primary regulation of growing sons. The
mothers, of course, continued to fuss and fume over them when they
were at home. Their letters to sons away at school or off learning a
trade reminded them to care for their clothing, guard their health, and
study hard. But boys in the pubescent years were understood to need
a father's supervision. Girls in their midteens, however, were particularly their mothers' concern. Mothers were essential sources of information and supervision. Informing daughters about the "delicate
matters" of sex and training them to perform the household tasks that
they would later perform as young matrons, mothers also guarded
those daughters from premature sexual activity and consequent social
disaster. Sometimes the interchange produced tension between them
and subsequent guilt if the mother died, as did Fanny Appleton's, in
this critical period. But on the whole the slow pace of change in
household techniques even in the industrializing economy of the
urban North made a daughter value her mother's experience and
skills as preparation for an adult role unlikely to be markedly different
from her mother's. Even if spinning and weaving were passing from
kitchen to factory, food preparation, child care and nursing, and the
maintenance and cleaning of a home were chores few women would
escape completely—whether or not they married, whether or not
they employed servants.[44]

In tracing the fairly uniform life cycle of the women who chose
marriage, we cannot ignore the tremendous variations they experienced in the quality of life. Some through luck or personality or
particular social talents were happily married and enjoyed the affection of children and spouse. Eliza and John Ravenel's correspondence
during a separation when John's business kept him in Charleston
while his wife and children visited her ailing father in New Jersey

shimmers with warm affection. Eliza confessed to great loneliness without John, felt "as if it were a crime almost" to be so "perfectly comfortable" in his absence—but also kept from him news of the alarming tumor she had developed until she had had it removed. Her silence on this occasion, like her advice to John "to go to all the parties & be happy," did little to assuage his loneliness during her absence. Others, like Robert and Adele Allston, kept up the pretexts and customs of married life but clearly were often miserable with each other. In justifying himself, the great rice planter and soon-to-be governor of South Carolina only laid bare the chilling source of marital disaffection. "Lying alone in our well-spread bed . . . I have thought much of you, of your occasional reserved, self-dependent manner, of your hard words." Knowing that Adele believed him "unjust, 'insincere & illiberal,'" he yet could not understand her misery, for he had provided her a "spacious dwelling," "costly pictures," and was himself a man of great wealth and high public standing.[45]

And if Adele was unhappy with a husband who could, apparently, examine a tense marriage only in the light of his possessions and repute, what of Charles Lowell's wife, whose husband's bankruptcy revealed that he had used up her fortune in riotous living, spending $8,000 a year just to keep the "notorious" Julia King in the style to which she—but not proper Boston—was accustomed? Or, at the other end of the social scale, what of the wife of Charles Jarvis who had fled her home to live with Margaret Bradley in Charleston only to be pursued there and threatened by her husband?[46] Advice books told such women to make the best of a bad situation. South Carolina law had no provision for divorce, and Massachusetts permitted civil suits for complete dissolution of marriage only on the grounds of proven impotence, adultery, desertion, and, after 1835, the imprisonment of one spouse for a period of seven or more years. A privileged few got around such restrictions through divorce by legislative action. But even where divorce was permitted, the process was costly and generally brought disgrace to those involved. Some settled for legal separation. But most could only endure.[47]

An extreme case of enduring marital wretchedness was that of

the Boston Tudors. Frederic, a freewheeling businessman, was nearly
fifty when he wooed and wed nineteen-year-old Euphemia Fenno.
The romance of their honeymoon ended when Effie discovered that
Frederic had shared "the marriage privileges" with another woman for
the preceding ten years. Then, only six months after her wedding,
Effie endured her first miscarriage. This she attributed, as she did the
serious illnesses that followed and several subsequent miscarriages, to
the "vitiated propensities and ungoverned passions" of her husband.
Then, when Effie tried to learn French, Frederic threw her books into
Boston Harbor. Such "cruel and unwarrantable treatment" was little
mitigated by her husband's efforts to please her without first consult-
ing her. He took a suite of rooms at the new Tremont House hotel,
although Effie, married now for two and a half years, wanted her own
home. And the lumbering, old-fashioned carriage he bought her was a
family bone of contention for twenty years. Yet they lived together for
thirty years until Frederic's death. As Charlotte Everett had said after
their wedding, "What a foolish girl to marry such an old man." And,
one might surmise, to trade youth and beauty for money.[48]

More typical and far happier was the life that followed Mary
Guild's marriage to Daniel Child, clerk and later treasurer of Boston's
Hinckley Iron Works. On the evening of their wedding in November
1839, they left Mary's family home in Roxbury for that of Daniel's
father in Boston, where they lived as boarders for a couple of years.
During the first few weeks their home was full of callers—sometimes
as many as ten a day. First family and kin paid their respects, and,
later, friends and acquaintances, including the wife of Daniel's boss,
called to acknowledge the change in the couple's lives.

As winter lingered on and the novelty of being married wore off,
Mary and Daniel settled down into a pleasant routine, mostly reading
at home in the evenings but frequently venturing out to attend lectures and concerts or small parties in the homes of family and friends,
where music and dancing set the mood. On Daniel's days off they
took long walks downtown or out to Roxbury and Dorchester.

This was their honeymoon. By fall, Mary was pregnant—Daniel
began to stop off downtown for warm baths; Miss Brigham, the

dressmaker, arrived to sew; and by March Mary was in "a *loose* gown."[49] But the major change in their lives that second winter was less Mary's pregnancy than the suicide of Daniel's older brother and the illness of Mary's mother. Daniel, as executor of his brother's estate, made daily visits to the widow in which Mary had little part. And Mary went ever more frequently to Roxbury to tend her invalid mother. By April, however, she was going out less, received fewer visitors, and had given up attending church and teaching Sunday school.

Finally, on May 27, the Childs' daughter was born. Mary's twenty-four hours of labor began in the night, and it was not until early morning that the doctor and nurse arrived to supplement the services of her friend, Mrs. Otis. Thus began a new phase of Mary Guild Child's life. For the first week she stayed in bed, and the doctor called daily. The next week she ventured elsewhere in the house, but it was not until yet another week passed that she resumed her place at the family dining table. Shortly thereafter she and Daniel took a cab to Roxbury to display the baby to Mary's mother and grandmother.

Still, Mary was none too sure of her new role. A nurse helped her tend her child for a full month. When she was dismissed, Mary and the baby stayed with her parents in Roxbury until September. Finally she plucked up "resolution enough"[50] to return home, to leave the baby occasionally with her sister-in-law while she took longer walks and resumed church attendance. Her life was now changed in many subtle respects. Often Daniel went to a lecture or concert with his sister, while Mary stayed home. Her circle of friends shrank. Evening entertainments gave way to afternoon activities with the mothers of other small children. Housekeeping, child-rearing, and the continual process of reproduction now governed her life.

In November 1842, eighteen months after the birth of her daughter, a son, Frank, was born. This time it was six months before Mary ventured out for more than occasional visits to her parents' home. Even though she nursed the new infant, she was pregnant again the next summer. And although that pregnancy ended in miscarriage, and she did not wean Frank until December of 1843, she was pregnant again early in 1844. The child she bore that August died shortly thereafter, and Mary experienced yet another spontaneous abortion the following summer.

Through all this, Mary managed children and household mostly alone. Daniel helped by taking the children for long walks—often in the early morning when he did the day's grocery shopping. Sisters-in-law still helped by babysitting. Intermittently Mary employed a cleaning woman. Once a year the seamstress came to sew. And when the second child had arrived, so had a nurse, who again stayed for a month. But the first five years of marriage had brought Mary five pregnancies, two children who survived, a significant deterioration of her health, and a marked limitation to her freedom. The sociability that had graced her courting and honeymoon days diminished—not just because she missed evening outings, but because she was left at home with the children when Daniel took his sister with him on a combined business and holiday trip to New York and Philadelphia.

Mary Child's was by no means a failed or even a strained marriage. She gave no indication of being miserable. Daniel perceived her to be a good wife and mother. Nonetheless her married life comports with Caroline Gilman's ironic observation that "there can be but few domestic trials, comparatively speaking, without children."[51]

For slave women, the trials that children brought were intensified by the tenuous nature of their family structure. The law did not recognize their marriages and their master could—and often did—separate spouses for their own economic purposes. Yet despite their legal uncertainty, many slave marriages embodied deep personal commitment and some even received institutional recognition. In Charleston the wedding ceremonies of black members of predominantly white churches were not infrequently performed by white clergymen or black class leaders. Some owners, when they sold their slaves, refused to part husbands from wives, just as most sold small children with their mothers. The experience of the coachman Peter is a case in point. His owner specified that neither Peter, age forty-five, nor his washerwoman wife, Tyra, age thirty-six, nor any of their six

𝔓𝔲𝔟𝔩𝔦𝔠 𝔖𝔞𝔩𝔢 𝔬𝔣 𝔑𝔢𝔤𝔯𝔬𝔢𝔰,

By RICHARD CLAGETT.

On Tuesday. March 5th, 1833 at 1:00 P. M. the following Slaves will be sold at Potters Mart, in Charleston, S. C.

Miscellaneous Lots of Negroes, mostly house servants, some for field work.

Conditions: ½ **cash, balance by bond, bearing interest from date of sale. Payable in one to two years to be secured by a mortgage of the Negroes, and appraised personal security.** *Auctioneer will pay for the papers.*

A valuable Negro woman, accustomed to all kinds of house work. Is a good plain cook, and excellent dairy maid, washes and irons. She has four children, one a girl about 13 years of age, another 7, a boy about 5, and an infant 11 months old. 2 of the children will be sold with mother, the others separately, if it best suits the purchaser.

A very valuable Blacksmith, wife and daughters; the Smith is in the prime of life, and a perfect master at his trade. His wife about 27 years old, and his daughters 12 and 10 years old have been brought up as house servants, and as such are very valuable. Also for sale 2 likely young negro wenches, one of whom is 16 the other 13, both of whom have been taught and accustomed to the duties of house servants. The 16 year old wench has one eye.

A likely yellow girl about 17 or 18 years old, has been accustomed to all kinds of house and garden work. She is sold for no fault. Sound as a dollar.

House servants: The owner of a family described herein, would sell them for a good price only, they are offered for no fault whatever, but because they can be done without, and money is needed. He has been offered $1250. They consist of a man 30 to 33 years old, who has been raised in a genteel Virginia family as house servant, Carriage driver etc., in all which he excels. His wife a likely wench of 25 to 30 raised in like manner, as chamber maid, seamstress, nurse etc., their two children, girls of 12 and 4 or 5. They are bright mulattoes, of mild tractable dispositions, unassuming manners, and of genteel appearance and well worthy the notice of a gentleman of fortune needing such.

Also 14 Negro Wenches ranging from 16 to 25 years of age, all sound and capable of doing a good days work in the house or field.

Richard Clagett's advertisement for a slave auction testifies to the exigencies shaping slaves' family life as well as to the attitudes of owners and brokers engaged in the trade. (Courtesy of the South Caroliniana Library) children, ranging in age from two to nineteen, should be sold outside city limits—although all were to be sold and not necessarily to the same owner. Indeed, at a public auction in 1842, an unsympathetic Yankee observer conceded, even in his shock at seeing the seven hundred slaves of a single owner put on the block, that "families were sold together" and "attachments between young people were respected."[52]

Yet such an occasion was the exception rather than the rule. No slave family could claim any protection from the law. Marriage ties usually went totally unrecognized when slaves were sold. Of 272 slave women who were individually advertised for sale with their children in Charleston newspapers between 1838 and 1844, only 8 were offered for sale as part of a family unit containing a husband.[53]

Under such circumstances it is scarcely surprising that even churches that taught that marriage was a bond dissolved only by death tolerated the remarriage of slaves whose spouses had not died. Accordingly the discipline committee of Charleston's Congregational church, noting that Mary Holmes's husband had been "removed from her for six years past," granted her permission to remarry with the church's blessing so long as her own conscience rested easy. And Dorinda Beach, whose husband lived in the country, was given similar permission in recognition of the common situation whereby women were kept in or sent to the city as domestic servants while men were kept on or sent to plantations as field-workers.[54]

Despite the exigencies imposed on slave marriages and their unrecognized and often unsettled nature, the minimal records we have confirm that many slave families were held together by lasting bonds, even though the roles that husbands and wives played differed notably from the definitions common in the dominant white society. Not surprisingly, on the other hand, slave marriages were at least as strife-ridden and marred by frustration as those of free people. Boston Fowler was excommunicated from the Congregational church for mistreating his wife and remaining at variance with her while he lived in adultery with another woman. And the wife of the slave Isaac died when her resentment at being pregnant led to a fight and severe beating.[55]

Whatever the variations attributable to class or region or race, to remain a spinster or become a wife was an option most women confronted—and answered by marrying. Yet even in this apparently most voluntary of decisions, the social expectation that men and only men proposed marriage limited a woman's choice as did the assumption that men would propose to women younger than they but of their own race and class—unless, of course, the woman had property or family connections that could improve her husband's standing. To what degree the women who, at the outset, remained single did so because they chose positively for spinsterhood or because no suitable man proposed, we can only guess. Nor can we know the number of women whose beauty, charm, or personality attracted men whose class or status exceeded their own.

What the evidence does suggest, however, is that courting was most encouraged within a relatively homogeneous group and that regional differences influenced that pattern very little. Whether Boston's more numerous spinsters and its more common advice that singlehood was preferable to an unhappy marriage are explained by a population slightly more female than male—and distinctly so during economic downturns and among its native-born, though not its foreign-born, population—is arguable. And while among Charleston's Afro-American and especially its free black population the pronounced gender imbalance mandated that many women could only be single, the slight imbalance of the city's white population in the other direction may have been either more or less important than cultural imperatives in determining women's greater proclivity there to marry—-and marry young. Overall, however, unless women were specially advantaged or disadvantaged, marriage and motherhood—either for personal fulfillment, economic security, or whatever else it promised—was a powerful lure.

In the end, class, status, and race, in addition to biological chance and public events, far more than region per se, remained major determinants of a woman's life cycle after her marriage. On the one hand, while many wished to control their own fertility, unwanted pregnancies were numerous. And while themes of republican motherhood vaunted women's careful cultivation of the next generation, mothers were helpless against infant and child mortality. On the other hand, if her class or status changed, it was a function largely of her husband's activity. Nor was it in her power to control the economic fluctuations or physical perils that could ruin her family or leave her a widow.

Yet the last stage of a married woman's life, as it turned out, was likely to involve the death of her husband. Many widows were left with children to rear and educate. Others, with families grown, could live with an adult child. Some were of an age to work and support themselves—running a boardinghouse, which might generate adequate income, or sewing in penury. Few enjoyed the same standard of living that their working husbands had provided—whether from wages, salary, professional fees, or profits. The law insured widows only the use of a third of their husbands' estates—though the wills of the men who made them were often more generous. For widows, in short, the most pervasive concern was relative or real poverty.

Some women solved the problem by remarrying—but there simply were not enough older unmarried men or widowers to go around even had every one of them chosen to be married in his ripe years. To those who were so inclined, the widow with resources was more attractive than one without—such as Mrs. Middleton of Charleston, frantically pursued to Saratoga and beyond by a Dr. Smith; or Mrs. McLean of Boston, whose second husband was not quite so wealthy a widower as she was a widow.[56]

What happened to the rest of the women when neither the late husband nor living children provided adequate support was largely a matter of the husband's class and lifetime associations. In Charleston, virtually every club provided pensions to needy widows of deceased members. Ethnic groups like the St. Patrick's Benevolent Association, the German Friendly Society, the Hebrew Orphan Society, and the

Brown Fellowship provided modest stipends. The more prestigious South Carolina Society spent over $5,000 a year taking care of "Widows & Children of deceased indigent Members" as well as "living decayed Members." The Society for the Relief of Orphans and Widows of the Episcopal Clergy in South Carolina awarded its annuities in amounts reflecting status as much as need, one bishop's widow receiving twice as much as the widows of most other clerics. The Fellowship Society, in contrast, tried to fit the stipend more nearly to the need. The aged Mrs. Ruberry, who also received $200 a year from the South Carolina Society and $60 from the Carpenters Society, got only $60 from the Fellowship Society. Mrs. Pearce, with "no property" and five children, received $150—no more and no less than Mrs. Gilbert with eight slaves but only one of them hired out and with four children to support. Where clubs failed, churches provided a mite for widows who were or whose husbands had been members. Finally, the utterly destitute with no other resources might receive cash and clothing as paupers supported by the state.[57]

The needy widows of Boston could also apply for public aid. If they were native-born and had lived long in the same ward and thus would be known to an overseer of the poor, they would likely become outdoor pensioners able to live in their own homes. Otherwise they had to move into a city institution—the house of industry. While come clubs, like the Society of the Cincinnati, provided for the indigent widows of former members, the most likely sources of private assistance were two benevolent societies designed specifically to meet their particular needs: the Widows' Society, which aided "poor and infirm widows and aged single women of good character"; and the Fatherless and Widows' Society, which sought out those living alone in hovels, destitute of resources. Reflecting unusual waves of public sympathy for those made widows under particular conditions, Bostonians raised funds for the relicts of men drowned when the steamboat *Lexington* exploded, and Charlestonians similarly provided for the widows of a longtime public school teacher and of volunteer firemen killed on the job.[58]

In sum, the belief that widows were more independent than

wives is mostly unfounded. Legally they regained their civil rights as persons. And, if they had inherited property or could earn enough to support themselves in comfort, they could control and spend their resources as they wished. But few, especially among older widows, could find such occupations, and none among the poor could depend on unearned income from inherited property. The childless young and those of middling or upper-class standing fared best economically, but at least among the latter this was largely a continuation of benefits they had also enjoyed in marriage. The rest were not unlike the unmarried Miss Odiorne, whose niece reminded her that "there is a provision for the poor, who are worthy and *amiable*." But the "friends" who assisted them "must judge for themselves, what they can do—and the person receiving their aid, must view it in its right light—in order to make it a mutual blessing." The old who received help from younger relatives or institutions were expected to respond "with gratitude" and not make further demands.[59]

Life as a widow, like that as a wife or a spinster, was shaped both by earlier conscious choices and by circumstances over which the individual had no control. Yet options remained—more, of course, to the fortunate than to others. Many found solace in religious or associational activity or in family life with children and grandchildren. Some renewed emotional intimacy in a new marriage or in close friendship with another mature woman. Eliza Cabot Follen, whose minister husband went down on the *Lexington*, and Maria Weston Chapman, whose merchant husband died of consumption two years afterward, formed ties so intense that when Eliza died some twenty years later Maria experienced a new "sorrow such as I thought never again to feel." "The joy & light & charm" of her life was gone.[60] But both these women had also inherited wealth, had been sufficiently educated to become published authors, and possessed the commitments that powered their activity in reform associations. They had ample resources and family assistance to care for and educate their children. And they became widows when they were young enough to reshape their lives and form new ties.

Few widows—or wives—or spinsters—were so fortunate.

3

Housework
and Paid Work

Although in the first half of the nineteenth century many women worked for wages, the priorities placed on marriage and motherhood decreed that the most acceptable employment for women was in their homes. Accordingly, with few exceptions, the sanctioned work for unmarried as well as married women was the unpaid care of family and house. Yet here, as in the marketplace, the particular nature of such gender-specific work was a function of region as well as of race and class. In Charleston there were two domestic servants for every ten residents, two slave domestics for every four white residents. In Boston, by contrast, there was only one domestic worker for every twenty-three residents. Indeed, well over 80 percent of all households in the city employed no help at all, while in 1845 a mere 1,069 of them—about 6 percent of the total—employed two or more domestics.[1] Since access to servants dictated the degree to which the housewife was either a white-collar manager or a manual laborer, the region in which she lived was a critical factor. Yet despite such differences, the variety of work performed in the home and its on-going, repetitive nature meant that in both cities housework was burdensome and endless.

The homemaker was chief overseer of the kitchen and often the sole cook and dishwasher. At a time when prepared food seldom encompassed more than baker's bread, when refrigeration in a northern urban home comprised a cellar or cold room, and when expensive ice, shipped in from Maine and Massachusetts, was the only coolant available during Charleston's torrid summers, daily shopping for most households was not just customary but unavoidable. The Charleston housewife might send a servant to market. Her Boston equivalent often relied on her husband's doing provision shopping while she prepared breakfast. This daily expedition, at least until well into the 1840s, generally involved going to a central market, since ordinances in both cities limited the sale of fresh goods to supervised stands and restricted peddlers where they did not prohibit them altogether. Moreover, regardless of who did the shopping and where, the offerings in the market set the day's menu. Dinner, the principal meal, was served midday. Men of middling status expected to come home to a hearty meal of meat or fish and a starchy pudding, with side dishes of vegetables in season and perhaps soup and dessert as well. Those less well-off consumed less meat but ate more soup, bread, and pudding, while the rich grew fat on elaborate dinners of several courses with more than one meat dish.[2]

The northern-bred but Charleston-domiciled novelist Caroline Gilman well understood the nature of the burdens thus imposed. Her *Southern Matron* portrayed the dilemmas of Cornelia Wilton and her father, who coped with the absence of both Mrs. Wilton and the family cook by going out and buying a new cook—allegedly expert in the high art of French cuisine. But, presented with an excruciatingly awful dinner, they quickly realized that they had not acquired a chef but a mason. Cuffee was put to work mending chimneys and the Wiltons settled for a less pretentious cook who "performed her duties better." And Cornelia continued to shun the kitchen house, believing it the territorial preserve of servants whom she neither wished nor really dared to oversee.

How different was the experience of Gilman's *New England Bride* who had been well trained by her mother. With the culinary skills she had learned in the country, Clarissa not only taught her Boston help and supervised her own kitchen, but she could fill in when a crisis occurred. It was, however, not solely a regional issue. Clarissa's city-born friend Emily Lawrence had been instructed by her wealthy mother only in the social amenities. Thus, when the servants she had hired in Boston all quit after she and her new husband moved to their country home, she was helpless. "You will spend your fortune to very little purpose," her uncle admonished after an especially inedible meal, "if, amid the abundance with which you are surrounded, you cannot procure a well-cooked dinner."[3]

Yet preparing even minimally palatable dinners with but few conveniences inevitably ate up the morning. The poorest families and many in the middling ranks had neither water piped into the kitchen nor wells or cisterns in the yard. Indeed, until Boston established a municipal water system in 1845, even the wealthiest Bostonians frequently lacked an adequate supply. Congressman Edward Everett's wife complained in 1834 that her home was the only one in the neighborhood still getting water from the private aqueduct company, which presumably served them all. And ten years later over half of the inhabited houses in Boston still had no access to potable water, and barely half had water soft enough to make soapsuds. In Charleston it was even worse, for the sea-level swampiness of its land and the density of its churchyard cemeteries condemned residents to drink a brew "not only [of] the soluble filth, and excretion of men and animals, but the very mortal remains of our citizens, who are interred in the city." As late as 1848 most Charlestonians still drew from their own cisterns and wells water "for the most part undrinkable, and hardly fit for washing or culinary purposes."[4]

Limited in basic supplies, the kitchen worker also struggled with minimal equipment. Although wood- and coal-fueled cook stoves were introduced in the 1820s and airtight ones were common in Boston homes of the 1850s, many cooks still worked over open fires. Either way, the heat so generated steamed the cook as well as the dinner. Happily breakfast was generally leftovers from the preceding day's dinner and the evening meal was a light one—often tea with bread and butter and homemade preserves when they were available.

Preserving foods plentiful in summer but sparse in winter was an activity common to urban as well as to rural New England households. The very frugal might lay down dozens of fresh eggs in hourglass solution and salt down whole beefs in brine as well as prepare the fruit jams that graced winter suppers. While the letters and diaries of Charleston women seldom mention such activities, they are full of thanks to country kin who shipped them fresh butter and eggs, poultry and meat, as well as preserves in return for the retail shopping their city cousins did for them. But running such errands—like laying down food, making clothes for family members, and undertaking a massive housecleaning each spring—had to be sandwiched in among the regular weekly chores—washing and ironing, sweeping and dusting, and baking pies and cakes if not bread.

Then, too, there were the less predictable wifely responsibilities. Although some overlapped chores that servants—where there were servants—might perform, others did not. It was the wife and mother who took charge of nursing ailing family members—young and old. Mrs. Samuel Prioleau, who had learned to shave her husband after the Charleston judge suffered a stroke, reportedly never left him in the last three or four years of his life. The wife was also hostess and personal secretary. Episcopal bishop Nathaniel Bowen's spouse was constantly engaged in the entertainments that her husband's post demanded. Margaret Adger Smyth, trying one summer to nurse three children through whooping cough, found she could scarcely do the writing and clipping and pasting assigned her by her absent Presbyterian-cleric husband and still give dinners to the visiting preachers who supplied his pulpit as well as attending to sundry requests from his parishioners.[5]

While such responsibilities might weigh down the more fortunate, they differed fundamentally from the physically exhausting work of Irish women packed into the tenements that lined Boston's Broad Street. In one such house, where fifteen families lived with neither a water supply nor toilet facilities, wifely chores included lugging tubs of dirty water and slops to the adjacent docks where they were dumped into the harbor. Doubtless these immigrant women neglected the economizing tasks recommended by such Boston-published handbooks as *The Frugal Housewife* and *The Young Housekeeper*. But the manly advice to all wife-housekeepers of whatever class resembled that which the hero of Sarah Josepha Hale's novel *Keeping House and House Keeping: A Story of Domestic Life* addressed to his wife: "I have given you the charge of the house, thinking the office of managing belonged to the woman. . . . Every married woman in good health should keep her own house; it is a sacred office, from which she has no right to shrink; it is a part of her marriage covenant—it gives dignity to her character." And, if this hero's wife replied that housekeeping also gave "littleness to her mind," others probably agreed with real-life Louisa Waterhouse, who believed that domestic responsibility "keeps one *on the Alert* & ever pleased with it as a source of knowledge" but still "hoping always that it will not last for ever."[6]

Women's work was not, however, confined to serving husband and children, house and home. Yet even the unusually full statistics of Boston's 1845 census are disappointingly thin about the work that women performed for pay. Lemuel Shattuck, who compiled the data, had instructed the census takers to obtain occupational data only for adult males. Nonetheless, employers voluntarily provided so much information about the women they employed on their premises that the city census does, although it omits outworkers and day laborers, reveal much about female wage earners. Indeed, even though he totally ignored the women who worked for pay at home, Shattuck nevertheless recorded occupations for nearly 20 percent of all women between twenty and sixty in the city. And it is probably safe to assume that, if those who did outwork in their own homes had been counted, the percentage of Boston women reported as doing paid labor in 1845 would have been close to the 40 percent reported in an 1837 tally.

Of those whose work Shattuck chronicled, a large number were engaged in manufacturing, but they were not employed in large mills, for the great Massachusetts textile factories were in fall-line towns beyond Boston. In the city itself, women, like the men engaged in manufacturing, worked in small shops. Some were highly skilled and comparatively well paid. In 1845, 45 percent of all bookbinders, 24 percent of all printers, and 9 percent of all typefounders in the city were women, who earned between $2.50 and $3.00 a week (albeit men in the same trades earned $8.80 to $11.00). Skilled female workers also comprised 10 percent of all furniture workers and half of all upholsterers. There were seventy-eight female shoemakers in the city, nearly one-quarter of the total, although some of them may have been only stitchers of uppers. And in the needle trades generally, women enjoyed a virtual monopoly of dress- and corset-making, while they predominated in cap, hat, and bonnet making.[7]

But the fact remains that most needle workers were not employed in such highly specialized and comparatively well-paid occupations. Rather they were the seamstresses, who, whatever their skills, were paid little for the garments they sewed in their own dwellings as outworkers. In 1830, Unitarian city missionary Joseph Tuckerman doubted that even those fully employed earned more than $1.00 or, at most, $1.50 a week, at a time when an unskilled male laborer was paid a dollar a day. Ten years later, according to Episcopal cleric William Hague, the situation was even worse. Only if a seamstress had the easiest items to sew and worked a full seven-day week could she earn one dollar. If she had to sew shirts and worked only five days, the seven garments she could make in that time would bring in only forty-nine cents. And this was in a city where charitable organizations estimated that a single adult needed three dollars a week to live decently.[8]

The knowledge that poverty was at its worst among Boston's female population was not confined to philanthropists like Tuckerman, and there was broad assent that such poverty resulted from the low wages paid females. The vast majority of the industrious poor, Thomas Thwing told the Consociation of Unitarian Benevolent Societies, were "unfortunate females, who are *made* poor, and *kept* poor by being obliged to pay unreasonable rent, and at the same time cannot get *half pay* for their work." Robert Waterston of the Society for the Prevention of Pauperism condemned the "starvation wages" paid the mothers of small children who had to work at home. Unable to support their families on as little as twenty-five cents a day, many of these outworkers with family responsibilities ultimately had no choice but to seek private charity or public welfare.[9]

Thus, even though most native-born white women regarded domestic service as degrading, its provision of room and board, in addition to money wages of $1.00 to $1.50 a week, attracted the

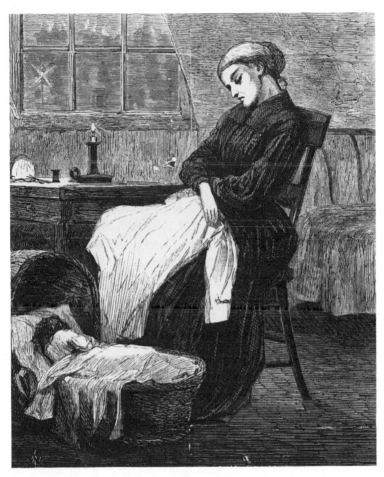

Stanley Fox's rendering of an exhausted seamstress in the small room in which she worked and lived and cared for her child was printed as part of a pictorial essay on women's work in Harper's Bazaar, *April 18, 1868. (Courtesy of the Schlesinger Library, Radcliffe College)*

second largest contingent of Boston's women workers. Yet the economic security it promised came at the price of personal restrictions. Servants were usually required to live where they worked and to be on call six and a half days a week. Most usually lacking peers and generally under the close supervision of their employers, servants could seldom control either their work or their private lives. Their only salvation from the tension thus produced was moving from one job to another in a city where the demand for servants was always greater than the supply.

The letters and diaries of their employers—mostly women—chronicle both the absolute subservience required of servants and the frequency with which they rebelled. Wealthy Mary Crowninshield Mifflin's diary wearily records servants' coming and going—usually without explanation. Julia Webster Appleton, daughter of a United States senator and wife of a merchant, almost broke down when her cook, to whom she had just given fabric for a new dress, quit on Christmas day. Unlike these young matrons with abundant resources to employ several servants was Louisa Waterhouse, whose husband, a distinguished doctor and an impractical politician, had lost so much money in the panic of 1837 that the family was reduced to a single servant. The first maid they hired was a mature woman, "a good Cook, good washer, good House maid," who also "attend[ed] to the Table" and "gather[ed] Berries." But she was careless—even extravagant—with firewood, and she had a fierce temper. Her gravest offense, however, was her independence, her determination to govern her own time off. Mrs. Waterhouse could not tolerate a servant who was not "willing to stay at home" and sew for the family when her assigned chores were completed. So, when the maid asked to serve tea early one afternoon so that she could go out on her own business, Mrs. Waterhouse fired her without notice. Yet the next help hired was even worse. A girl of nineteen with little experience, she saw no reason to interrupt her housework to answer the door when Mrs. Waterhouse was seated at her desk ostensibly doing nothing. Before long she too was dismissed when she cut her own generous portion from the family's beefsteak before it was set on the Waterhouse dinner table.[10]

All these quittings and firings were tests of will across class lines. All reflect antagonisms between servant and mistress so persistent that both the advice manuals and the fiction written by Boston women often gave extended attention to them. Presented from the employer's perspective, these texts nonetheless provide insights into the lives and tribulations of the "help." The employer for her part had the power to hire and fire; she was on her own home ground, surrounded by family and empowered to control the live-in servant's full time. The maids were of varied types: the simple country girl who had learned the basic skills from her mother but was now far from home; the child taken from the orphan asylum or almshouse whose honesty was questionable and knowledge minimal; the mature woman whose private failures, not infrequently related to drink, had driven her to seek paid employment. Nonetheless, the servant had effective weapons in the ongoing tug-of-war with her boss. She could deliberately shame or embarrass her employer by displaying ill manners or providing shabby service when guests were present. She might choose holidays or family festivities as the time to demand changed conditions of employment, threatening to quit without notice if the demands were not met. In sum, because she lived so intimately with her boss, the servant acquired and used the power that knowledge of her employer's weaknesses gave her. And underlying the interplay between them were the realities of conflicting economic and social goals—the mistress manipulating her maid to enhance her own role as lady; the maid refusing to play the role of dependent inferior.

Given such stress and having other options, American-born women avoided domestic service whenever they could. Increasingly it was Irish immigrants who were understood to comprise Boston's most likely pool of domestic workers. Yet, if they more readily endured the indignities of live-in servants, they were also less likely to be familiar with the work required of them. How, one reformer asked, could a young Irish peasant, ignorant of any American "cookery except that practised in a cellar in Broad street, know how to prepare a dinner for a gentleman's family?" But no schools of "Domestic Industry" were founded to teach them. And Societies for the Mutual Benefit of Female Domestics and Their Employers were less mutual than they claimed to be. Acting primarily as employment bureaus, they filed character references for servants—but none for mistresses—and urged employers to reward faithful servants with bonuses designed to keep them on the job rather than to improve their lot. Underlying all were assumptions similar to those of Charlotte Brooks Everett, who allowed that *"Colored help"* was preferable to *"trap-door help"* but that either was better than Irish servants—for of "all trials laid upon mortals, there is none so difficult to bear as the temper of an Irishman." Race and ethnic hostilities thus mingled with class to intensify the proclivity of Boston ladies to think of their servants as feckless wenches.[11]

In Charleston race was the predominant determinant in the servant-mistress relationship. Yet, as a fictional conversation between northern and southern vacationers at Saratoga in an 1828 story suggests, the results were not all that different. The young Yankee heroine observed that southern women "complain of their *servants*, and we of our *help*. They talk of selling the *blacks* because of bad behaviour, and we of turning away our *whites* for similar faults." That observation, however, oversimplified Charleston reality. While most residents of the southern city owned their servants, many in fact hired the slaves of others. In such cases, written agreements between the slave's owner and her temporary employer provided for greater continuity of employment than did northern maid-mistress agreements. They also, of course, altered domestic politics. Generally it was the owner who collected the slave-servant's wages, ranging from as little as two dollars a month for a young and minimally trained girl to five to seven dollars for a housemaid and upwards of ten dollars a month for a good female cook. While these wages were not inconsonant with Boston pay for similar work—and may indeed have been slightly higher—they offered little incentive to the slave, while her owner was probably reaping annual returns of 10 percent to 25 percent on her capital.[12]

On the other hand, a significant number of slaves used the hiring-out process to expand their personal freedom. Some managed their own time and paid a sizable portion of their wages to the masters and mistresses whom they thus relieved of managerial responsibility. Others granted the right to hire their own time paid their owners only a token fee. And a few took matters completely into their own hands. Bess, a twenty-year-old washer and houseworker who disappeared from her Charleston employer's house in the fall of 1840, apparently used the city license that her owner, John Stuart, had bought in order to be able to hire her out to acquire a false legitimacy for quite other arrangements. That some slaves managed quasi-independence for long periods of time is borne out by Thomas Calvert's advertisement seeking information about his slave Jane Prentiss. He had, he said, lost all contact with her during the years she had lived on her own. Other slave domestics, lacking such full control over their lives, nonetheless exercised a real veto power. Twenty-one-year-old Amelia, sold to a planter, resisted doing fieldwork so effectively that her former owner in Charleston had to refund the buyer's purchase price and bring her back to the city.[13]

Such situations were, of course, the exception; most urban domestic slaves even more than their plantation sisters contended directly with almost omnipresent owners. If they did not sleep in their owners' domicile, they lived in kitchen and carriage houses within the walled yards that, as much as piazzas, characterized Charleston's vernacular architecture. Even their leisure hours were not really free time. To venture out in the evening after nine o'clock in winter or ten o'clock in summer, they had to carry a written, explicit, and dated permission ticket from their owners. Neither secular amusements nor religious services involving more than seven people were permitted them by law unless a white person was present. And for defiance of a private order as of a public law, the slave could be sent to the city workhouse for correction.[14]

Yet for all that apparent control, Charleston women's frustrations in managing their slaves—whether they were lazy and feckless or hardworking but set in their ways—were as common as Boston employers' complaints. Their lamentations attest that domestic servants working directly for their owners were not devoid of power—though such power depended on the special skills they brought to their work, on longtime relations with their mistresses, or simply on their mistresses' dependence on slaves to do the work that would otherwise fall to them. Some servants practiced outright defiance that, if it gave them no respite, could drive their owners beyond the minimal restraints the law imposed on slaveholders. Lindy was an extreme example. An alcoholic and often sick, she sorely tried her mistress, who, over time, whipped her ever more severely and frequently until she died of so "great Cruelty and Neglect" that a South Carolina Court of General Sessions fined the owner $214.18.

Still, instances of this sort were rare, for most slaves were protected from fatal beatings—though not from whippings—by the owner's economic self interest. On the other hand, having an unusually humane owner did not guarantee protection since death or abrupt financial loss could force the sale even of those slaves who had been efficient or highly regarded servants. Moreover, if heirs disputed the terms of a will sheltering slaves from disruptive sale and dispersion, the court of chancery might intervene, as it did in the case of Elizabeth McCall, by ordering the sale of twenty-six servants and the equal distribution of the proceeds to her family members.[15]

More fortunate slaves were better protected by their owners' wills, often to the full limits of Carolina law. Ann Smith left to her slave Nancy, her two children, and any future children she might bear the right to hire their own time, paying Smith's estate only a token three dollars a year. Moreover, Nancy inherited all her mistress's furniture and one hundred dollars in cash, and she could look forward to emancipation if state law ever changed to permit it. Rare was the Bostonian, by contrast, who bequeathed as much as five or ten dollars to a longtime servant. Nonetheless, even those slaves promised a compensatory inheritance like Nancy's might find, as did the servants of Elizabeth King, that a codicil absolutely reversed the original will, specifying their sale at public auction to provide benevolences to the Charleston Orphan House, the Methodist church, and the Ladies Benevolent Society. The irony of such philanthropy only highlights the importance of wages and the right to quit.[16]

But, beyond all this, it was primarily in the wide availability of domestic workers that slavery shaped the work world of Charleston. No one can overlook the impact on white women of living in a city where nine out of ten female slaves did domestic work and where virtually all adult black women, as opposed to only 15 to 20 percent of white women, were in the labor force. On the other hand, domestic service excepted, the distribution of women in various occupations resembled Boston's. Charleston women employed in manufacturing worked chiefly in the needle trades. All the city's mantua makers, milliners, and seamstresses were female in 1848, although their distribution within the clothing industry was further shaped by race and status. Three-quarters of the mantua makers and more than one-third of the seamstresses were free blacks. All the milliners were white but so were half the seamstresses. Thus, although many slave women doubtless did sewing as part of their work as domestics, they were barely visible as part of clothing manufacturing, in sharp contrast with free blacks who comprised over 60 percent of all such workers. Yet, whatever the racial divisions, seamstresses in both cities fared least well. The condition of slaves was, of course, governed by their status regardless of the work they did. But free seamstresses—whether black or white—were paid wages insufficient on any scale. Charleston-born Sarah Grimké observed, as much about the South as the North, that any woman, no matter what her work, was paid only a third to a half as much as a man engaged in the same or comparable work. So the long hours the least well-paid women worked not only eroded their physical well-being but returned them little, if any, more economic independence than did the unpaid labor of women who worked in their own homes for family members.[17]

For a minority of women, however, gaining independence through earning their own living was no delusion. And it was for such women that regional cultures most shaped particular opportunities. Eleven percent of Charleston's white working women, for example, were engaged in commerce, while in Boston fewer than 1 percent of all women workers were so employed. Indeed, Boston's white women were only as likely as Charleston's black women to engage in trade. This situation doubtless reflected the minimal prestige attributed to retail trade in the low-country, where Dr. Samuel Dickson pointedly advised young men to leave shopkeeping to women because it was an effeminate occupation. Even so, the opportunities shaped by such an attitude did, he thought, offer southern women a rare chance to profit directly from American productivity by earning an income adequate "to sustain life and procure . . . clothing, fuel, and shelter" more abundantly than was the case for most other self-sustaining females. Nor, despite the law of coverture, were such opportunities reserved to spinsters and widows. South Carolina was unique in permitting a married woman to separate her business from her husband's control by advertising herself as a "feme sole trader" who intended "to carry on business on her separate and exclusive account and benefit." So it was that white women—single, married, and widowed—sold china, clocks, mirrors, engravings, vases, clothing, fancy goods, and dry goods while black women peddled fruit, fish, and milk. A few entrepreneurs produced the products they sold. Dorcas Sutcliffe operated a bakery. Sally Berry made and sold ice cream. Mrs. Wittpinn ran a greenhouse. Free black Barbara Barguet made and sold umbrellas. And places of public accommodation were probably more likely to be operated by women than men. Free woman of color Eliza Lee was famed first for her Carolina Coffee House and then for her Carolina Hotel. Susan Wilkie was the proprietor of the Farmers Hotel. White Mary Ann Main ran a tavern. A group of black women operated an oyster emporium. Indeed 80 percent of all boardinghouse keepers and hoteliers were women. If these women clearly did not enjoy the same prestige or the financial rewards of those women who at the time comprised one-fifth of all planters listed as residents of Charleston, they did enjoy an autonomy unusual among women.[18]

In Boston, on the other hand, where retail trade was well regarded as a suitable first step for young men out to make their fortunes, the entrepreneurial opportunities for women were limited indeed. Women did, it is true, dominate the artificial flower and corset business, operate a quarter of all bonnet shops, and, in very small numbers, manage other kinds of clothing stores. Yet so inconsequential was their role that the R. G. Dun credit ratings for Boston businesses in the 1840s listed only two women shopkeepers—one a good and one a poor risk—and, in some hundred closely written pages, commented only once that a firm employed a female clerk. Furthermore, because Shattuck's census of Boston failed to record the occu-

"Selling Sweet Potatoes in Charleston," printed in the London Illustrated
News *at the beginning of the Civil War, demonstrates racial stereotyping as
well as the entrepreneurial activity of black women in the southern city. (Courtesy of the Schlesinger Library, Radcliffe College)*

pations of women working in their own homes, we have no idea how
many ran boardinghouses. But given literary references to the practice
of boarding out, we know there must have been many. No woman,
however, was listed in 1845 as a hotelier or innkeeper, even though in
the 1820s Lydia Vose had owned and managed the French Coffee
House. Nonetheless, women's role in Boston's service sector appears
to have been less varied than it was in Charleston.[19]

Also visible among the occupations that promised women more
than mere survival wages was health care. Nurses in both cities were
almost always female because nursing was assumed to be a uniquely
feminine activity, whether performed within the family or for pay. In
Charleston, both in public institutions and in private employ, white
nurses generally were better paid than domestics or seamstresses,
earning six to twelve dollars a month in addition to room and board.
The city's five midwives and its single female practitioner of botanic
medicine in 1848 doubtless earned still more and could live in their
own homes as well. The Boston census, in which all nurses listed in

1845 were women, mentions no midwives; and the other female health-care workers Shattuck noted were in categories of minimal prestige—truss-makers and leechers predominantly. Nonetheless, we know that at least three women practiced medicine there at some time during the 1840s. Still, although conservative Judge Peter Thacher praised Mrs. Ruth Wheeler as a woman "skilled in the healing art" whose service to women and children won her "considerable celebrity and some property," he called her "Mrs." and not "Dr." Furthermore, the powerful Boston Medical Association and the Massachusetts Medical Society did not grant her any professional status in their records. In South Carolina, by contrast, midwives were licensed by the medical profession.[20]

Considerably more visible than the few women physicians were those who went on the stage as dancers, singers, or actresses. Louisa May Alcott's novel *Work*, whose characters engage in most of the occupations available to midcentury Boston women, portrays acting as the most remunerative and exciting, and this seems to be as true of Charleston as it was of Boston. Even though few women who chose such a career won fame or fortune and many were tainted with the stigma of prostitution, widely associated in the public mind with theaters, significant numbers of talented women did succumb to its appeal. Among the stars whose performances brought public plaudits and financial rewards were Clara Fisher, whose final performance, climaxing her first season in Charleston, attracted sixteen hundred people. If Fisher managed to overwhelm southern critics and escape the social ostracism that polite society generally imposed on actresses, Fanny Kemble was still more warmly accepted—welcomed even—in polished drawing rooms on Beacon Hill. Her first Boston season not only attracted audiences "of the first class" but also invitations from the city's cultural elite—former congressman and mayor Harrison Gray Otis and physician-professor John Warren among them.[21]

More typical of the equivocal reception accorded even popular entertainers was that given Fanny Elssler. A marvelously agile dancer with a sensuous style, she commanded prices that Bostonians had never paid before, boxes for her performance in "La Sylphide" selling for as much as $288 in 1841. Although her effect on Charleston was not so inflationary, she nonetheless doubled the usual demand for tickets whenever she danced. But Elssler's popular performances typed her as a sexual object as much as an artist. After decent Bostonians had successfully demanded that she lengthen her skirts, the Charleston press lamented that their length impeded her performance. Nonetheless, the *Mercury* announced that her effect there on old men was so titillating that they "dyed their whiskers" and took "to capering and declared they had not felt so much like boys for half a century." And, despite proper Boston, prominent politician Caleb Cushing's name was only one of those linked with Elssler's—in no way portending matrimony.[22]

Whatever gossips might imply or moralists condemn, nineteenth-century Americans agreed that female roles on the stage should be taken by women—whether in opera, ballet, or play. That the women who took them should be admired and rewarded for their performances in public, however, was at odds with all those theories that consigned women to private roles within their families and homes. An entertainer's position was, therefore, a paradox, for it was her very gender that made possible her success, whether through public acclaim or financial reward, and thus negated the very distinctions gender theoretically imposed.

When being female was not essential to her accomplishment, however, the entertainer was as disadvantaged as other working women—paid less than men yet expected to equal or excel them if they were to be employed at all. Mary Strobel was a case in point. Organist at St. John's Lutheran Church in Charleston in the mid-1830s, she earned significantly less than her male predecessor. When she protested to the vestry, they replied only that it was not expedient to increase her salary. After another four years she quit.[23] And there is no record to indicate that she was subsequently hired by any other church. She had encroached on the male world, well outside the limited natural monopoly that made stars of sopranos and ballerinas.

The women who entertained through the printed page rather than on the stage were in a more secure position. Male authors, of

course, complained about "lady scribblers," and many female authors
hid behind pseudonyms. But women novelists surely enjoyed special
attention from their predominantly female reading public. Furthermore, women writers did not confine themselves to fiction. Several
gained success as editors. Caroline Gilman's Charleston-based *Rose-
bud*, like Lydia Maria Child's *Juvenile Miscellany*, attracted a profitable
readership among young people. Sarah Josepha Hale's *Ladies Magazine*—both when she herself published it in Boston and later when
she edited it as *Godey's Lady's Book* in Philadelphia—was for forty
years the most widely read women's magazine. Nor were editorships
limited to periodicals specifically designed for juvenile or female
readers. For five years the *Boston Daily Transcript* throve under a
woman's direction after Cornelia Walter succeeded her brother as
editor in 1842. For three years in the early 1840s Lydia Maria Child
edited the *National Antislavery Standard*. And, in William Lloyd Garrison's absences, Maria Weston Chapman frequently put out the
Liberator.

Nonetheless, poems, stories, and novels primarily defined the
lady scribblers' domain. The pseudonyms under which poems appeared in *The Magnolia* suggest, if they do not prove, that southern
women wrote most of them. In the 1820s Lydia Maria Child was
among the first of the women novelists to earn a comfortable income
and also among the few to win critical acclaim as well. Likewise, with
an eerie similarity in the diversity of her literary career, Charlestonian
Caroline Gilman flourished as novelist, editor, short-story writer, and
purveyor of household advice. Significantly, however, neither Gilman
nor Child suffered the isolation of Margaret Fuller who eschewed
fiction for essays and edited the *Dial*, a journal for intellectuals. She it
was who fit the stereotype of the bluestocking, that homely spinster
unable to live a "normal" woman's life, the intimidating Zenobia
among Boston's transcendentalists.[24]

The inconsistencies within the female labor market force us to
consider why women chose the work they did. There can be no doubt
that slave women worked at the jobs assigned them because they had

no choice. There is also little doubt that the free servants, seam-stresses, and washerwomen, those who worked in the sectors with greatest demand for female workers and could barely live on what they earned, did so because most women, North or South, had no meaningful employment choices. They could anticipate neither psychological fulfillment from their work nor the extrinsic rewards with which generous pay could enhance their free time. Thomas Cooper, president of the South Carolina College, was as vocal as Joseph Tuckerman, Boston's city minister to the poor, in condemning the destitution common to the lives of most working women in the 1820s and 1830s and proposing that more remunerative trades be opened to them. Both men understood that most women took ill-paid jobs simply as a matter of survival.[25]

Nor should we assume that only single women worked for such meager returns. Infant schools, charitably supported day-care facilities that gained fleeting popularity around 1830, offered supervision and instruction for very small children of working mothers. They were, by their very existence, a public admission that significant numbers of mothers did have to work to support their families as well as themselves. And sometimes those families included men who were unable or unwilling to work—often manual workers maimed on the job or petty entrepreneurs who had failed in business. Temperance literature singled out still other men: they were the alcoholics who drank all they earned until they were fired or bankrupt and then earned not at all and still drank. Relatively little contemporary attention went to the repercussions on women of the increasing number of male urban workers who lost their jobs as a result of economic fluctuations, and who, unlike rural folk, had no homestead, garden patch, or cow to ease their families through hard times. Indeed, even those private letters and published stories that related the impact of business failure or unemployment on a man's family largely ignored the demand it made on wives and daughters to seek gainful employment.

Therefore, the letters of the very articulate Lydia Maria Child, chronicling a marriage strained by one financial crisis after another, are an unusual exploration of a working wife's responses to a husband consistently unable to support her. In her youth Maria—she was never called Lydia—was sufficiently schooled to become a teacher and at eighteen proclaimed her intention to be self-reliant and financially independent. After five years of successful teaching and one year after having published her first novel, *Hobomok*, she opened her own school just outside Boston. Three years later she married David Lee Child, a Harvard graduate who had gone to Spain in 1817 as secretary of the American legation, only to leave his post to fight in the unsuccessful revolution of 1823. No less quixotic when he returned to Boston, he read law, only to represent clients too poor to pay for his services. So, when they married in 1828, it was Maria who bought the furniture for their modest home. And it was Maria who supported them by editing and writing as David subtracted from their resources when, almost simultaneously, the paper he was editing failed and he was sued for libel. Even in their first year of marriage, Maria so feared "losing all the little" she had earned "by years of hard exertion" that she took in boarders, wrote constantly, and contemplated reopening her school.

Somehow they struggled through, sustained in part by her *Frugal Housewife*, written, so gossip had it, "to keep herself from starvation" and embodying her own housekeeping necessities. Then the Childs, who took part in William Lloyd Garrison's abolitionist campaign, grew still poorer, for in 1833 the publication of her controversial *Appeal on Behalf of that Class of Americans Called Africans* doomed her profitable popularity as an author. Romantics at heart, the Childs patched together enough to keep living in Boston, Maria still sure she preferred being David's wife "without a cent in the world, than to possess millions," until in 1838 David decided to fight slavery by raising sugar beets and refining "free labor" sugar in western Massachusetts. Unfortunately he proved to be as poor a farmer as he had been a lawyer and editor. Cut off from her life and friends in Boston, Maria became ever more desperate as she coped for three years in a house—little more than a shack—which was further crowded when her father, who, having provided the capital for the venture, came to live with them, albeit he soon left in disgust.[26]

Then she too left to edit the *National Antislavery Standard* in New York. Although she took the position as much to help the family exchequer as to further reform and gained little personal satisfaction—or money—from the venture, being alone for three years in New York made up for other deficiencies. So, when David, having lost his farm and gone through bankruptcy, came to New York to replace her as editor, Maria had reached the end of her patience. Writing to her close friend, lawyer, and longtime financial advisor Ellis Gray Loring, she asked him to separate her financial affairs from David's. "To pump water into a sieve *for* fourteen years is enough to break down the most energetic spirit. I must put a stop to it, or die."[27] For the rest of the 1840s, Maria lived alone, wrote her popular *Letters from New York*, and enjoyed a series of sentimental attachments to young men.

Finally, in 1850, Maria rejoined David on a small farm they bought together in West Newton, close to Boston. But when that also failed, they moved in with her father, who was, by then, a demanding invalid. "I have done building castles in the air," she observed as much of her isolation and lost independence as of her marriage. "All my dreams have settled into a stoical resignation to life, as it comes."[28] And that dead-end life, relieved somewhat by an inheritance from her father and the earnings that her renewed Civil War popularity brought, she lived and shared with David until he died in 1874. What differentiated her marriage to a husband who earned little and failed often from those of most other women in that predicament was that she was one of the lucky few whose work brought personal fulfillment and, occasionally, an income adequate to her needs.

Clearly Child was atypical for, besides having both talent and unusual opportunities to exert it, she had neither children to tie her to David's home nor a husband who refused to separate his finances from hers. For her, and for a number of actresses and other authors in both North and South, individual advantages and exertions opened paths closed to other women.

More characteristically, however, it was race and class that most determined women's vocational choices if they either wished or were compelled to gain their own livelihoods independent of the men in their families. Most severely limited were Charleston's slaves, though even they, if they were lucky, could mold the work expected of them to their abilities. Those with most choices were the relatively few who had the education, apprenticeship training, or capital resources to permit them to do work of intrinsic interest and also enjoy incomes sufficient to meet their obligations. Yet in almost all the occupations open to them, these women garnered fewer rewards—whether in pay or prestige or power—than did men. Generally it was the married women who worked unpaid in their own homes and were thus economically dependent on their husbands who enjoyed the greatest security and social prestige. On the other hand, those women who gained financial and personal autonomy through their own efforts were mostly spinsters or widows, although some few indeed were wives. Being a single mother of small children provided fewest alternatives to free women, even to those possessing more than basic household skills.

As urban dwellers, however, these women of Charleston and Boston had more occupational choices than did their rural contemporaries. Ironically, but also logically, it was in Charleston, where retail trade was scorned, that women's entrepreneurial opportunities were greatest and that unique laws routinely permitted feme sole traders to separate their business affairs completely from their husbands' control. And although Boston in the 1850s opened a women's medical college, it was in Charleston that the medical society voluntarily recognized midwives as part of their professional structure. Nonetheless, as a group all women had fewer choices than did all men. And whether they were financially dependent on men or not, overwhelmingly they did or oversaw housework wherever they lived.

4

Learning
and Teaching

Ic Charleston provided greater business opportunities
for females, it was Boston that most freely offered public schooling to girls and teaching opportunities to women. Indeed,
no arena better reflected regional cultural differences than did education. The importance that Bible-reading Protestantism had long given
to education in Massachusetts intersected in the nineteenth century
with commercial and manufacturing demands for a literate and nu-
merate work force, creating a combination that propelled the rapid
extension of free public schools from a groundwork already well
prepared. Traditional piety, women's increasing presence in the paid
work force; and, last but not least, the new public schools' demand for
an affordable teacher corps were strong forces for expanding female
education.

In Charleston, however, where traditional higher education was
just as venerated as in Boston, there was no comparable development.
The state legislature, responding to growing antiabolitionist fears in
the 1830s, extended its earlier prohibitions against teaching writing
to slaves to forbid their instruction in reading. Nor did state-funded
free schools, specifically reserved to the poor, encourage the city to
assume responsibility for a broader-based public system until 1856.
And those conditions, in turn, created only a limited demand for
women sufficiently educated to staff primary and grammar schools.

There was, furthermore, no consensus in either city about what
young women—and especially young ladies—should know, could
learn, and might profitably use. For their part, few Bostonians denied
that all citizens should be literate and that girls should have a good

general education. Here, in that American Athens, which in 1829 provided its sixty thousand residents a choice of thirty-four newspapers and twenty-five magazines, readers were valued. That very year, a ladies literary room was proposed, whose three-thousand-volume library soon provided women not only the latest literature but also the best in reviews, magazines, and journals. Here, Sarah Josepha Hale began her *Ladies Magazine*, written by as well as for females. Here lived many of those "lady scribblers," whose poems and stories Nathaniel Hawthorne scorned but whose commercial success he envied. But here too the aging Hannah Adams was reduced to poverty despite her multivolume history of New England, her extensive studies of religion, and her school history text, whose sales were undercut by questionable competition from the Reverend Jedidiah Morse.[1]

Not all Boston women were avid readers, and even fewer were writers. But many were visible in the city's intellectual life. They filled public lecture halls in even greater numbers than did men to hear the lyceum speakers who, in yearly series, provided a diverse if unsystematic program of adult education. A luckier and more select few improved their minds by attending Margaret Fuller's famous "Conversations" or the private lectures on English literature that Richard Henry Dana the elder presented to young ladies eager to cultivate their still-unshaped intellectual capacities. Indeed, Dana explicitly addressed the special needs of girls at that "period of life at which school instruction commonly ends," which seemed to him "to be that at which the regular study of our literature should begin."[2]

That there was no boundary to women's self-education is also evident. Young Frances Appleton, whose intellectual attainments as well as her father's wealth attracted her future husband, Henry Wadsworth Longfellow, recorded her year's reading in 1840. The list embraced such diverse writers as Cicero and Jared Sparks, Sir Francis Bacon and Mrs. Trollope. She read as well essays by John Locke, three Jane Austen novels, and the published letters of both Samuel Taylor Coleridge and Abigail Adams. That same year she began Dante's *Divine Comedy* and finished Goethe's *Faust* (however "vague, unsatisfactory, chaotic" and coarse all that German's work seemed to her).

Not so different was Mary Peabody, whose avid curiosity did nothing to impede Horace Mann's wooing and who believed that "no one has read more novels than I have, and novels of every description." Yet she also agonized over the romantic proclivities that she feared might have deterred her from more serious learning about "men and things" and thus have reduced her intellectual acumen.[3]

Was that a form of unconscious self-protection? Many men were put off by brainy women—no matter how romantic. The literary enthusiasm that attracted Professor Longfellow and State Education Commissioner Mann made merchant Amos Lawrence uneasy. His sister-in-law Katherine so kept his brother Abbott on the run with her overactivity that Amos felt obliged to warn his adolescent son against "the nonsense quackery that is *dignified with* the name of *intellectual*, among people" when "old *fashioned common sense* is a deal better." And historian-politician George Bancroft only scorned the "squad of blue-stockings" who dominated several Boston social circles. It is not surprising, therefore, that few men joined Unitarian cleric William Ellery Channing's lament that women harmed their minds by reading too much light fiction rather than headier and more serious works. And fewer, too, were those of either gender who commended Lydia Maria Child's praise of the "real love of reading," which would necessarily drive women to study the history and classical literature now so foreign to them.[4]

Because Frances Appleton and Mary Peabody defined one extreme of a spectrum that at the other included growing numbers of untutored immigrant women and their offspring, differences over women's appropriate education were not confined to private observations. During the 1820s and 1830s it was a significant political question as Boston sought to harmonize its public school system with newly perceived needs—both social and economic. It is true that public education was already well established in the city on a hill. By the 1790s its grammar schools were opened to girls as well as boys. Then in 1818, when public concern arose about the children whose parents could neither teach nor afford to pay others to teach their

The Franklin School, first established as a boys school in 1785, had become a public grammar school for girls only by the time this picture was published in the Boston Almanac for 1849. (Courtesy of the Massachusetts Historical Society)

children basic reading skills required for admission to the grammar schools, the city established public primary schools that, from their inception, were open to girls and boys alike.[5]

By the 1830s girls were as likely as boys to attend Boston's public schools. Moreover, girls were competing successfully for the Franklin medals that the city awarded to the most able and diligent pupils in the various grammar schools. But the studies so satisfying to medal winners like Edith Adams at the Hancock School, Sarah Mitchell at the Bowdoin Street School, Elizabeth Willard at the Adams School, and Lydia Sweetser at the Franklin School ended at the grammar school level.[6] Indeed, nowhere were the limits that prevailing ideas of woman's place set on educational opportunity better defined than in the debate over the short-lived public high school for girls.

That Boston should offer its boys advanced education was a long-honored commitment. The Latin school had been founded in the seventeenth century to prepare male youths for Harvard and the social and professional advancement that a college education then promised. Nearly 150 years later, and thirty years after the old Latin school had been reorganized as the Latin High School, Boston's commercial interests demanded a high school to provide courses more suited to careers in trade than the traditional classical preparation for Harvard. In 1821, therefore, the English High School opened its doors—but to boys only. Then, in a seemingly logical expansion, the school committee voted in 1825 "to place women in respect to education upon ground, if not equal, at least bearing a near and honorable relation to that of men." When the Girls High School opened the next year, it was unclear whether the resolution had intended only to prepare young women more extensively for their future roles as wives and mothers or had sought rather to create a source of teachers for its steadily expanding school system. In any case, competition for admission was fierce: 286 girls applied for its 133 places. And, under the respected administration of Ebenezer Bailey, the school's quality justified its popularity.[7]

Yet within two years its doors were shut when Major Josiah Quincy, the pioneer of Boston's remarkable reorganization of municipal government, challenged its practicality. His decision to close the school was openly political, one in which both class and gender assumptions played roles. In the Age of Jackson, Boston could justify spending as much as one-quarter of its total budget on education only on the grounds that its public schools served "the mass of the community." Yet more than half the students at the Girls High School came from privileged families who could afford to pay for their daughters' education elsewhere and, indeed, had already been doing so, for private school pupils had comprised the majority of those applying for admission. Why then should public funds be spent on them when the soaring costs of modern city government already alarmed economy-minded citizens?[8]

Responding to taxpayers' ire, the school committee tried through-

out the 1830s to stretch the educational budget and accordingly
embarked on experiments to lower expenditures for teachers' salaries.
One device popular at the time was the monitorial system. Under it,
more advanced students, supervised by the schoolmaster, instructed
their juniors in return for their own instruction. If it were adopted by
the public grammar schools, each school could either accommodate
more pupils for the same expenditure or cut costs by operating with
fewer assistant teachers. The existence of the Girls High School,
however, would curtail such a program, for it was just those girls who
left the grammar schools to attend the new high school who would
have been most qualified to assume the monitorial role. Regardless,
therefore, of any presumed educational virtues inherent in this so-
called Lancastrian system of learning by teaching, the school committee's experimentation with it, like their decision to close the Girls
High School itself, turned largely on economics.[9]

It was true that the annual cost of educating a girl in the high
school was only eleven dollars, compared with the twenty-eight dollars spent on a boy in the English High School or the thirty-one
dollars laid out for a lad attending the Latin High School. But how
could even eleven dollars be justified if spent to no public purpose?
Prevailing opinion held that public schools were there to prepare
young people for productive work lives. But unlike young men who
turned their advanced education to practical use in business and
professional careers, young women would, it was assumed, marry and
contribute nothing to the city's economic life. In short, the Girls High
School promised no economic return and, to make matters worse, it
was likely that with no career beckoning, girls would stay in high
school longer than would boys and thus impose an even greater as
well as a more unjustifiable burden on urban taxpayers.

Quincy had put the case clearly when he argued that a high
school education for girls was ornamental, for boys, practical. And it
was what fueled economic growth rather than individual fulfillment
that determined public school policy. When the subject came up
again, this same argument prevailed. In 1836 the common council
rejected reinstituting the Girls High School specifically on these

grounds. "The future destination of Boys, as to their pursuits and professions, among which may be reckoned services to the community in public stations, requires a difference in their preparation." That reason for maintaining high schools "does not apply. . . for Girls." So, however much class interests, democratic rhetoric, and republican values shaped the public school system, so too did gender. Females needed no higher education than that offered by grammar schools. Those "commodious buildings, with able and well educated teachers at their head," were open to girls from age seven to sixteen. They provided an "enlarged" range of studies, "all the learning, of a substantial character, necessary for a female in order to fill with dignity and propriety any station, however elevated, in domestic life."[10]

If class and gender intersected in the arguments over the high school, so too did they over coeducation. Unlike their rural contemporaries, whose schooling was still scheduled to comport with agricultural seasons—boys filling the schoolroom in winter and leaving it free for girls in the summer—Boston young people attended grammar schools together, though usually separated in the classes they attended. Until 1830 it was unquestioned policy that every grammar school employed both a reading and a writing master (each of whom was college educated and paid a salary of $1,200) as well as several male ushers (paid $600 each). While boys were taught by one master in his classroom, girls were instructed by the other. But as the number of schools increased to accommodate the growing numbers of youth attending them, budgetary pressures—and perhaps educational policy—dictated a single master; an assistant, paid $600; and other assistants, paid only $200 each. Built into this plan was a provision for single-gender schools to avoid mixing boys and girls approaching puberty in the same classroom. At least part of the rationale doubtless derived from the savings that filling all the assistant slots in the girls schools with women teachers would accomplish, for, while few men would teach for an annual salary of $250, that was the established pay for primary school teachers, all of whom were female. But in those wards that voted heavily Democratic and that were peopled primarily by artisans and laborers, the new plan was understood to threaten the quality of education offered their children. It was those wards that pressed the school committee hardest to retain the "old" system with two masters and two sexes in each school. The resolution of this debate reflected differing class priorities within a school committee still elected by wards. Except for South and East Boston, which each had school-age populations too small to fill more than one school, the city's only remaining coeducational grammar schools in 1845 comprised the all-Afro-American Smith School and five others in the predominantly working-class districts of the North and South End and around Fort Hill. The rest of the city was served by six grammar schools solely for boys and five exclusively for girls.[11]

The arguments offered by each side elaborated the interacting values rooted in class and gender concerns. Those who resisted gender segregation took the same ground as did those who, a few years later, challenged racial segregation. A group of petitioners argued in the fall of 1830 that if girls were forced to attend separate schools, they would have to go so far to attend classes that they would effectively be denied their right to a public school "within convenient distance" of their homes. Furthermore, the time spent in long treks to and from their classrooms would curtail the work that girls customarily performed at home—a service particularly important to humble families. So ending coeducation, like watering down the quality of schools long vaunted for enabling "every individual in the community, however poor, to have his son educated for the particular profession, or pursuit in life, for which his talents destine him," was a class issue. As for gender per se, proponents of the old way saw no reason why boys and girls should not attend the same schools.[12]

The largely middle- and upper-class proponents of the new plan, however, thought differently. It was only suitable, they argued, that young girls be taught by women—even though all-female grammar schools were to be headed by a master, not a mistress. So, too, it was clear to the innovators that girls required a gentler sort of discipline than did boys, a coddling that one hostile critic called "candy government and gingerbread apparatus." But why? These adolescent virgins, who were destined for the cult of domesticity if not the pedestal of ladyhood, must be preserved from the corruption that encountering boys, "not only rude in speech and manners, but of immoral dispositions and habits," might well entail. There was, so a school subcommittee reported in 1837, "an impropriety and danger of girls and boys, at an age approaching to that of maturity, going every day, for years, to the same school."[13] And in so protecting them it reinforced a new emphasis on female delicacy, the propriety symbolized by a pedestal elevating the ladylike above coarser males.

If such arguments framed the public school debate, they also underlay the success of private schools for older girls. Indeed, after as well as before the city so briefly provided them a public high school, the daughters of Boston parents who could afford school fees enjoyed a wide variety of alternatives. William Fowle's Monitorial School, with the support and blessing of Harvard professor George Ticknor, provided its older pupils practical courses in bookkeeping "suitable to the wants of American females," enabling them "to avoid the reproach, inconvenience, and loss to which females are so often exposed from their ignorance of accounts, and the ordinary transactions of business."[14] At the other extreme, there was the genteel finishing that M. and Mme Bonfils offered young ladies likely to use the social polish that their particular emphasis on reading and speaking French provided them. More in the male academic tradition, Harvard-educated Ebenezer Bailey pursued the direction he had set for the public Girls High School in his subsequent proprietary Young Ladies High School. There, young women might add to the usual branches of learning the study of Italian and Spanish as well as French. There, too, penmanship was more important than needlework and, although drawing was offered, dancing was not. At Mrs. Inglis's select school, advanced students thrived on astronomy, history, and elocution, they could choose among four modern languages, and they could learn Latin if they wished. Equally thorough but European in style and more traditionally female-oriented in content was the Ursuline Convent school in neighboring Charlestown, which attracted daughters of prominent Protestants.[15]

Although this is but a small sample of the private schools that provided Boston's most fortunate young women with educational opportunities generally reserved to their male peers, and although many girls spent the years between infancy and late adolescence attending such classes, the truth was that many others studied only intermittently and for brief periods. Critics were more right than wrong when they scorned the superficiality of women's education. Too often it focused on polishing young ladies' manners rather than providing their minds intellectual content. Too often it sent sixteen-year-olds off to the presumed real business of life—marriage and domesticity—ill prepared even for that restricted sphere. It was the exceptional private school that proved such critics wrong. Yet counterbalancing Catharine Beecher's complaint that most teachers purveyed superficialities, relied on rote recitations, and turned out pupils whose time and labor were "spent in acquiring what is lost about as fast as it is gained," was Hannah Jackson's complaint about the headmaster of her school. He had refused to allow her to concentrate on the subjects she preferred, arguing that her education must lay a foundation in various "branches of study" so that she could both discover her interests and be able to pursue them further on her own as an adult.[16]

Regionally determined values influenced the interplay of race, class, and status to produce a contrasting educational structure in Charleston. If in Boston black children were crowded into a single segregated school, in Charleston state law denied them access to any school. Moreover, slavery and the city's anxious response to growing northern abolitionism virtually precluded a school system designed for the universal basic education that would produce a literate work force associated, in the North, with economic growth. Charleston, therefore, spent its educational dollars to open its first public high school in 1839, a classical institution specifically intended to prepare boys for the College of Charleston, which the city had taken over in 1838. Thus attitudes nurtured by a slave society and the social structure it imposed significantly limited, however unintentionally, the educational alternatives it offered girls and young women. The half of the city's female population that was black was totally excluded because of race rather than gender. Very poor white girls, even if they attended the state-funded primary schools, had little hope of going further. Those who were orphans were somewhat more extensively instructed in the city-funded orphan asylum. The others who were white but neither poor nor orphans were, of course, not doomed to the illiteracy that was relatively more common in the South Atlantic states than in New England. But necessarily they relied on schools operated either by benevolent societies—a few of which were fully subsidized—or by private proprietors whose only income came from student fees. Yet however much such restrictions on women's education grew out of distinctive regional characteristics, female Charlestonians were also limited by commonly held views about the mental cultivation appropriate to their sex.[17]

In 1841 several correspondents, writing pseudonymously in the *Charleston Courier*, sketched the boundaries governing women's education there. Answering "Eugene's" denunciation of the city's vapid and ill-educated young women, "Pickwick" argued that "their education is not as much neglected as you seem to imagine." The young ladies of Charleston "read well, dance well and converse as brilliantly as your Boston favorites." The difference, he alleged, was that "they are not as 'blue,' . . . they make less parade of their attainments." Here, "Caroline," perhaps a Yankee bluestocking in disguise, entered the fray. "You are perfectly correct," she told Eugene, "in your remarks on the sad deficiency of our education, and by no means too 'sweeping.'" The problem, it seemed to her, lay with their city's institutions and values, for "there is not in the Union another city as large and as populous with so few facilities for women to acquire a 'finished education.'" Then, assessing the limited local alternatives, she continued. "You cannot more easily provoke the laugh of derision than to ask a man, who sincerely wishes his daughter to become an accomplished scholar, why he sends her away to school."[18]

The much respected lawyer James Petigru was a case in point. Yet his decision to send his eldest daughter to a New York finishing school and then bring her home after a single year illuminates the ambiguity with which even the most intellectual Charlestonians handled their daughters' schooling. Having sent his gifted child to New York for an education that he believed was superior to that which she could obtain at home, he nonetheless brought her back home when she was only fifteen. That she had learned much and well, Petigru admitted. Her music was well begun, her drawing was "very creditable," and her French was "beyond what she would have obtained at home." Still, he knew that her education was far from complete. "Fifteen," he admitted to his sister, "is not an age to finish one's education and in taking her from school I do wrong, and do it knowingly." And Caroline Petigru's world shrank accordingly.[19]

Even so, there was in the southern city persistent if institutionally unrealized support for women's intellectual cultivation and growth. In 1830 a reading room and library for ladies, modeled on a similar institution in Boston, was proposed, and the public press cheered it on as "highly useful and convenient for the purposes of literary improvement and social intercourse." A pseudonymous letter writer urged that a ladies literary society could only improve the tone of a city already blessed with more literary merit than any other in America. And although neither the literary society nor the reading room seems to have been established, the city did provide alternatives. Some women had access to the extensive private collections in the Charleston Library Society. Much more evident and extensive, they attended lyceum lectures in numbers proportionate to their Boston sisters. Moreover, there is considerable evidence to suggest that, in an age when natural history was the major activity of American scientists, southern women were unusually active collectors and classifiers. Henry Bruns, teacher at both the College of Charleston and the city high school, observed that the Misses Annely's shell collection was far superior to that of medical school professor Dr. Edmund Ravenel. Moreover, the "young ladies . . . knew all about their [shells'] history, and localities, and afforded me much information as well as amusement, as they pointed them out to me." The German scientist Frederick Leitner gave botany lectures at Mme Talvande's academy for young ladies while the German Friendly Society's female school provided its pupils the same scientific program and identical "philosophical apparatus" that made the courses in natural philosophy at their boys school distinctive.[20]

On the other hand, in scientific as in literary pursuits, prevailing opinion insisted that such study not interfere with women's proper domestic sphere. A "Friend to Female Education" argued that girls should study chemistry because, unlike ancient languages or political controversy, it was a branch of revealed religion as well suited to female as to male minds in giving "an expanded and elevated idea of our Creator, who, in the air we breathe, and the light we enjoy in the regulation of the Animal, Vegetable, and Mineral Kingdoms" has made a "harmonious whole." And even author Caroline Gilman, who, in praising a girls school that not only taught Latin and Greek but chemistry, astronomy, and botany, openly challenged "the masculine gender['s] . . . dominion over the realms of science and literature," did so in the context that such study would promote "domestic peace and improvement" by providing "intelligent companions for life, who will adorn and dignify [men's] homes."[21]

It was that wifely justification that, in the eyes of Sarah Grimké, undermined the very learning it allegedly promoted. Born to a socially prominent Charleston family and seemingly destined to marry and marry well, she had been allowed to share in her brother's study of mathematics, geography, history, Greek, and natural sciences as well as to undertake the more traditional girl's fare of French, singing, and fancy needlework. Moreover, her practical mother had insisted on her daughter's acquiring the household skills necessary for running a large domicile and supervising its slaves. But to the rebellious Sarah, it was a "butterfly" education, one made "miserably deficient" because, like the other young women of her class, she was "taught to regard marriage as the one thing needful, the only avenue to distinction." Those as well educated as she soon found "that where any mental superiority exists, a woman is generally shunned and regarded as stepping out of her 'appropriate sphere,' which . . . is to dress, to dance, to set out to the best possible advantage her person, [and] to read the novels which inundate the press, and which do more to destroy her character as a rational creature, than any thing else." Indeed, even middle-class women in the southern city were "brought up with the dangerous and absurd idea, that *marriage* is a kind of preferment" and trained to acquire a husband in ways that "necessarily exalt[ed] . . . the animal above the intellectual and spiritual nature." As a result women came "to regard themselves as a kind of machinery, necessary to keep the domestic engine in order."[22]

Though it was a bitter analysis of woman's lot, there was much truth in it. Anna Hayes Johnson, who wrote out of immediate experience rather than with Grimké's mature reflection, complained to her cousin that a girl had only to appear to have intellectual interests to acquire the "bar blue" and be neglected by every eligible young man. "I verily believe," she commented wryly, "that you have nothing more to do than to start a literary subject to make them run from you as if you had the plague." And so, despite those who would have had it otherwise, most female Charlestonians were educated according to their city's *Gospel Messenger's* encomium that "home is the sphere of woman." Indeed, that Episcopal journal contended that only necessity should cause a girl to be sent to a day school rather than pursue her education at home and that only necessity most dire should separate her from her family by an exile in boarding school. It was a value system shared by Charles Fraser, lawyer, trustee of the College of Charleston, amateur painter—and a bachelor. Women's education, he wrote, should be directed only "to the development of the moral and intellectual qualities suitable to the becoming discharge of the peculiar duties designed for them by nature." Though this might encompass some study of literature, history, and geography, it would be unnatural for a woman to achieve "literary distinction," for it was a self-evident truth that "for every success [thus] obtained some appropriate duty has been neglected."[23]

Thus even parents who could afford to send their daughters to the schools that would challenge their minds hesitated to do so. Young girls like Harriott Horry Rutledge, who preferred the study of Latin and ancient history to playing with dolls because "it has life and spirit in it" as no "pretty smiling doll" ever did, caused aunts to worry. Yet even for young rebels, the likelihood that they would conform as they reached the age to be courted was great. And, as soon as they married, as an unsympathetic character in Susan Petigru King's *Lily* pontificated, even the remnants of their schooling would vanish as they would inevitably "shut the piano, never open a French book, give their paints away, and might a great deal better have had all the money spent on these accomplishments put in the Savings Bank instead." So a real father might, like Mr. Wilton in Caroline Gilman's novel of southern courtship, be happy to have a daughter learn from a talented teacher, but he would be equally well "satisfied" just to pay "round sums of money for [her] education."[24]

Not many papas, of course, had the round sums to dole out for their daughters' education. Those girls who were very poor but white could attend one of the state-funded free schools, which re-mained relatively unchanged in nature and number from their initia-tion in 1811 until a new state law passed in 1852 opened the way for a more inclusive city public school system, begun in 1856. Therefore, throughout the 1820s, 1830s, and 1840s free schools taught only the 250 to 550 pupils each year whose parents complied with a means test. Moreover, unlike Boston, where roughly half the public school pupils were female, only one-third to two-fifths at any one time were girls. Taught in coeducational surroundings (in 1841 one school— apparently the single grammar school—was set apart for boys only), these charity schools did provide a basic primary education in read-ing, spelling, arithmetic, grammar, and geography to students who, on average, attended them for five years.[25]

In sum, the free schools of Charleston instructed, at most, some 20 percent of the city's white children—or less than 10 percent of all children from five to fifteen—while Boston's public schools educated about 55 percent of its school-age population. And within those populations, girls in the southern city were disadvantaged both pro-portionately to their total numbers and in being absolutely excluded from the municipally supported high school and college, which, in this respect at least, was not unlike Boston. Even in the city-funded orphan asylum school, girls, after they mastered the three "r's," completed their education with instruction in domestic arts, while their male equivalents, largely destined for artisanal apprenticeships, were introduced to other academic subjects of potentially practical use to them. So it was that while boys at the orphan house might continue in the classroom until the age of fourteen, girls attended only until they were twelve.[26]

Yet here as elsewhere class advantages varied the regional patterns. Charleston girls whose parents had some, if only moderate, means fared considerably better in schools operated and subsidized by private social clubs. The Fellowship Society used income from its $50,000 endowment to operate a coeducational primary school. In the 1820s the South Carolina Society, which had previously operated a similar school, replaced it with academies offering secondary-level education to both boys and girls. While its female academy did not offer the classical languages and mathematics available in the boys school, it nonetheless provided an English education the equivalent of that offered young males. But, although they were subsidized by annual grants from the society ranging from $1,500 to $2,500, these schools did charge tuition fees according to whether or not pupils' fathers were society members and whether or not the pupils were orphans. But in all categories, girls paid a quarter less than did boys—perhaps because their teachers were paid less.[27]

The situation was somewhat different at the German Friendly Society's academies, where the male teacher of the female academy was paid more than his alter ego in the boys school even though tuition for both schools was the same. Whatever that implied, even here the curricula differed with Latin and Greek reserved for the boys, albeit the commitment of John Bachman, pastor of the German Lutheran church, to science largely eliminated other distinctions. In any case, as the society's minutes read, if education for boys was "an advantage & a Credit to the Society," then a girls school could not "fail to be equally so, since we consider the education of Daughters who are required to fulfil the various relative Duties of life, as of equal importance with that of Sons."[28]

However much ethnic and religious proclivities shaped an unusual gender egalitarianism in the German Friendly Society schools, the tight control that Bishop John England wielded over Catholic schools had different results. It was he who directed the largely Irish Sisters of Charity of Our Lady of Mercy to limit their teaching to subjects suitable for females of the "middling classes of society"— whether they were tuition-paying students or inmates of their society's orphanage. But it was clearly to acquire social polish that young ladies were sent to the Ursuline academy, a school every bit as expensive as any private school in the city. Their papas paid dearly to "finish" their daughters in foreign languages (including the Latin of their liturgy); in musical performance on piano, harp, or guitar; and in that giveaway to the decorative superficiality of such institutions, painting on velvet.[29]

Then there were the private proprietary schools—some of which lasted less than a year, a few of which spanned decades. Reflecting an understanding that schools lay primarily in the private sector and following as well the commercial pattern that encouraged women to engage in small-scale entrepreneurial ventures, Charleston spawned a profit-oriented educational structure in which teachers of both sexes and varied specialties competed openly for students. A few, like the Female Seminary and the Institute for Young Ladies, were corporate, with trustees drawn from the city's clerical and secular leadership. Some with a religious orientation, like that of Episcopal priest J. Stuart Hankel, who taught the higher branches of female education "on Christian principles," or Miss Lopez's school, which was kept in Beth Elohim synagogue, had at least a loose connection with a denomination.[30] But mostly the private schools were wholly owned and directed by one or more individuals acting independently. More often than not situated in rented rooms or private homes, they might be operated by a man but more frequently by a woman or sometimes by a family group—a married couple, a widow and her daughters, a pair of sisters. These schools were minimally capitalized, and the constantly changing complement of self-proclaimed teachers who operated them glutted the market, advertising their wares in a stream of newspaper advertisements. Mr. and Mrs. King, strangers to town, first opened their school in rooms above Hussey's Bookstore, then moved it around the corner to a private house in which, for several years, they ran their Seminary for the Education of Young Ladies, which offered a program of music, drawing, modern languages, mathematics, and elocution. Longer lasting was John Bruen's school at his Pitt Street residence, where he taught young ladies the "branches of an ENGLISH education," while his employee, a M. J. J. Delissa, instructed them in the "Oral and Louvanian system of the French language." Mrs. Murden, a longtime teacher in the Fellowship Society school, was, soon after opening her own school, sufficiently patronized to erect a building specifically designed for the establishment that she and her daughters operated. Indeed, the structure may have been its strong point for she advertised "large and airy" rooms and gardens "sufficiently spacious to allow exercise and recreation to the Boarders within the enclosure."[31]

Other schools were so short-lived that they are difficult to place in any setting. R. McHelm, probably escaping the failure of his former Poughkeepsie, New York, Collegiate Institute, set up a Charleston academy in 1841 to provide a practical education emphasizing penmanship and double-entry bookkeeping for young women. Lucy Holmes was obviously struggling to make ends meet when she advertised not only the English education her seminary offered but also her boarding facilities for students attending competing schools. The Misses Stewart, recently arrived from Scotland in 1842, supplemented income from their regular boarding school in the city by offering summer courses in French, music, and drawing at the nearby summer resort of Sullivan's Island. And so it went as Mrs. H. Blome, Mrs. Jones and Mrs. Prince, Messrs. B. Jenkins and J. Rosenfeld, and myriad others proffered their educational wares through the local press.[32]

For Charleston girls this meant a wide variety not only of offerings but of price tags, but with no guarantee of quality, be their education scientific, business, plain English, academic, or genteel finishing. Yet there was consensus that a few schools whose French proprietors gave them special strength in language instruction were the equal if not the superior of most northern institutions. James Campbell, former Brown University student, a lawyer, and a somewhat prickly Yankee migrant to the South, wrote his sister that were she to visit him, she could attend "a French school much better than any in Boston even."[33]

Two schools, each run by Santo Domingan refugees, stood above all others. Julia Datty, who had come to Charleston after the Haitian revolution, maintained her school until the early 1830s, when she joined the Sisters of Charity of Our Lady of Mercy and organized their school. Thereafter Mme Talvande's was unique until 1850 in its reputation for excellence. Best remembered as the institution that Mary Boykin Chesnut, the diarist, attended, the school was described in letters home from the thirty or so boarders that it accommodated each year along with its Charleston day pupils. There they learned their French and music, their drawing and dancing, a little better than their English, geography, astronomy, or history. But study them all they did. And parents willingly paid the "round sums" Mme Talvande charged. William Kincaid, whose daughters Nancy and Rebecca were boarders in 1831, paid $420.875 for five and a half months of entrance fees, tuition, board, washing, books, play tickets, concert admissions, spending money, and other requisites of a private education. Compared with the South Carolina Society's Female Academy fees of twenty-eight dollars for half a year, the expense was great. But as Charleston factor Alexander Robertson observed, "Mad T's is the best school," however much he, as a staunch Episcopalian, had religious reservations. He advised that city girls attending the school live at home, for Mme Talvande had "too many Catholic priests about her . . . performing Mass rather too often for me."[34]

Charleston parents who did send their daughters to boarding schools generally chose ones either in the North or nearer to home in the South Carolina up-country. Finishing schools in Philadelphia or New York were social meccas for the parents who could afford them; Episcopal bishop George Washington Doane's St. Mary's Hall in rural New Jersey perhaps seemed safer to those with strong religious ties.

The Barhamville Academy, known for its extensive curriculum and academic rigor, attracted girls from throughout South Carolina to its campus near Columbia. (Courtesy of the South Caroliniana Library)

But probably most Charleston girls who left home to attend school went no farther than their native state. Nor did their education necessarily suffer from that choice. Dr. Elias Marks's no-nonsense South Carolina Female Institute in Barhamville, near the state capital, was among the most demanding. Married first to a Charleston native, Julia Barham, and then to Troy Female Seminary graduate, Julia Pierpont Warne, Marks, with his wife, operated the school, which he had founded in 1820. By 1832 it had the faculty to offer nearly thirty courses embracing classical languages, science, and mathematics as well as the more customary modern languages and the standard reading and writing of an "English" education. If, in the depression years following the panic of 1837, families strained to pay the $200 to $400 tuition fees for a year at the school, charges varying according to the courses taken, its cost compared favorably with the $500 to $600—in addition to travel expenses—that Miss Binsee's much-patronized New York academy charged. Moreover, Barhamville's commitment to an academic education so solid that its scientific curriculum embraced chemistry, botany, geology, and astronomy reflected a respect for women's intelligence and their need for intellectual discipline as they assumed adult responsibilities in a society they were bound to influence either directly or indirectly. Responsive to Marks's insistence on understanding over rote memorization or "polite learning," students might, however, complain about the food or the school's isolation. But young Miss McAliley—who did so—went on to confess that she puzzled and fretted over her lessons so much that she had little free time, but that she really enjoyed what she was doing. Her observations in 1852 echoed sentiments of one predecessor who had admitted that she worked hard sometimes "because I wished to please my teachers and parents and again because I thought I would show off when I was grown." But best of all, "I have sometimes studied because I loved to."[35]

Nor was Marks alone in trying to create this milieu. Mary Bates (whose father had presided over Vermont's Middlebury College) established a seminary for girls in Pendleton, South Carolina, where she struggled valiantly against the "butterfly" pressures that had so bothered James Petigru when he withdrew his daughter from school long before her education was finished. Herself a product of the schooling available in the best northern academies, Bates implicitly criticized the social pressures propelling immature girls toward early marriage. Writing in 1843, she noted the "difficulties of a peculiar nature" that impeded girls' education in the South. "The early age at which many scholars are taken from school, ere the mind has reached maturity, is a source of deep regret to those who feel the value of a systematic course of education." By contrast, New England's daughters "are now reaping its benefits, while the equally gifted children of the South are too often interrupted in the early stages of education, and thrust into society, long before they are qualified to adorn it."[36]

Many women, however, were thrust into the adult world not to adorn society but to earn their daily bread and support either children or other family members. For them, learning readily marketable skills was crucial. In both cities public-spirited citizens recognized this need, yet in neither did either private or public institutions offer such instruction to more than a small number of those who needed it. The Charleston Orphan House, like the Boston Female Asylum, bound out young girls in their charge to learn housework. The former also employed a seamstress to teach the skilled sewing that would enable those who left its shelter to do tailoring, millinery work, and the dressmaking that Harriet Martineau believed was "almost the only employment in which a white Southern woman [could] earn a subsistence." But the Boston institutions giving sewing lessons prepared both children and adults to sew the ready-made clothing that was least likely to produce incomes above mere subsistence. On the other hand, the city missions and similar church programs as well as the Seaman's Aid Society reached many more women, and the latter also provided a nonprofit slop shop, which sold the sailors clothing their students made and thereby raised their wages. Nevertheless, the persistent destitution of seamstresses in an oversupplied labor market nullified the good intentions of most such occupational training.[37]

Additionally there was little instruction in the practical business affairs that women of all classes needed to manage their household budgets. Louisa Lee Waterhouse, wife of a Boston physician so impractical that she had to conduct almost all the family's business affairs, lamented this deficiency. Spurning Latin and Greek as useless, she argued the centrality of "Arithmatic [sic]—which is always wanted, *every where* & in every station [for m]ost women . . . cannot make to advantage the necessary purchases for their families or themselves, because of their slow calculation." And, more specific to her own class and condition, she lamented that women were "not sufficiently instructed in the management and care of Property. . . . How many wives [there are] of thriftless or more literary husbands who are thrown into a state of dependence & awkwardness by not understanding what is commonly called *business*, & they must pay others to do what they ought to do for themselves, & what they are as well able to do as men." Indeed, even a knowledge of banking and commerce would be useful, for "a woman by knowing the risks to which property is liable, would be more careful in spending it." And spinster author Catharine Sedgwick pressed publicly for a business education that would prepare women for jobs more remunerative than sewing.[38] Because, however, women were more likely to be shopkeepers or clerks in Charleston, it was there, rather than in Boston, that classes in bookkeeping and commercial writing were more available to women.

But of the jobs widely available to women, teaching was paramount in applying school learning to employment. This was especially so in Boston where the expanding public school system created an ever-increasing demand for teachers and where in 1838 all the primary school teachers and two-thirds of all grammar school teachers were female. Even here, however, the question of how teachers should be taught to teach was an issue. In 1838, Boston's school committee rejected point-blank a proposal for a city-operated normal school—perhaps because its teacher turnover rate was nearly 40 percent per annum. Yet it did institute special classes, lectures, and teachers' meetings to discuss pedagogical matters. And it willingly accepted instruction in special courses sponsored by the Boston Academy of Music.[39] Nonetheless, its primary reliance was on girls whose formal education was completed in the public grammar schools. It is true that young women aspiring to teach in the grammar schools were urged to attend the normal schools that Massachusetts initiated with an all-female institution in Lexington, and a number of them did so. But they were also excluded from the college education that qualified men—and men only—to administer those schools.

Because, however, it was almost the only profession open to females and because it provided a more nearly adequate income than most other options available to them, teaching attracted women to its ranks. It was true that the $200 to $250 paid women teachers in Boston schools was but a third of the salary paid their male colleagues. Yet it was also four times as much as a seamstress was likely to earn and somewhat better than the wages generally paid skilled female workers in the city. And it was fully compatible with the cult of republican motherhood, which assigned to women the exclusive care of and responsibility for training young children. So, if it is not surprising that by 1860 2 percent of all native-born white women in Massachusetts between the ages of fifteen and sixty were teaching school, the fact that one in every five had, at some time in her life, done so strongly testifies to the role that education played in molding the lives of Yankee women. Nonetheless, long-term professional commitment was far less common. For most, teaching was an occupation pursued for only a few years. Yet if a teacher was sufficiently qualified and enterprising and if she also had a good reputation, operating her own school could produce, even in Boston, earnings uncommon for women. Anna Jackson made $1,500 in a single year. Caroline Weston ran a school that, over a ten-year period, brought her nearly $15,000.[40] Such women made teaching a profession and running a school an entrepreneurial venture. In so doing they achieved autonomy by their own efforts. But they were very few in number.

Because in Charleston the city employed no more than three female teachers in the free schools and two in the orphan house, the numbers engaged in public school teaching were minuscule compared to Boston. Indeed, in one ten-year period, only four women taught in the state-supported free schools. On the other hand they enjoyed longer tenure and were also better paid than their Boston equivalents, earning $750 a year.[41] Consequently, it was in the private sector that women teachers came and went with great rapidity and that many earned too little to continue. In stark contrast to Mme Talvande's fabulous school, which lasted for some forty years, was the short-lived and troubled school that Mary Hort ran. A middle-aged woman who had come to Charleston in 1842 after her Florida school had folded, Hort lacked the personal characteristics as well as the public connections to succeed. Obese and frequently depressed, she spent three harrowing years attempting to run a day school. Constantly moving from one location to another, always pressed to find enough students to fill the classes, or, when they did materialize unexpectedly, seldom successful in finding a suitable assistant, she was so badly in debt when she left town to teach in a Mr. DuBose's country school that she had to sell the piano she had brought with her from Florida. Recognizing that her personal problems—"self-indulgence," "worldliness and vain-glory," and "habitual irritability"—had contributed to her defeat, she also blamed parents unwilling to make a lasting commitment to their children's education and their long delays in paying tuition fees.[42]

Between the two extremes of Talvande and Hort were the many good, solid teachers who did their work well, were respectable members of the community, and earned a decent if not a generous living. It was of them that James Petigru wrote his sister: "To be the governess of a respectable female school, . . . although not the very highest prize in the lottery of life, nor even the most brilliant part which a woman may play under the democracy, (when a very invidious distinction is made by excluding them from the benefits of the general suffrage,) is nevertheless after all depreciating considerations of that kind, still an honorable independency."[43]

How an individual girl was schooled and the uses to which she later put that schooling were determined in part by broad underlying cultural characteristics of the city in which she lived. The degree to which education was either primarily a public responsibility or a parental obligation reflected value systems of which it was but a part. Boston's positive commitment to economic growth dependent on a knowledgeable labor force led both to its spending as much as a quarter of its city budget to provide an elementary education free to all and to its denying girls access to any public high school. It also provided an American schooling for the growing number of immigrants' children, designed to control their youthful behavior and assure their assimilation into the work force as self-supporting adults. To insure that this process would be long lasting, it not only educated future fathers and voters but also future mothers and teachers, who only thus would be equipped to instill American virtues in the children they both taught. Within this broad social context, a girl and her parents made choices reflecting the size of their purse as well as their personal aspirations.

In Charleston, where the labor of half the city's population was involuntary, where the transformation of black slaves into economically independent workers and responsible citizens was not a goal, and where universal literacy threatened rather than reinforced stability, education was shaped accordingly. Here self-conscious ethnic and social organizations more often assumed responsibility for teaching their members' children—perhaps with less immediate insistence on assimilation than on positive respect for diversity. And because there were few free tax-supported schools and others charged tuition, the purse and aspiration of a girl and her parents were somewhat more consequential in shaping her education. But in both cities, the education of young females was shaped more by public policy and private preference than by pursuit of social justice or gender equality. Girls in both cities had fewer and different educational options than their brothers—differences that reflected as much as they perpetuated their more limited choices of the work they would do as adults. Consequently they contributed also to making marital choice a greater determinant of all aspects of life for women than for men.

As Massachusetts author Catharine Sedgwick argued, however, it was also education that could free a woman from the restrictions imposed by men's control over the public sphere and women's consignment to the private sphere. Yet she, no more than James Petigru, proposed revolutionary change when she urged girls between ten and sixteen to pursue their education with vigor. Those who married and had children, she told them, needed to learn not just domestic economy but that more extensive knowledge that would "enable them to unfold the minds, and preserve and fortify the health of their children." Those who inherited property, she continued, needed to know how to manage it. Those who remained single and had no property must use their education to be self-supporting. In all cases, it was education that promised women the tools with which to lead a life of their own. Unmarried herself and addressing especially those who would never marry, she nonetheless limned a truth for all women. With a good education, she promised, "you will not be the *old maid* touched by every ill word, and dependent on every chance kindness, but you will secure an independent existence, and the power of dispensing to others."[44]

Chances are that Charleston teenager Minnie Hooper never read Sedgwick's *Means and Ends of Self-Training*, but she sensed its message in her own experience. Thanking her "dear papa" for the money he had spent sending her to boarding school, she justified this temporary dependence as the necessary preparation for an autonomy she hoped would enable her to assist "my dear parents by my own exertions. . . . In Nov[ember] or a little later I shall if I can get scholars & commence *teaching* directly and *thank you a thousand times for thus putting it in* my power to earn a subsistence[.] How much I shall rejoice to [be] independent and to cease to be a burthen."[45] In its psychological effects at least, the self-respect with which education endowed well-taught women could overcome regional and even class disparities.

5

Property,
Privilege,
and Power

No matter what her self-image, a woman's ability to retain, use, or bequeath the property she had either earned or inherited was, like contracting or dissolving her marriage and gaining or losing custody of her children, limited by laws that vested familial authority in men. Being part of a wealthy or simply prestigious family generally endowed daughters, wives, and sisters with social privilege denied the less fortunate. Owning significant property, more likely inherited than earned, empowered women to fund philanthropies, reward—or punish—family members, or simply enjoy financial independence. Yet, in all these respects, they were more restricted by public law as well as by customary usages than were men. The ways in which they altered or circumvented those restrictions were also as varied and complex as their circumstances. Among kin and between spouses, the personalities and priorities of individual women doubtless molded family politics. But when that failed and women had to confront a legal structure that gave men both the power and responsibility to support and govern their wives and children, they necessarily acquired a new understanding of how private and public spheres interacted.

Nowhere was this clearer than in matters of property law. Early-nineteenth-century American usage was largely fixed by Blackstone's dictum that in marriage the husband and wife were one—and that one was the husband. This was coverture, the legal doctrine that at marriage a woman ceased to be an independent legal entity and that, consequently, her property was his. But, like most else in the law, changing social values as well as the increasing importance of equity jurisprudence and the passage of new statutes encroached on the common law tradition. The widow's traditional claim on her husband's estate, enshrined in dower rights, was steadily lessened in response to changing economic priorities imposed by growing commerce and industry as well as by new social values that increasingly favored a man's children over his wife.

As judges handed down new interpretations of coverture shaped by the economic and cultural imperatives of their distinctive jurisdictions, legislatures too responded to pressures for and against redefining women's property rights and extending their access to separation, divorce, and alimony.[1] Some of the changes benefited women; others only subverted traditional protections. In either case, their overall impact challenged old assumptions. Even in South Carolina, where agricultural values continued to dominate the economy, John C. Calhoun's observation in 1811 that, in marrying, a wife placed "both her honor and property" in her husband's custody had long been only partially true. And in Massachusetts, where the pace of economic change was both swifter and more overt, so too was the pace of legal change affecting women. Yet, as Marylynn Salmon has observed, women in both situations "often chose not to utilize the safeguards designed for their benefit," especially when those safeguards involved separating their property from that of their husbands.[2]

The fact remains, however, that some women—generally only a fortunate few—did use the law to maintain control of a property sufficient to guarantee them autonomy regardless of their marital status. Others resorted to marital separation and divorce to free themselves from a husband's economic as well as physical control. And, if it was more often the rich than the poor, the propertied rather than wage-earning women, who so benefited, there were also less privileged women who used the legal devices available to them to enhance their power both within their homes and outside them.

For women, the laws governing marriage, separation, and divorce were of vast personal importance because marital status shaped the whole of their lives far more than it did men's. Yet, despite society's common prescription that matrimony and motherhood defined women's full role, South Carolina and Massachusetts laws governing marriage differed markedly.[3] Because the former did not recognize binding legal ties between slaves, half of Charleston's female population lacked both the legal protection and the subjection to a husband that marriage promised. And, although white owners and black associates alike recognized long cohabitation as a special tie that imposed obligations on both partners, they also assumed that a forced separation cleared the way for each partner to enter another such union. In Massachusetts, on the other hand, society generally followed the courts in denying any legitimacy to a union, no matter what its duration, when it had not been contracted according to law.

When it came to divorce, the patterns were equally dissimilar. In New England, where Puritans had defined marriage as a civil contract rather than a religious sacrament, secular law had provided for divorce even in the seventeenth century. Like any other contract, the marriage bond could be broken when either of the contracting parties failed to meet the obligations it imposed. In 1786, in fact, state law specifically empowered Massachusetts courts to grant absolute divorce with the right to remarry if the suit of one spouse could demonstrate adultery, impotence, desertion, or conviction for serious crimes on the part of the other. Moreover, wives, though not husbands, could obtain a divorce on the grounds of nonsupport.

It was not until 1868, however, that South Carolina granted a divorce with the right to remarry. Yet neither a strong, religiously based understanding that marriage was an eternally binding tie nor a secular culture rooted in male honor and female dependence barred the state from providing some relief in the case of an unbearably bad marriage. An 1822 statute provided for divorce from bed and board in cases of "intolerable ill-temper" or adulterous behavior in either of the parties. Furthermore, a wife so abused might, at the discretion of the court, be awarded alimony. Yet this meant only separation within a continuing marriage. Eleven years later, Judge John Belton O'Neall pointedly ruled that "the marriage contract, in this State, is regarded as indissoluble by any human means." And in 1847 he emphatically reasserted that the court must follow the prevailing popular consensus that marriage was a divinely sanctioned institution. How could courts do otherwise when the legislature uniformly refused to annul the marriage tie by private bill even when "the most distressing cases, justifying divorce . . . upon scriptural grounds, have been . . . presented"? Surely the courts could do no less for, as O'Neall intoned, "the working of this stern policy has been to the good of the people and the State, in every respect."[4]

Yet, even when the law apparently offered no relief, some women not only extricated themselves from intolerable marriage ties but also occasionally managed to defy the enshrined principle that the father was the natural, and thus the sole, legal guardian of his offspring. The saga of Ellen Sears D'Hauteville, unique though it probably was, attests to a rather startling elasticity when the law was confronted by a determined woman of property and powerful family connections.

Taking the grand tour in 1837 with her father, David Sears, a Boston merchant with extensive real estate holdings, her mother, an heir to the great Mason fortune, her two brothers, and a sister, eighteen-year-old Ellen was the epitome of innocence abroad. And her being laid low in Paris by an extended bout of rheumatic fever probably only increased her vulnerability to the polished attention of a European suitor. Attracted to Paul Daniel Gonsalve Grand D'Hauteville, a Swiss Protestant, who would, reputedly, inherit the title of baron and, more immediately, receive a marriage settlement of a million francs, Ellen succumbed to the romance of Paris in the spring. Furthermore, her parents' ostensible commitment against "interfering with [their] children's affections in matters of marriage"[5] and, perhaps even Mrs. Sears's fascination with having a titled son-in-law helped create a new world for their naïve daughter. Yet, when Gonsalve first proposed, Ellen refused to commit herself. Only when his parents arrived in town and pressed his suit did she accept him.

Then followed a period in which the parents negotiated and Ellen equivocated. David Sears, aware of European practice in such matters, insisted on the marriage portion he had understood was to be Gonsalve's; but the elder D'Hauteville refused to increase his smaller proffered settlement and consequently broke off the engagement. Troubled at this turn, her father pressed Ellen to state her real feelings. "Astonished . . . at the depth of the impression which her heart ha[d] received," he backed down on his demand for the marriage contract he had originally expected, sure that the D'Hauteville parents could "do a great deal" and that "they will do it—not by contract, perhaps, but by voluntary contribution."[6]

So plans for an August wedding at the Swiss family's estate in Vevey went forward despite David Sears's growing awareness that the D'Hauteville property to be settled on their son was, even nominally, worth only a fourth of its rumored value and, still worse, produced an annual income of barely $1,600. Neither that nor the $20,000 that Sears gave the couple in their marriage contract promised the young couple the life-style he believed was appropriate. So, for the twelve years before the trust fund he had already established for Ellen would begin to pay her $2,000 a year, her father committed himself to provide an annual stipend to enable the young couple to spend their winters in Paris—an arrangement not included in the marriage contract but made to meet Ellen's expressed need to be part of the American community abroad.[7]

Even so, just before the marriage took place, Ellen anticipated a homesickness so intense that Gonsalve released her from her engagement. It was only the elder D'Hauteville's report that the break had made his son gravely ill that made Ellen relent. And to assuage her sense of ominous isolation, Mrs. Sears and the other children arranged to spend the next six months at Vevey to keep Ellen company. Whether the newly married couple would have made their own adjustments without such interventions by their parents is an open question. As it turned out, however, the marriage was an unhappy one. Pregnant by January, depressed by her mother-in-law's domination of Gonsalve, and angered by the D'Hauteville family's rudeness to Mrs. Sears, Ellen insisted that Gonsalve honor their premarital agreement to spend the winter in Paris—where her mother would also be. The elder D'Hautevilles, contending that there was no such agreement, announced that both generations would winter in Geneva.

Amid considerable stress, therefore, Ellen returned with her family to Paris while Gonsalve remained in Geneva to be with his ostensibly ailing father. Yet, within weeks and without prior notice, he arrived in Paris and ordered Ellen to be ready to leave with him the next day for Switzerland. Fearing that her husband would kidnap her if she resisted, Ellen took shelter in the home of Lewis Cass, the American minister to France and a family friend.

The young D'Hautevilles' marriage was thus already a cause célèbre before Ellen sailed for America with her family in late May. Although her husband had spent the spring living in the Sears's Paris apartment, he had insisted that, except for meals, Ellen spend her every minute with him alone. His view of spousal relations was that the wife must "conform to the views of her husband." And because he was "responsible before God for the happiness and conduct of [his] wife," he thought it his "duty to address sharp reproaches to her, so long as she shall not live for her husband above every thing else." Under this regime Ellen had grown pale and thin and, in the opinion of her uncle, the eminent Boston physician John C. Warren, would either die or go insane if it continued.[8] Faced with this diagnosis, Gonsalve reluctantly had agreed to Ellen's going home to have her baby—but had refused to accompany her.

Although, when she had left, both assumed that Ellen would return after the baby was born, a month at home freed Ellen to declare her independence. Almost at the very instant that Gonsalve was writing David Sears and asserting that when Ellen returned to Switzerland she must confide in him alone for only thus would he be "master in my own house,"[9] Ellen was writing that she would never, under any circumstances, return to that house. Although Gonsalve instructed that the baby be baptized Alois in a Presbyterian church, Ellen, shortly after his birth in September 1838, had the child christened Frederic in the Episcopal church. The summer following Frederic's birth, when Gonsalve arrived in Boston without notice to collect his wife and son, Ellen heard of his pending arrival and disappeared to her family's summer home in Nahant. And when Gonsalve arrived there, she had already moved again. By June 1840, she was living in

Philadelphia because Pennsylvania law favored the mother's guardianship when a child was still an infant. So it was there that D'Hauteville
sought the writ of habeas corpus that would enable him to assume his
son's guardianship and remove him to Switzerland—with or without
his mother.[10]

In public hearings, which dragged on all summer, each side
rehearsed its case, submitting to public view the correspondence that
preceded and followed their marriage, the rival interpretations of
subsequent events, and the mutual allegations of fraud and deceit.
Ellen's case rested ultimately on her claim that, because of the child's
age and tender health, a mother's care was "indispensably necessary
for his present and future welfare." Gonsalve's was that American, like
Swiss, law gave the father sole guardianship of his children—indeed,
that when the Sears family had pushed the New York legislature to
pass an act denying such guardianship to any foreign father of an
American-born child, Governor William Seward had vetoed it explicitly because it violated that prevailing fundamental of family law. But
whether it was because the infant did indeed need the nursing care
of its mother or because she had "ample means to support and
educate the said child in a manner befitting his station" or because she
pledged to hand the child over to the father when he was of suitable
age, the Philadelphia court refused to grant D'Hauteville's petition for
a writ of habeas corpus.[11]

If her testimony in the Philadelphia hearing had presented Ellen
as young, meek, and a victim, her response the next year to D'Hauteville's petition to be exempted from a Rhode Island law protecting the
mother's guardianship in cases like hers demonstrated intellectual
and emotional growth. At eighteen, a girl reticent even with her
parents and a young lady more afraid of being thought a jilt than of
contracting a dubious marriage, at twenty-two she was a woman who
had been forced to reassess the social and legal prescriptions that
denied women the rights and the power they granted men. She was
still, of course, extraordinarily privileged. Not only did her parents'
wealth allow her to move from state to state to take advantage of the
laws most advantageous to her case, but her father's connections with

men of power had convinced the legislatures of three states—New Hampshire and Rhode Island as well as New York—to pass legislation under which she might retain custody of her child.[12] Yet her husband also had the resources to press his claims in courts and legislatures and to force this once-fragile young lady to lay bare the intimacies and disgraces of her most private life.

The result, however, was not surrender nor even just a determination to keep her child. The public battles had not only bred open hostility to her particular spouse but also an articulate formulation of the rights and principles she thought should shelter all women. To Gonsalve's demand that the wife devote herself entirely to her husband's happiness, she now argued that marriage was a contract from which either party's failure to meet the conditions set in pre-nuptial arrangements freed the other. "The duties of marriage are," she insisted, "reciprocal," and as for coverture and the unrestrained power it granted the husband, she rejected the role of "subject and slave" and the whole "doctrine, which no American, man or woman, [could] ever voluntarily submit to." And if Gonsalve could use the laws of Switzerland to file for divorce with no notice to her and to keep as his own the $20,000 her father had staked on the marriage contract, why should not she and her friends, as American citizens, make "known her particular wrongs, or grievances, . . . by all lawful and honorable ways and means of suggestion to any legislature, or to any individual members of any legislature, as all other sufferers do" and seek "any modifications of the general laws of the land, which she and they, for their own protection, might desire"?[13] To that extent, at least, she had established her rights. But although D'Hauteville appears to have given up on American courts and legislatures after 1841, Ellen Sears D'Hauteville was still obliged to maintain her legal residence in New Hampshire to insure her continuing guardianship over her son.

Few cases were so dramatic, but similar circumstances were common enough to nourish the creation of various legal shields that protected women from the harshness of the common law. Operating within a system of equity jurisprudence, which Massachusetts lacked, South Carolina courts, in Marylynn Salmon's words, did "everything in their power to protect women. The intent of settlements, gifts, or wills, however haphazardly designed, governed judicial decisions" in their favor. The southern state also made special provision—as Massachusetts again did not—that women might surrender dower rights to their husband's property only after a court, by private examination, determined that the woman was acting knowledgeably and voluntarily. Finally, South Carolina statute had also, since colonial times, provided for governmental enforcement of written marriage contracts, whereas Massachusetts law did so only after 1845.[14]

This unusual protection of women's property rights in South Carolina extended to those of modest as well as substantial property. Moreover, the kind of protection that marriage settlements afforded changed over time to accommodate the shifting economic needs of Charleston women. In the 1830s probably about 10 percent of all marriages involved contracts registered with state officials—a provision not legally required for their enforcement. But, if their numbers remained fairly constant (31 in 1829, 27 in 1839), their content reflected different purposes in the boom years before the 1837 panic and the depression years that followed. Post-nuptial contracts, rare before 1836, increased markedly as the danger that a wife's property would be subject to her husband's creditors increased.[15]

That this shift was for the benefit of both husband and wife was demonstrated in 1842 by the case of Eliza Black, whose trustees intervened to protect her interests when her real estate developer husband, Alexander Black, failed in business. Faced with his creditors' claims against all his property, her trustees sued in the court of equity to shelter the proceeds from the sale of their ten-room home with its extensive outbuildings and furnishings and their six domestic slaves, which Mrs. Black had apparently brought with her when she married.[16] Otherwise the proceeds from the sale of their home would, like Black's commercial real estate and corporate stock, have benefited the creditors to whom he had assigned all his property the previous year and would have left his wife and children destitute.

Less obvious changes also occurred in these years. Settlements that left management decisions and the disposition of income to husbands alone fell from 22 percent of the total in the late 1820s to a mere 7 percent in the mid-1830s—before the panic could have had any effect. But this decline, like the increase in post-nuptial settlements, betokened mutuality since the compensating increase was not in settlements providing for the wife' sole use of income but rather for joint use by both spouses. There was, on the other hand, a marked decline in restrictions placed on the woman's power to bequeath her property by will.[17]

Other subtleties, while too few to be of statistical interest, illustrate class and racial variations in marriage settlements. Of four settlements involving free blacks in the mid-1830s, only one allowed for the husband's disposition of his wife's income, and two reserved her income for the wife's exclusive use. And Maria Chapman, who gave her husband joint use of her property, including real estate, slaves, corporate stock, and household furnishings, reserved to herself the sole right to buy, sell, and manage that property and any other she might acquire. Nor was that provision an exclusively black pattern. The parents of Eliza Schnierle, daughter of Charleston's second ethnically German mayor, who was about to marry Henry Horlbeck, son of a wealthy building contractor and brickyard operator, made sure that whatever property she might inherit from her father, like that which she brought with her in marriage, would be not just for her sole and separate use but without any "controul, intermeddling or interference" from young Henry.[18] The previously married Mrs. Penelope Somers, owner and operator of several establishments in Charleston's red light district, was even more explicit. She was not about to surrender her independence to John Rehpenn, grocer and intended husband. Indeed, she would use her property quite directly to control him. Their marriage settlement read "that if the said John Rehpenn, be a good faithfull and loving husband, and have the interest of himself and spouse properly at heart; be no spendthrift, or any ways alienate the affections of Mrs. P. Somers, his intended wife or in any manner ill treat her, that then and in such case, he shall be possessed of and enjoy the emoluements, profits, and income of the said Estate thus settled on him, and be the only heir of his intended Wife Mrs. P.

Somers, in case he shall survive her." But while she was still alive, John Rehpenn, no matter how faithful or loving, would have no power over her. He would have no right to "let or lease" any of her properties without her approval, nor dictate where she should have her "place of dwelling" nor how she should conduct her business, which she would carry on "according to her own will and pleasure, and at such place and pleases as she may from time to time think most proper for her own use and benefit."[19]

More distinctly ethnic were the Jewish marriage settlements, often written in Hebrew but nonetheless recorded with the civil authorities. They were, in fact, ketubas enforcing traditional religious requirements that at marriage the bride (as long as she proved to be a virgin) was secured an income from property contributed by her husband as well as her father. More esoteric was the French couple who registered a similar marriage settlement both with Charleston's Registry of Mesne Conveyance and the French Consulate. Their contract, combining resources from both families, however, was a substitute for the wife's dower rights.[20]

In any case, women of all sorts and degrees of wealth used marriage contracts. At one extreme was Margaret Campbell, whose property included the three-hundred-acre plantation and $30,000 in other investments that she brought to her marriage with the even-wealthier lawyer Mitchell King. At the other extreme was Hagar Simpson's one small city lot, her single slave, her horse and cart, and her simple furniture, which she brought to her marriage with William Johnson who was, like herself, a free person of color.[21]

It was indeed a matter of region more than race or class that determined how a married woman's property was protected from her husband and his creditors. Charleston women were benefited by equity, which, precisely because it treated them as dependent persons who needed special protection, encouraged an especially favorable interpretation of all legal documents—whether wills or marriage settlements—to afford women maximum protection. Additionally, although South Carolina law banned divorce, the state had, over time, developed a system of legal separation with alimony. In both cases, the law's special protection came from the assumption that women—because they were women—were incompetent to look after their own welfare.

By contrast, although Boston women had access to divorce with the right to remarry, they had a far less certain claim on property. Their state's rapid transformation from an agricultural to a commercial and manufacturing economy pressed its courts to curtail dower rights by removing many kinds of business and personal property from the widow's entitlement. Thus the apparent legal advantages that Massachusetts women enjoyed often seemed nugatory, and specific legislation was necessary to give them the protection of property rights that their Carolina sisters had long enjoyed. So it was that in 1833 they welcomed a new law that protected a married woman's property against the depredations of deserting husbands and in 1845 were cheered by a married women's property act that protected married women's right to enjoy a separate estate of both real and personal property. Like Charlestonians' increased use of post-nuptial marriage settlements, this law was as much a response to the 1837 panic and subsequent bankruptcy proceedings as to the particular needs of women. Nonetheless it did shelter wives as much as husbands from creditors' stripping the family of both spouses' property. Like its immediate predecessor, it also responded to fathers fearful that errant husbands would make off with funds they had provided for their daughters' and grandchildren's well-being. Significantly it was only in 1855 that Massachusetts, moving well ahead of most other northern states, legislated protection for the wages of working married women, protecting for the first time those whose property had not been given them by others.[22] It was only then that, on balance, Massachusetts law promised more protection to married women's property than did South Carolina's equity tradition.

The extent and kinds of property that women did, in fact, own reveals as much as the law about its peculiarly domestic nature. Estate inventories in both Boston and Charleston list the property that widows, spinsters, and those wives empowered to make wills actually possessed.[23] In addition to their clothing, household furnishings and kitchen equipment were their most frequent possessions. Next were silver utensils ranging from a few silver spoons to extensive silver services. Yet not even these possessions were uniquely or assuredly women's property, for men's wills often left such property to wives or daughters—property that the wills occasionally noted had been the wife's possessions before her marriage.

Even when inventories extended beyond household furnishings, the property that women owned was, more often and more exclusively than men's, identified with consumption rather than production. When Boston women willed real estate, in two cases out of three it comprised only their residences. Not one of the forty-four sampled inventories of women's property, which the probate court required of intestate estates as well as of those conveyed by will, included the stock-in-trade or artisanal tools that were often left by men of middling or limited means. Of the sixteen inventories listing investment portfolios, ten consisted primarily of bank and insurance stock, which paid safe but small returns. Although six did include more risky but also more remunerative textile and railroad shares, the paucity of women directly enriched by the transportation and industrial revolution is striking. Few women reaped direct benefits from Massachusetts's burgeoning textile manufacture. In an 1833 tally of the 160 shareholders of the Merrimack Company, twenty-six women—fifteen spinsters and eleven widows—owned a mere 121 of the 1,500 outstanding shares. The eight women stockholders in the Jackson Company in 1838 owned only twenty of its five hundred shares.[24] In addition, even when they owned stock, women had no role in corporate decision making. Dividends on their shares were customarily paid to male trustees or guardians; their stock was always voted by male proxies.

The kind of property that Charleston women owned, however, gave them greater managerial opportunities. Although South Carolina did not, as did Massachusetts, require that real estate be inventoried, probate records nonetheless reveal considerable female ownership of income-producing real estate that was more likely to be plantation land than urban rental property. Even more prevalent among women—as it was among men—was slave ownership. While this observation reminds us again that half of Charleston's women were slaves and legally devoid of all property, it also substantiates the greater potential for managerial control that slave property gave Charleston's free women. Their decision either to use their slaves to enhance their own domestic leisure or to hire them out to provide income was shaped by several factors. Those owning slaves on plantations doubtless worked most of them as agricultural laborers. Wealthy women who owned urban slaves—often twenty or more—seem to have employed most of them as domestics in their homes. But those whose urban slaves were their only or their major property were likely to hire them out to produce income. Thus, although the stock that Charleston women owned gave them no managerial scope since it was confined even more than that of their Boston counterparts to bank shares, their plantations and slaveholdings did. Moreover, five of the forty-five inventories in the Charleston sample listed either business property or stock-in-trade among the decedent's possessions. These data reinforce the supposition created by women's occupational patterns in Charleston that the southern city's free women had more varied opportunities for economic independence than did Boston women.

In both cities, however, women owned quantitatively less property than did men. Indeed, if property owners are ranked in an ascending scale, at each level women comprise an ever smaller proportion. Of those who at death left property worth no more than $5,000, men in both cities outnumbered women by a ratio of three to one; but of those whose property exceeded $5,000 in value, men outnumbered women five to one in Boston and six to one in Charleston.[25] And among those for whom public records give evidence of significant wealth, only 10 percent of rich Bostonians and 13 percent of similar Charlestonians were female.[26]

Formal government documents tend to obscure, if they do not hide altogether, those married women whose property was assessed and taxed as part of that of their husbands. In the 1840s, however,

Bostonians' consuming curiosity about the rich and the sources of their wealth sparked two popular pamphlets that melded information from public tax records with common gossip and that, however anecdotal, shed still more light on women's wealth. Thomas Wilson's *Aristocracy of Boston* reported that 10 of the 183 richest Bostonians were women: 8 were widows of wealthy men and 2 the spinster daughters of very rich fathers. The implication is clear. Women of vast wealth came to their riches not through their own exertions but through inheritance from the males in their families. But of equal interest is that some of Boston's richest men gained much or all of their wealth from marrying the daughters of rich fathers or the widows of rich husbands. This pattern is elaborated in Richard Hildreth's *"Our First Men": A Calender of Wealth, Fashion and Gentility.* Here were paraded Boston's 400—398 to be exact—who were taxed on property assessed at $100,000 or more. Of them, 44 had either created or enhanced their standing by marrying daughters of other first men—offspring of such worthies as Jonathan Mason, Gardiner Greene, David Sears, "Wicked" Jonathan Amory, and "Gentleman Bill" Bordman. And 4 had married a deceased first husband's wealth as well as his widow.

And if the property of 48 of the first men came from wives not listed independently for their "wealth, fashion, and gentility," an additional 41 of the first "men" were, in fact, women. Every single one of the women for whom such evidence is given had inherited her fortune from a male family member. The spinsters were their fathers' or brothers' heirs. Moreover, of the 18 who were widows, 6 had inherited their riches not from husbands but fathers in amounts ranging from $100,000 to $300,000. And that was true as well for the 5 (perhaps 6) married women whose property, ranging from $100,000 to $400,000, was taxed separately from that of their husbands and was, in at least 2 cases, explicitly held in trust for their sole use. And then there were the 2 divorcées. Ellen Sears D'Hauteville, who was not technically a Bostonian because she had to keep her legal residence in New Hampshire to retain safe custody of her son, was one. The other was Mary Mason Parkman, who, in divorcing her forger husband now exiled in Italy, had saved the fortune she had inherited from her father.[27]

The fact remains that these women were even less typical of their gender than were very rich men of theirs. The reality in each city was that women simply had less property than did men, whether its amount was determined from tax and probate records or from anecdote and rumor. Among all the propertied, women were almost as distinct a minority as were rich women among all women. Moreover, by their own decision if not by legal prescription, few married women actually controlled the property they brought to a marriage, and even fewer controlled the wages they earned. In Charleston Alicia Russell Middleton watched her planter husband dissipate her merchant father's estate as well as his own in an open display of the grand style. And Bostonian Mrs. Charles R. Lowell learned only after the fact that her husband had wasted her father's beneficence on another woman. Yet, in all probability, most husbands did apply such funds to the family's "joint use," even when marriage settlements did not mandate it. And if they diminished the capital, it was more probably as Samuel Gridley Howe did the fortune of Julia Ward Howe—out of ineptitude and unanticipated financial reverses rather than conscious intention.[28]

In both Massachusetts and South Carolina, the law gave widows the life use of one-third of their husbands' real property and daughters the right to inherit equally with sons. That most men died intestate, thus giving mute assent to public law, and that the wills of those who made them generally conformed closely to its mandates demonstrate that most men did provide for their wives and daughters. Some, it is true, grumbled that dower rights gave wives too much and wrote wills settling on them only the bare minimum. In a sample of eighty-four wills written by married men and probated in Boston between 1825 and 1843, exactly one-half adhered strictly to the legal minimum, providing their widows no more than the life use of one-third of their estates. But more than one-quarter left their widows in absolute possession of their entire estates—albeit those estates more often than not were small ones. On the other hand, eleven husbands provided for their wives only so long as they remained widows, stripping them of part or all of their life-use inheritance should they remarry. Whether or not the testator's intention was primarily to protect his children's future inheritance from a stepfather or to exercise power over his widow's behavior from beyond the grave—or, as one will explained, to shelter his widow from fortune hunters—such restrictions imply that it was a woman's dependence rather than her wifely contributions to the family economy that entitled her to a share of her late husband's property.

Similar patterns appear with somewhat different frequency in a sample of sixty-nine wills drawn by male Charlestonians with living wives and probated during the same period. Over one-third conveyed property to their widows absolutely. The rest settled for life use in conformity with dower rights, but five husbands withdrew life-use provisions should the widow remarry. The major substantive difference was that six wills, as did none in the Boston sample, openly provided for common-law wives, five of them free blacks and one a slave.

There was even less substantive difference between the two cities in how fathers divided property among their children. Sixty-one percent of Boston fathers and 79 percent of Charleston fathers bequeathed their children property in equal portions regardless of gender. On the other hand, sixteen of the seventy-six Boston wills in which fathers provided for children gave daughters preferential treatment, and three were especially generous to spinster daughters unlikely to receive future support from a husband. An equal number, arguing similar assumptions about need, explicitly curtailed the shares given daughters whose affluent husbands could supply their needs. No Charleston will avowedly reduced the share left a married daughter, although three did make special provision for spinster daughters. And while in neither city was there an apparent desire to favor sons over daughters, Charleston wills are likely to note that sons had already been given plantations by inter vivos deed.

If regional differences in men's wills ran parallel, the variations among individual wills illuminate the distinctions that amounts of property and differing bonds of affection could make. Reflecting a deep concern for his widow's future freedom as well as her security, John Jacob Schnell of Charleston not only left all his modest real and personal property to Cordelia Schnell's absolute ownership but also provided that should she remarry that property would be put in trust to protect it against all claims of her new husband or his creditors. Similarly, coach and chair maker Robert Ling left his wife Jane all his property remaining after paying his just debts "for her own sole and separate use without being in any manner subject to the contracts or control of any husband whom she may have." A husband concerned more exclusively for his wife's security might bequeath his widow, as did the fabulously wealthy Gardiner Greene of Boston, absolute ownership of a set share of his property equal to the specific bequests left to each of their children and then add on for her an additional annual income should she remain unmarried. Both his absolute and his provisional bequests to his widow comported with his further intention to divide the residue of his estate so equally that the children of a deceased daughter shared property equal to the amount given each of his eight surviving children.[29]

Still more complex was Thomas Hanscome's will. A wealthy Charleston merchant, he left $150,000 to maintain and educate the eight children born to him and Nancy Randall, a "free colored woman," and a further $15,000 as well as his furniture and linens for her to use in the house he had built for her behind his mansion. More humbly, John Weston recognized obligations to his former common-law wife, Mary Furman, like himself a free person of color, and to his present wife, Sarah Weston. To Mary Furman and their three children—Furman, Elizabeth, and Sarah—he left a house and lot; to his present wife he bequeathed the home in which they both lived and all his business property. Most nearly unique was the provision made in the will of Joe Rogers, a free black, for Mrs. Sarah Jones, "a white person." To her he left his furniture, the use of his horse and of his slave Dinah, and a monthly payment of five dollars so long as she remained "single and unmarried," while to the free black mother of his daughter Joanna he left only money enough to buy mourning clothes.[30]

The disposition that women made of the property they inherited or accumulated on their own was notably different from that of men. First of all, married women had to take special steps to secure the right to make wills—a right more common to South Carolina women because of their marriage contracts and their state's equity system than it was to their Massachusetts sisters until an 1842 statute there gave all women the right to make bequests. Thus in Charleston Mary Magdeline Prioleau Ford, whose considerable property inherited from her father, Samuel Prioleau, was held in trust, passed that property on to her daughters with the same provisions that were in her own trust. The husband of either girl might have no more than a life interest in her estate—exactly the benefit Mr. Ford had enjoyed.[31]

Such transmission of property through the female line was common in the wills of both Boston and Charleston women, who were almost twice as likely to leave property to their daughters as to their sons. In so doing, they made wills notably different from men's, for while fathers might make distinctions in the kind of property they left daughters as opposed to sons, giving the latter business property and the former residential property and home furnishings, they almost never wholly ignored daughters for the sole benefit of sons. And, if writing wills rather than relying on the public law that distributed the property of intestates equally among all children implies discontent with the law, the sizable proportion of wills written by the women of both cities suggests that women were less easy than men with that law. Because women's access to property was limited and their property holdings generally small, it is especially significant that almost half of Charleston's and a third of Boston's testators were women.

If the amount of property to be conveyed cannot account for this phenomenon, the power that property gave women within their families may explain their proclivity to make wills. For instance, Eliza Pinckney used her property and her ability to will it as she liked to defuse a potential family dispute. Perplexed that one of her two daughters would refuse to take her inheritance in slaves, Pinckney tried to establish the precise monetary value of all her property so that her will might distribute it equitably and save her daughters from financial transactions that might produce disharmony between them. Similarly, Esther Palmer, concerned to avoid future wrangling among the children and grandchildren of her two marriages, made a will that would disinherit any child who raised a legal challenge to its distribution of property. In a third Charleston case, widowed Ann Drayton Perry used her will to shelter as much of her property as she could from the control of her only child, a wastrel son. While she did bequeath him her residual estate, she left this errant young man with only the use of her two plantations, whose ownership she put in trust for as yet unborn grandchildren. To insure that there would be grandchildren reared according to her lights, Perry provided as generously for Edward's fiancée, whom clearly she liked, as for her own mother. And she used her will not just to forgive the debt that Edward Perry had refused to repay in a manner that at one point had caused the mother to take the son to court, but to remind him of that unpleasant contretemps. And finally there was Harriet Hockley Bampfield, whose will cut off her husband without a sou and left the extensive property she had inherited from her mother and an unmarried sister to two adopted daughters and two female friends.[32]

It may have been that it was easier for women to assert power within their family circle posthumously than within their lifetimes. Not infrequently, indeed, when the daughter of a rich and well-entrenched man married one less well endowed, the disparity between her father's and her husband's positions created divided loyalties and unanticipated tensions in ways that subverted the influence she had over either. The dilemmas that the daughters of two wealthy and powerful Charleston men faced in their marriages are cases in point.

Margaret Bennett had been wooed and won by James B. Campbell, a promising young lawyer who had left his native Massachusetts in the 1820s. Certainly there were, for this ambitious young man, powerful attractions, in addition to the charms of plain and bespectacled Margaret, to marry into the family of Thomas Bennett, whose rice mills cleaned much of his state's second crop and whose political career had included service as intendant/mayor of his city and governor of his state. The Bennett family, of course, was reassured when this young stranger's origins were vouched for by no less a Carolinian than Joel R. Poinsett, the first United States minister to Mexico and soon to be Martin Van Buren's secretary of war. Moreover, in the Charleston whose politics in the 1830s were shaped by the nullification controversy, Campbell, like Poinsett and Bennett, was a conspicuous unionist.

So when Campbell thought of postponing marriage until he could support his wife in suitable style, Poinsett urged his young protégé to marry as soon as possible, for his wedding day would bring him the property, prestige, and political connections which Thomas Bennett could bestow. "Once a member of the family," Poinsett wrote, "every one would be interested in promoting your views; and Mr. Bennett[,] who is as generous as he is able[,] would place you in a situation at once to render you independent of him & all others by the exercise of your own industry & talents." And so, in January 1837, James and Margaret became husband and wife in a ceremony that James thought was the beginning of the "happiest era of [his] life."[33]

Whether or not it was Margaret's wish to remain in her father's home after her marriage, we do not know. But James's still small law practice probably contributed to the Campbells' decision to do so. And whether or not it was Campbell's pride rubbed raw by semidependence on his father-in-law or whether it was his loyalty to his old mentor Joel Poinsett outweighing new ties, he not only backed Poinsett's candidate against Bennett's choice of Hugh Legaré in the congressional election of 1838 but also publicly alleged that the Bennett faction had deliberately misrepresented Poinsett's position.

So offensive was this slur on gentlemanly honor that knowledgeable men predicted James Campbell's ruin. Surely he must either face a duel or "quit the Country." But his father-in-law, more committed to family than faction, intervened to save Campbell's future in Charleston. Nonetheless, his description of the domestic scene that it precipitated suggests the emotional price that Margaret, a pawn in the affair, as well as James paid for the latter's "passions excited almost to madness."[34]

Of the contretemps before the crisis, "poor Mag knew nothing." Her father had hidden from her view the newspapers containing Campbell's denunciatory letter and the attacks it had provoked. When "at midnight . . . Her Husband told her the circumstances," she at once rushed to her father's bedroom where, "her anguish unutterable, she complained of me, and vindicated him on the ground that I had rejected him from the Legare ticket." Explaining the "facts in the case" to her, her father then promised to do what he could to "avert the impending evil" and sent her back to James. She then relayed to him Bennett's explanation of how the ticket had been chosen. "A moment more" and James was at Bennett's "bed side almost sobbing. I hope never to pass through such a scene again."[35]

Whatever the dynamic of this scene, for which we have only Thomas Bennett's report, Campbell pulled back and remained in Charleston. Rumor had it that Bennett had forced his son-in-law's retraction "by a threat to cut him off from any share in [his] property." The repercussions of this family drama for Margaret, as much as for the two men, are summed up in Bennett's lament to Poinsett. "My own domestic condition—communicates to my mind a forceful & incessent disquietude, which deeply affects its tranquility."[36] Shortly after this trauma, the Campbells moved into a nearby house that Thomas Bennett gave his daughter. There their son was born and died, and there James reared their daughters after Margaret's death in 1851.

The not dissimilar tale of a wife and daughter who was caught between the two men on whom she was economically and emotionally dependent emerges from the letters that Margaret Adger Smyth wrote her absent clergyman-husband during his summer sojourn in the North and in Great Britain. Like Margaret Bennett, Margaret Adger had grown up in a home marked by strong family bonds as well as wealth and power. If her father lacked the political career of Thomas Bennett, his economic role in the city's commercial life was even greater, for as agent of the Baltimore banking house of Brown

Brothers and as the most active director of Charleston's largest bank, he controlled much of the credit on which his fellow merchants depended. He was also the most powerful layman in the Second Presbyterian Church when its pastor, Thomas Smyth, married Margaret in 1832.

A native of Scotland and not acclimated to semitropical heat, Smyth left Charleston every summer for travel and relaxation in healthier climates, while Margaret stayed behind to cope with their increasing family and the continuing demands of her husband's parishioners. During his absences, Margaret's parents, her sister, and her brothers and their wives provided the adult companionship and practical assistance that, in 1844, the often-harassed clergyman's wife particularly needed. That summer Margaret not only had to manage the usual household and church routines to which she was long accustomed, but also had to care simultaneously for her three-month-old daughter and two young sons sick with whooping cough. Moreover, it was in an atmosphere of uncertainty: Thomas had written about a call from a New York church that, if he accepted it, would separate Margaret from her family bulwark in Charleston. While such an important affair was brewing, her husband, notorious for his extraordinarily long sermons, wrote only "little scraps of letters with *three* words in a line." "My heart sickens," she wrote him, "my eyes overflow, & I feel inclined to throw down the pen, with a feeling akin to despair" as she contemplated a long summer of uncertain correspondence. When, for a while, Thomas wrote more frequently, his letters still had a "hurried" quality, "as if you could not spare me a little more of your time." And then for the six weeks after he sailed from New York for Liverpool, Margaret heard nothing at all.[37]

Without guidance from him, she was called on to address an acrimonious church dispute in which Thomas had been engaged but had not settled before he left. As the summer lengthened and the strains increased, Thomas's uneasiness with the Adger generosity and close family ties that sustained his wife were revealed in his sparse communications, which, in turn, spurred Margaret to lay bare her discontents. Why should he who left her alone so regularly resent the dynamics by which his brother-in-law James took the absent Thomas's place at meals or by which her brother William purchased the fine English stockings his sister had requested? Never so explicitly mentioned but implied was the ominous shadow cast by a father-in-law who dominated the practical affairs of a church whose spiritual leader was frequently at odds with his parishioners. Most immediate for Margaret, however, was the apparent deficiency of her own home life as compared to that of her brothers. Even when Thomas promised to "be less of a student, & to cultivate more [his] love for [his] wife & children," Margaret contrasted their marriage to those of her brothers. "It is the want of this *home companionship* which makes me seek in others that which I cannot find in you and makes me jealous, & almost envious when I see Robt & Wm with their wives & children." She could not live "without love & sympathy & when you drive me from you as you so often have done, I must seek it where I can find it, in mother & Susan."[38] Her romantic illusions were gone. After twelve years of marriage, the birth of six children, and the death of three, Margaret Smyth relinquished her early "ambition to be loved as no other woman was loved, & *humbly* desire[d] to be loved *as* some others are loved."[39]

If such women were seemingly powerless over familial tensions created by having a wealthy father and a proud husband, their experiences do not negate the greater options their privileged positions gave them. Yet the short and simple annals of the poor, though recorded more briefly and only in public documents, attest that similar family complications could arise from ownership of even a little property—particularly property in persons. But those records also show that ownership created options that those with absolutely no property did not have. Tenah Glen, for example, left her son, Cudjo, "whom I purchased," to the care of her freeborn daughter. Thomas Gates bequeathed his "mulatto butcher John" to John's wife, Abby Mitchell, a "free woman of color." While in both cases the power inherent in owning a family member doubtless loosened the bonds of slavery, it also muddied relationships created by kinship and affection. But it was the circumstance of Mary Douglas, a free woman of color, and her husband and slave, William, that best illustrated the ultimate irony. William, allegedly the son as well as the former slave of a Dr. Irvine, was a barber by trade. In August 1832 he was executed for "grievously wounding, maiming and bruising" two white men—stabbing one in the arm, the other in the ribs—while he was on a drunken binge. Five years later, in December 1837, the South Carolina legislature responded to Mary Douglas's petition to be compensated for her court-imposed loss. The legislature appropriated $122, "the amount usually allowed on such occassions [sic]" to pay Mary Douglas, who was both the widow and the former owner of William.[40]

The ways in which property and privilege defined women's roles in a male-dominated society were thus anything but simple. Great wealth, high social rank, inherited property could not guarantee meaningful power to married women, though it could provide them, as it did some widows and spinsters, a significant measure of independence. Yet even for those with only a small property, its possession might modify a marriage relationship or reshape other family ties. Although its management was more often than not limited by law and custom, property did promise the women who possessed it a greater chance for autonomy, whether by allowing them to remain comfortably unmarried, by creating a more equal balance between spouses, or by providing an escape route from an unworkable marriage. Moreover, much of the power that women did wield outside their homes stemmed, like social privilege, from property ownership. For most, however, the property that determined their status was either owned by the men in their families or given them by such men. Few women could achieve ownership of significant property by their own efforts, but they could keep it and convey it to whomever they chose by using the law to its full advantage. The laws governing them varied by region and the property they possessed varied by class, but the will of women to use both to their own best advantage was an individual matter.

6

Piety,
Philanthropy,
and Reform

Of all the spheres in which nineteenth-century women were active outside their homes, those that violated no canon of domesticity were religion and charity. The attributes inherent in the model of true womanhood—having greatness in suffering and a soft and tender heart, relieving misery, acting as an angel of mercy—all comported with the woman who found solace in her prayers, tuned her sensibilities to the needs of others, and comforted strangers, as she did her own family, in illness or distress.

Moreover, although Ann Douglas and others have recognized a distinctive nineteenth-century pattern in the feminization of religion, Cotton Mather reported as early as 1699 that the vast majority of communicants in his church was female. He concluded that "the Curse in the Difficulties both of Subjection and of Childbearing" had become instead a blessing that propelled women to religious observance. So pervasive was this pattern that women, although they were generally barred from church governance and excluded not just from the clergy but from acting as deacons, moderators, or vestrymen, nonetheless made religion their fortress and their mission. Barred from public preaching, they effected conversions among family members—husbands and sons as well as daughters and sisters.[1]

Indeed, Catharine Sedgwick personified religion as a goddess who strengthened women to carry on their domestic tasks as she also made them docile, faithful, persevering, and patient. Personal piety enriched their emotional life, bolstered their endurance, and aided them to achieve self-discipline. So great was her need for warm ritual rather than the cold rationalism of Unitarianism that Mrs. William

Brooks convinced her merchant husband to leave Boston's First Church for the Episcopal fold. And Brooks went readily because "women make religion much more a matter of conscience & the heart than men do." For socially prominent Boston matron Mary Amory it was her son's failure to make religious observance a greater part of his life at Harvard that made her write him that piety was not only the only sure support in adversity, but also the best control over human passion. And for tormented Charleston schoolteacher Mary Hort, it was both a bulwark against a hostile world and a solace to her troubled conscience. Tortured by her "*horrible iniquities*," "desperate corruption," and "*temptation* on *all* hands," as well as her uncertain livelihood, this mature spinster filled her diary with an antiphony between her "*utter weakness* of purpose" and the consolations she derived from throwing herself upon the bosom of the Lord Jesus. No less guilt-ridden, young Frances Appleton recorded the traumas of adolescence in a journal whose remaining pages—many have been torn out—pray for divine intervention to "soften every warring passion" in her heart and to "pardon her for this constant repining against what Thou hast appointed as her lot."[2]

That religion promised the means of self-control, that its divine sanction made women's burdens more bearable, and that it proffered forgiveness for rebellious emotions explain its powerful attraction for women of all ages and sorts—to which church membership patterns in nineteenth-century cities attest. In Charleston's leading Episcopal churches, St. Michael's and St. Philip's, the ratio of female to male communicants was ten to one; in the Circular Congregational church, for every man there were five women who had confessed their faith; St. John's Lutheran counted six women for every man in full membership; and in the Second Presbyterian, the ratio was three to one.[3] Boston churches showed similar patterns with five female to every three male Congregationalists in the city. The same ratio held for St. Paul's Episcopal and the Second Universalist churches. And women were four times as numerous as men in both the Baldwin Place Baptist and the Hanover Street Methodist churches.[4]

The very evident disparity in gender distribution meant that ministers vying for followers played on women's special susceptibilities. Thus, in the winter of 1841–42, when Baptist Jacob Knapp, Congregationalist Edward Kirk, and evangelical Presbyterian Charles Grandison Finney competed for Boston converts, all developed special appeals to women's emotions. The *Boston Morning Post* voiced concern less about the means by which young, handsome, unmarried Edward Kirk attracted "immense audiences" to the Park Street Church than that he preached extensively in private homes in an intimacy more "agreeable to the ladies." But so extreme was the Elder Knapp's church activity that mobs surrounded his meetings and threatened him with violence, while the press repeated their angry accusations that he had driven weak women "frantic by religious terror," detailing specifically how one convert had lost her reason. Similarly, a Charleston pastor used fire and brimstone to terrify women who left his church for the promise of universal salvation that Theophilus Fisk preached. Fisk himself reported in 1836 that Baptist cleric Basil Manly had invaded the sick room of a woman parishioner who had slipped the fold and, despite her serious illness, had threatened her with the "*dangerous condition*" in which her apostasy had placed her soul. Moreover, when she recovered but did not repent, Manly excommunicated her without the ecclesiastical trial customarily accorded male apostates.[5]

Such events were, doubtless, aberrations. Nevertheless, they reflect general assumptions typified by Charleston's Second Presbyterian Church. While it protected female delicacy by not requiring women to make the public confessions demanded of men who sought full church membership, it excluded women members from the conduct of church business for the same reasons. In virtually all Protestant churches in both cities, it was not the confessed members or communicants but rather a corporate body comprised of all male— and only male—pewholders who chose church officers, selected the pastor, allocated resources, and made all but the spiritual decisions governing the congregation and its church building. Women pewholders were quite explicitly excluded from voting in such meetings even when they were a sizable minority—30, for instance, among the 203 pewholders of Boston's Trinity Episcopal and 13 among the 162 of Unitarian King's Chapel.[6]

There were, however, exceptions. At Episcopal Christ Church, Boston women were allowed to vote their pews when a controversy flared over the Reverend William Croswell's alleged neglect of parochial duties. Significantly all five voted with the majority of twenty-one to defend their rector. Similarly, when, for more than three years, the Unitarian Hollis Street Church pewholders battled to fire their pastor, the few women pewholders, reflecting female communicants' overwhelming support for their pastor, struggled unsuccessfully to retain John Pierpont. It was also true in Boston, as it was not in Charleston, that women were visible in organizing new churches to meet the needs of the city's soaring population. Ten women and six men, for example, signed the charter that launched the Twelfth Congregational Society in 1825.[7]

These exceptions to the rule, however, do not negate the general expectation that women would find solace in religion but would not exercise power in church affairs. On the other hand, they were not merely passive church members. If few women played a visible part in church politics, many joined Bible study classes, frequented prayer meetings, taught Sunday school, and participated in a panoply of religious organizations. When such organizations embraced both genders, it is true that women's membership seldom involved more than financial contributions to societies run by men. This was true of both cities' Bible and Tract societies and of Charleston's Society for the Relief of Orphans and Widows of the Episcopal Clergy in South Carolina. But it was not so in Charleston's most unusual Methodist Benevolent Society, which engaged both genders in the same activities by insisting that visiting be done in pairs, each comprised of a man and a woman.

It was, however, primarily in those religious associations with no male members—except the ministers—that women contributed substantially to organizational decision making. There were many women's groups formed within single congregations to carry out social activities within their particular church's structure. Of these, the Maternal Association and the Circle of Industry of Bowdoin Square Church and the Social Circle of Hollis Street Church in Boston, and the Gregorie Society of St. Philip's, the Unitarian Ladies Society, and the Female Lutheran Society in Charleston were all representative. There were also ad hoc groups that organized bazaars to meet special needs of their churches or denominations, selling fruit, flowers, objets d'art, and needlework made by the ladies to raise sizable sums seldom less than $1,000, on occasion as much as $4,000. Then there were, in Boston, the Female Society for Promoting Christianity among the Jews and the Ladies Association for Evangelizing the West and, in Charleston, the Female Bible, Prayerbook, and Tract Society and the Protestant Episcopal Female Domestic Missionary Society, all of which drew membership from several churches and, lacking a single focal clergyman, were, accordingly, less subject to male supervision.

Yet the pattern well characterized by the Channing Circle of Boston's Unitarian Federal Street Church points to the limitations inherent in many church-sponsored women's groups. An entirely female organization, with a membership of 121 in 1842–43, the Channing Circle rarely made its own unassisted decisions. Their guiding light was their pastor, Ezra Stiles Gannett, who attended all their meetings, set their agendas, proposed the charities that the ladies should support, and otherwise dominated the society so much so that when he could not be present at a meeting, no business was transacted. Nonetheless, the minutes record an undercurrent suggesting that the women not only were more relaxed at such times, but also discussed their society's affairs with greater interest. Probably Mary Clark exaggerated when, in 1837, she observed that Boston clergymen were "losing their influence over female minds & hearts by their overwrought efforts to retain it,"[8] but tensions between the two are borne out in the records of several organizations—most notably where teaching the young was at issue.

In both cities, although women comprised the majority of Sunday school teachers, it was men who administered and presided over the schools. Perhaps it was because these men were out of touch with the rewards that women volunteers got in their church-sponsored classrooms that gender friction reverberated through the minutes of teachers' meetings. On the one hand, we have sixteen-year-old Hannah Jackson, who enjoyed teaching her charity sewing class because it was "interesting to see these children together, & have authority over them. You know," she concluded, "we all like power." On the other, the superintendent and the male assistant superintendent "together with the male Teachers" of Charleston's Congregational church bluntly asserted their dominance. It was they who were "authorized to adopt rules and regulations for the government of the school, and to alter and amend the same." And this was true even though their fellow parishioners lamented as did their city's Episcopalians that while there were "many amiable and pious ladies" teaching Sunday school, there were very few men.[9] Fearful that the situation thus created might get out of hand, church organizations, like the clerics who presided over them, made sure that Sunday school teaching was not the first step to women's entering the pulpit.

With rare exceptions, however, women did not protest openly. Both the Hollis Street Church Sunday school and the Howard Sunday School, which Boston Unitarians ran for the children of the unchurched poor, kept full records of Sunday school teachers' meetings. Rarely did women speak when both genders met together—or at least rarely did the inevitably male secretary find what they said of sufficient interest to record it. The committees the teachers appointed were almost always exclusively male. Yet it was in this setting that the Howard school's women teachers moved to secure for themselves more of the power that Hannah Jackson so valued. First they established a sewing circle to provide clothes for children who, without such assistance, could not attend their school. Before long, however, the sewing circle was the women's caucus, which discussed issues of consequence and proposed policies that a Mrs. Edmonds, a distinct maverick in speaking openly and frequently at the general teachers' meetings, then pressed. Yet, when some of the Howard school teachers presented essays they had written for these teachers' meetings, the only essay read aloud by the superintendent rather than the author was that by a female teacher.[10]

Equally fraught with tensions over male authority, female submission, and a religious commitment to teaching was the experience of Charleston's Sisters of Charity of Our Lady of Mercy, an order established in 1829 by the city's Catholic bishop, John England. During the first two decades, the order attracted more than forty women, most of them Irish by ethnicity if not nativity, who devoted themselves to nursing the sick, operating an orphanage, and running a girls school. Its first superioress was Julia Datty, the Santo Domingan refugee who had for many years kept one of Charleston's most respected secular academies for girls. Sixty-seven when she joined the order, she turned at once to establishing its school for young ladies. Its enrollment grew under Datty's tutelage until it was chartered independently under South Carolina law. But following her death in 1837, Bishop England ordered the sisters to curtail their educational efforts, to offer only the basics to the daughters of middle-class parents, and to leave teaching music, French, and social graces to a new school operated by the long-established Ursuline order.

Dismayed, the sisters, caught in a hierarchy that concentrated authority at the top more than did any Protestant church, obeyed their bishop. But their records betray a tension as they accepted their curtailed mission with "all the resignation they possibly could." The suppressed resentment that phrase implied came into the open only after England's death in 1842. Unable to renew their vows because appointment of a new bishop was delayed, the sisters threatened mass resignations. Neither their new convent and orphanage, for which England had raised funds in 1840, nor the arrival of a new bishop stilled the turmoil—in part because both provided them substance for a new autonomy for which they were unprepared. Allowed for the first time to elect their own officers, they so foundered in the unfamiliar intricacies of church politics as to require intervention from Bishop I. A. Reynolds. And it was not their own assertiveness but rather the Ursulines' decision to leave Charleston in 1847 that restored to the Sisters of Charity their educational function and the status that teaching French and music to young ladies accorded.[11]

For many women, the same cultural values that limited the scope of their church-related activities determined the measures they undertook for secular organizations. Most visibly they raised funds for essentially male-dominated causes by organizing fairs. The Charleston ladies whose gala benefited seamen stranded in Charleston, like the Boston gentlewomen whose bazaar garnered funds to complete the Bunker Hill monument, were scarcely charting new courses. Nor did the independent charitable societies that they organized and ran on their own violate either city's limiting definitions of women's proper role. In Charleston, where women's associations like those of men reflected a value system rooted in the belief that the whole social fabric is "but a chain of reciprocal dependence, the poor hanging upon the rich, and the rich upon the poor," rich women were, unlike rich men, restricted by the expectation that their activities on behalf of the poor would be "limited to those purposes which are appropriate to the sex." They were advised to act in "the meek and quiet spirit, the humility and desire to profit by the counsel of the wise and good" for which women had "ever been distinguished." Their advantage in this respect over other women, as the young Episcopal priest Daniel Cobia observed, came because they had many servants, who freed them from women's customary household labor.[12]

It was within these boundaries that the Ladies Benevolent Society aided the sick poor; the Female Seamen's Friend Society provided sailors a temperance boardinghouse; the Fuel Society distributed wood—free in winter, at cost in warmer weather—to distressed families supported solely by a woman; and the Juvenile Industry Society, like the Ladies Garment Society, clothed the infants of poor mothers. Their membership lists included the names of Charleston's commercial and professional men—preceded, of course, by Mrs. The Ladies Benevolent Society, whose records are most complete, rather resembled a modern-day Junior League. Led by Mrs. John Faucheraud Grimké, it organized the daughters and wives of the city's leading clergymen, lawyers, and merchants to serve the less privileged. Other organizations, albeit with less prestigious memberships, were usually led by the same or similar women. Thus Mary Grimké served also as president of the Female Seamen's Friend Society and her daughter Angelina, the future abolitionist, was its secretary. Of the sixty-six Charleston women who were leaders or visibly active in either secular or church-related philanthropy during the 1830s, 43 percent were married and 42 percent were widowed. The occupations of their husbands tell us that at least 40 percent were the wives or widows of professional men; 20 percent, the wives or widows of merchants. Only four were married to planters, although two were planters in their own right. And of them all, including the never-married, a quarter had enough property to make them wealthy in their own name.[13]

Partly because Boston was larger but partly also because its social structure and cultural values tolerated more fundamental dissent, its residents generated rather more diverse benevolent organizations. Accordingly, women in the northern city not only engaged in diverse philanthropy, some also dared venture into reform efforts that, if they succeeded, would change the very society of which they were part. Therefore the kinds of women drawn to voluntary associations differed markedly from the Charleston pattern. Even if we confine ourselves to purely philanthropic groups, the difference is clearly visible. A distinctly smaller proportion—a mere 5 percent—of benevolent Yankee women were independently well-off. Proportionately more were single, far fewer were widows, and over two-thirds, as opposed to Charleston's two-fifths, were married to living husbands. Their spouses were more likely to be merchants, less likely to be professionals, but lumped together were, like their Charleston equivalents, primarily either in commercial or professional occupations. Then there were the reformers, who differed from the simply philanthropic in both cities. None was independently wealthy. Slightly more had occupations outside their homes. Nine-tenths of them were married and to husbands slightly less likely than those of philanthropists to follow high prestige occupations.[14]

These data are subject to various interpretations, none of which can be proven conclusively. But viewed in the context of their distinctive urban cultures, their different meanings become more comprehensible.[15] Much of the activity carried on as private philanthropy in Boston was handled through public or quasi-public institutions in Charleston. In the latter city the hospital for the sick poor was part of the municipal poorhouse; the dispensary for home health care was, like its privately endowed orphan asylum, administered by a board appointed at city hall. In short, Charleston's benevolent activities were very likely to fall within the political sphere, a realm reserved to men. Moreover, because the voluntary associations to which Charleston men belonged were largely clubs that included charity among many other activities, there were few men's groups that resembled the exclusively philanthropic organizations run by women.

In Boston, by contrast, the care of the sick poor was handled largely through privately funded and managed institutions—the Massachusetts General Hospital, the Lying-In Hospital, and the Boston Dispensary among them. It therefore followed that Boston husbands and fathers were more likely than Charleston men to engage in the same kinds of associations as their wives and daughters did. Men, for instance, operated the Boston Asylum for Indigent Boys; women, the Boston Female Asylum. And, although the charter of the latter held the husbands of its married officers accountable for the society's funds handled by their wives, that provision deterred neither men known for their wealth and good works nor their wives, for the Female Asylum's officers included Mrs. Thomas B. Wales, Mrs. Amos Lawrence, and Mrs. William Prescott.[16] In short, it seems likely that Boston husbands, unlike their Charleston counterparts, better understood the private benevolent groups of which their wives were part and actually encouraged their participation. (Significantly, in Charleston, the constitutions of women's benevolent groups uniformly required that the treasurer be single.) And the remarkable similarity of the surnames of the mostly male membership of the Massachusetts Anti-Slavery Society to the Boston Female Anti-Slavery Society roster suggests an even greater community of reform interest within individual homes and families. How much this organizational structure explains the higher proportion of married women active in Boston's benevolent groups is hard to say. Doubtless the fact that proportionately more Charleston women were widows accounts for some of the difference. Nonetheless, it cautions us against assuming that women's associational activity was inherently or necessarily a rebellion—or even a protest—against ties of home and family.

The differences in membership, however, must not obscure the similarities among women's charitable organizations in both cities. In Boston the Fragment Society gave clothing especially to poor women in confinement and to their infants; the Dorcas Society clothed the necessitous and deserving poor; the Female Philanthropic Society pledged "immediate relief" to the "sick and destitute"; and the Ladies Shoe Society shod the feet of indigent children. But in providing charity to still other groups, different urban structures molded different sorts of female philanthropy. While in Charleston churches and men's clubs provided for indigent widows of their former members, in Boston women's groups took much of the responsibility for aiding "deserving widows." There the Fatherless and Widows' Society helped underpaid women working to support their children. And, although its longtime president was Mrs. Ann Amory McLean, whose late husband had endowed the McLean Asylum, its leadership and membership drew middle-class as well as upper-class women from all parts of the city. More elite in both membership and objectives was the similarly named Widows' Society, which sustained "poor and infirm widows and aged single women of good character, who had seen better days, and who were reduced . . . by misfortune."[17] Its leadership in the late 1830s all lived within blocks of the Common; most, in fact, on Beacon Hill. Nevertheless, whatever the source of membership, the institutions founded by such societies were, like their sponsoring groups, run by women. The Children's Friend Society, founded in 1833 to care for the neglected children of indolent and intemperate parents, operated a home that could care for forty children at a time. Admitting 242 youngsters in its first nine years, its annual budget of $3,000 to $4,000 was managed under the supervision of a board headed by the remarried Mrs. Ann Amory McLean Lee and her successors. Similarly managed but less well endowed were the institutions run by the Children's Aid Society and the Samaritan Asylum for Indigent Children.[18] Boston women, as it turned out, were thus more likely to aid the sick and the poor through institutions under their own management than were their southern counterparts, whose similar charity usually focused on fund-raising, visitations to the afflicted, and the direct distribution of largesse. It was here that northern women most visibly exercised the administrative talent that Charleston women used to manage slave property or small businesses.

Furthermore, Boston women, unlike those in Charleston, extended philanthropy to the realm of reform. Two major societies engaged in such work had started as adjuncts to men's groups. The first was formed as an auxiliary to the Seaman's Friend Society, which had, since 1815, furnished sailors "regular evangelical ministration [and the] . . . means for their spiritual and temporal welfare"; and which provided, in the pastor of its Mariners' Church, Edward Taylor, the model for Melville's Father Marple. Then, in 1829, the Female Seaman's Friend Society was founded. Like its Charleston counterpart, it was at first committed only to supporting temperance boardinghouses convenient to the waterfront. But within three years it had become the fully independent Seaman's Aid Society, directing its efforts to bettering the lives of the widows, wives, and daughters of seamen, largely by working to raise the wages of Boston seamstresses. In 1833 it organized a nonprofit store to compete with the privately owned slop shops that made large profits on seamen's clothing. In so doing the society also increased the wages it paid its seamstresses from 33 percent to 100 percent above the going rates. Even so, the maximum weekly wage it paid could not provide a full-time seamstress the three dollars a week she needed for a minimally decent living. Nonetheless, as the society's shop attracted customers, it did improve the economic well-being of the women who sewed for it; and its annual payroll increased from $514 in 1834 to $2,000 in 1840 and, after a depression-connected slump, to almost $3,500 by 1844.[19]

Simultaneously the society's members became ever more aware of the economic exploitation of all women. Its 1836 report, probably written by its president, Sarah Josepha Hale, editor of her own *Ladies Magazine*, asserted that "the profits [created by the work of women] . . . ought to be secured to our sex." But pressing further, it linked the lot of privileged women to that of seamen's wives, attacking the common law that gave "the husband uncontrollable power over the personal property of his wife." "Though she possessed a million dollars before she marries," the report went on—more for the women who sustained the society than for its beneficiaries—"she cannot, after she is a wife, dispose of a dollar in her own right, she must go to her husband to beg money for her charities."[20]

Efforts to redeem prostitutes generated a still more explicit recognition of female bonding across class lines. It started with the 1825 organization of a women's auxiliary to assist the four-year-old, male-operated Penitent Female's Refuge Society. Defying the social conventions that proscribed contact between decent women and their fallen sisters, the new society attracted a solid board of officers, which again included the indefatigable Ann Amory McLean. Nonetheless, in the following years, the parent society severely limited the auxiliary's activities until, in 1835, women formed the independent Boston Female Moral Reform Society, a group free to shape its own program. While the Penitent Female's Refuge Society had confined itself to the moral regeneration of the penitent, the new society not only undertook preventive programs to inform and protect country girls new to the city but also addressed the economics of prostitution. Soon it, too, expanded its concerns to become a voice for the economic rights of all women. All its work was conducted in terms of male exploitation rather than female sin, weakness, and repentance. "Come then to the rescue," read their second annual report, "and let us combine our influence to redeem woman from her wrongs, and her captivity to the caprice of man."[21]

The perceptions of female bonding among presumed equals that committed members of the Odd Ladies Mutual Aid Society "to be sisters not only in word, but in deed,"[22] when they intersected with women's gender-determined responsibility to aid the weak, made northern women address the plight of southern sisters held in bondage. Also, because antislavery reform became a major issue in national politics, it cast women into the public limelight as did no other reform. But overt organizational activity to end slavery was, almost necessarily, forbidden to Charleston women, living as they did in a city whose population was half slave and where, therefore, abolitionism signaled treason to whites and rebellion to blacks.

In Boston, however, criticism of slavery was open and public, though admittedly often unpopular. In 1832, even before the Boston Female Anti-Slavery Society was founded, black Maria W. Stewart had denounced slavery from a public platform and defied, as only Frances Wright had dared do previously, the sanctions against women lecturers. Two years later, urged more by William Lloyd Garrison's *Liberator* than Stewart's single lecture, Boston women formed their own antislavery society and brought to it the techniques that women had developed for blander philanthropy. The society, in sponsoring the first antislavery fair in 1834, initiated an annual event that soon became a major source of funding for abolitionist lecturers and journalists. They also issued annual reports that, like those of the Seaman's Aid and Moral Reform societies, offered pungent propaganda. In 1835, the society invited the highly controversial British abolitionist George Thompson to address their annual meeting and, by so doing, produced Boston's first antiabolitionist mob. Frustrated by Thompson's failure to appear and inflamed by the society's biracial membership, the angry crowd surged against the building in which he was to have spoken until Boston's mayor, Theodore Lyman, arrived. Convinced to allow the women, who left their hall in an orderly double column, to go unharmed, these "gentlemen of property and standing" then vented their wrath by nearly lynching Garrison, whose office in an adjacent building made him an easy target.[23]

The threat of terror, in this case, proved a mother to growth. By 1836 the society's membership reached nearly three hundred; two years later, the Boston Female Anti-Slavery Society raised sufficient funds to employ its own agent and to sponsor as well a regular series of public lectures.[24] Yet some women found its stage too narrow and sought roles in the male-dominated antislavery conventions and the organizations that ran them. The response was an increasingly vocal animosity from those who believed that speaking or acting publicly in men's presence transgressed women's appropriate sphere.

At this point, the Female Anti-Slavery Society members, like those of its counterpart male organizations, factionalized. Radical Garrisonians, regardless of gender, supported women's right to take part in "mixed" meetings; their more conservative, religiously oriented colleagues denounced women who dared serve on "mixed" committees or speak from a public platform. Some of the latter even debated whether there should not be male control over the female society's activities in the familiar pattern in which a minister so often supervised the activities of church-related women's groups. Conversely, radicals suspected that ministers indeed were already manipulating conservative members of the women's society in order to control it.[25] In any case, the more that women sought a larger role, the more did clerics invoke St. Paul's encomium against women's speaking in public.

Specific targets for much of this debate were Angelina and Sarah Grimké.[26] Born in Charleston in 1792, Sarah was the daughter of a prominent, plantation-owning family. Her father was a distinguished lawyer who had codified South Carolina law; her mother, Mary Smith Grimké, was a leader in philanthropic activity. Her favorite brother, Thomas, who shared with her the education she so envied, still could not admit her to his world of college and legal study any more than he could open to her his active role as a lay leader of St. Philip's Church. Denied his options, Sarah's critically inquiring mind made her challenge the status quo. She doubted slavery's morality. She drifted from the family's Calvinist-tinged Episcopalianism to Quaker pietism. Finally, in 1821, a twenty-nine-year-old spinster, she left her native city for Philadelphia, joined there the Society of Friends, whose practice encouraged women's speaking out in church, and came to overtly

Charleston-born Sarah Moore Grimké had, by the time she was fifty, left her native city, become a Quaker, lectured mixed audiences on the evils of slavery, and written her Letters on the Equality of the Sexes, and the Condition of Women *(Wendell Phillips Garrison and Francis Jackson Garrison,* William Lloyd Garrison *[1885], vol. 2)*

antislavery views. Eight years later, her youngest sister, Angelina, whose education Sarah had overseen, arrived in Philadelphia, having traversed a similar religious path.

By 1836, both sisters had plunged into antislavery advocacy. That year the American Anti-Slavery Society published Angelina's *Appeal to the Christian Women of the South* and Sarah's *Epistle to the Clergy of the Southern States*. Each played on the sisters' southern birth and direct experience of slavery—characteristics so rare among vocal abolitionists of either gender that they were both appointed agents of the society. Within a year, they were deluged with invitations to divulge the realities of slavery at local meetings and regional conventions. Even ministers who damned women's presence on a public platform urged their female parishioners to hear the Grimkés' message, and, of course, they themselves attended as pastors. But as wives told husbands, sisters told brothers, and daughters told fathers about what the Grimkés had said, growing numbers of men joined their womenfolk at the lectures. Socially conservative but still antislavery clerics were increasingly uncomfortable with the situation as 1837 wore on and the Grimkés' audiences became noticeably more "mixed." One Boston minister, so Angelina reported, "recommend[ed] our desisting from our present course and confining our labors to our own sex."[27] Yet even he, praising the immediacy that Angelina, the better speaker of the two, brought to the case, wrote his wife spoofing the panic these women were stirring up among his fellow clergy. "Poor souls! they would do well to put on petticoats & [be] done with it. Indeed I suspect *diapers* would not be amiss on some of them! It is really humiliating to see *men* behave as some of our good ministers do."[28]

Nonetheless, this observation reveals a gender anxiety common to clerics, who must be men in the world but whose work lives must be lived largely among women, many of whom were seeking ever larger roles in the churches, of whose membership they already constituted a majority. Ministers' constant allusions to St. Paul's strictures against women's usurping men's place in religious service reveal their underlying fear that women, in asserting themselves as Christian reformers, were threatening to move from pew to pulpit. In any case, it created an open battle within antislavery ranks in which clerics preponderantly chose one side and women activists the other. Because of this, female abolitionists are often credited with having launched the feminist movement in America. So acutely did Sarah Grimké see the issue in these terms that in 1838 she published her *Letters on the Equality of the Sexes* . . . , which likened women's lack of civil and political, as well as religious, rights to the rightlessness of slaves. And here, at least, her antipathy for slavery was overshadowed by her plea for women. "Whatever is *morally* right for a man to do, is *morally* right for a woman to do." And so, "if it is the duty of man to preach the unsearchable riches of Christ, it is the duty also of woman."[29]

But in 1840 when this issue produced a clerical and conservative exodus from the American Anti-Slavery Society, the Grimkés retreated from public reform to a domesticity new to them both.[30] Angelina, then thirty-five, married fellow abolitionist Theodore Weld and, in so doing, embarked on a union that in the following decade brought both spouses close to psychological breakdown and introduced Angelina to the physical traumas of bearing three children, enduring at least as many miscarriages, and suffering the prolapsed uterus that ill-treated pregnancies inflicted on so many nineteenth-century women. This time it was Sarah who followed her younger sister, not into matrimony but into the Welds' Spartan farm home where, at times, she almost usurped the ailing Angelina's maternal role. That in the 1850s the Weld marriage turned around, that Angelina began teaching, and that during the Civil War and after both sisters resumed, in a minor way, the reform activism they seemed to have deserted in 1840 cannot shroud the toll that marrying and mothering took even on women maximally free from the traditional shackles of family and social propriety.

Yet it was not necessarily so. Under the most favorable conditions, marriage and reform were not inherently incompatible, as the dynamic life of the Boston Female Anti-Slavery Society's major voice demonstrated. Born in 1806, Maria Weston[31] was the eldest of five sisters, all of whom became teachers or reformers or both, and two brothers, who were notably less distinguished. Educated largely in England, where she lived with her uncle Joshua Bates, a partner in the vast English banking house of Baring Brothers, Maria returned to Boston in 1828 to teach in the city's new Girls High School. It was then that she met and, in 1830, married Henry Chapman, a Harvard graduate and a partner in his father's extensive mercantile business.

Economically secure in marriage after having been economically independent as a teacher, this beautiful and intelligent young matron seemed to have the world at her feet. Admiring her many attributes, that quintessential Boston snob Edmund Quincy truly believed that she stood "at the head of the human race—men or women."[32] But she was too active simply to be admired—or content with the pleasant social life to which her husband's resources and social standing entitled her. As members of William Ellery Channing's Unitarian church, she and Henry responded to weekly sermons exhorting parishioners to recognize their moral obligations and act out their consequent duties in the world. In the early 1830s, that was a world stirred by William Lloyd Garrison's damnation of slavery, inspired by British emancipation in the West Indies, and startled by the American Anti-Slavery Society's call for the immediate abolition of slavery in the United States. By 1834 both Chapmans had joined the abolitionist crusade. In 1835 Henry, who as an undergraduate had embraced temperance reform, was elected treasurer of the Massachusetts Anti-Slavery Society, the same year in which Maria was made secretary of the Boston Female Anti-Slavery Society. Rapidly her reform role overshadowed his. Her *Right and Wrong* pamphlets were less the annual reports of the Female Anti-Slavery Society than independent polemics rallying those doing right as Maria defined it and chastising all others as wrong. The Chapman home on Summer Street soon became the informal meeting place for Boston abolitionists. The antislavery bazaars she organized were major money raisers for the cause. So visible was she that in 1839 she actually received several write-in votes for lieutenant governor in state elections.

But none of this unsexed the extraordinary, slender, graceful

When this daguerreotype of Maria Weston Chapman, which "falls short of the rare beauty of the original," was made, she was a widow, the mother of three adolescent children, and a propagandist so passionate and fund-raiser so extraordinary that she dominated the inner circle of Boston abolitionists, who had long made her home their meeting place. (Wendell Phillips Garrison and Francis Jackson Garrison, William Lloyd Garrison [1885], vol. 2)

woman with her golden hair, brilliant complexion, and deep blue eyes. In ten years of marriage, she and Henry had four children. Indeed, it was Henry's health that declined, as his consumption worsened until, by 1839, he was an invalid. All this Maria took in stride without interrupting her reform commitment. Only once was she overwhelmed—on her single appearance as a public lecturer before a large, mixed audience. After a spectacular performance at the Women's Anti-Slavery Convention in a hall surrounded by a hostile, howling mob of proslavery Philadelphians, she succumbed to a "brain fever" that nearly killed her.

Her narrow escape from a mob set on arson and her desperate bout with an illness that threatened her sanity defined limits of which she had not previously been aware. Nonetheless, the experience seemed to make her tougher and more committed to the cause. Yet so active a commitment was made possible only by family. One or another of her maiden sisters was almost always on hand to free Maria from child-care responsibilities. The elder Mr. Chapman made adequate housing and servants available even when Henry could no longer work. When the latter's health demanded travel to a warm climate, the Chapmans could go to Haiti where, in a land made free by slave revolt, they could continue their antislavery activity, taking part in the Port-au-Prince antislavery society and writing semipublic letters to friends at home.

Her opportunities and her accomplishments as an abolitionist thus only made Maria Chapman demand a broader field of action. "We once verily believed we were in the way of duty, when we carefully eschewed every enlarged and comprehensive purpose, as masculine, and unsuited to our sex. Our eyes being opened to our error, we cannot be expected again to close them to the value of the christian character as it may and ought to be exemplified in woman."[33] While Henry still lived, he encouraged Maria's claim to act in the public sphere usually reserved to men. When, in 1842, he died, her crusading only intensified. She became a dominant power among the Garrisonian abolitionists as their chief money raiser and planner of campaigns. When Garrison was sick or out of town, she frequently edited the *Liberator*; when the *National Antislavery Standard* fell into ideological error, she became its coeditor. Indeed, her activities expanded so much after Henry's death that one may question how important his support had been. Apparently so did Maria in her later life when she came to doubt the wisdom of talented women's marrying at all. While men "in situations of peril and difficulty . . . looked up for aid to women superior to themselves in ability," they also preferred that the women they married be "inferior to themselves" and shaped the institution accordingly.[34]

Very few women, even among reformers, either enjoyed the personal independence or achieved the public power that Maria Weston Chapman did. Indeed, few created, even for a part of their lives, the visible public role of the Grimkés. Together these active abolitionists and feminists mark one pole of a spectrum whose other extreme lay with the many women whose church participation gave them only the spiritual strength to bear things as they were. Yet the trinity of piety, philanthropy, and reform were, in mid-nineteenth-century cities, not merely static categories but a dynamic pathway that led women out of their homes. Churches that offered weekday prayer meetings or the opportunity to teach in Sunday school provided pious fulfillment broader than that enjoyed by most rural women. Although few poor or working-class women had the free time or financial resources to do so, middle- and upper-class women might go from participation in a church-connected and clerically supervised sewing circle or fund-raising bazaar to other benevolent activity in which women themselves set and controlled the program. But at that point, regional differences began to mold the options available to urban women of each city as prevailing social values and existing institutions established the philanthropic structure within which they must act. The private nature of Boston's social service encouraged women's operation of charitable institutions—whether orphanages, shelters, or cooperative slop shops—far more than did the governmentally operated charity of Charleston and its men's clubs that mixed charity with other activities. The distinctions were even more evident when it came to reform, which the rapid economic changes in

Boston more readily fostered than did Charlestonians' determination to preserve social values that were increasingly under attack. Nonetheless, the Grimké sisters demonstrated that Charleston women could, at the cost of exile, follow the dictates of Christian conscience into a reform that challenged the very basis of their society. There is no better illustration that piety need not produce passivity in women any more than it does in men.

7

Propriety, Sexuality, and Self-Control

Maintaining propriety, limiting sexuality, and promoting self-control in their own lives, like instilling those values in their children, reinforcing them in their social circles, and imposing them on their gender at large, were central to women's socially defined role. Yet within those expectations of behavioral decorum, there was latitude. A woman's age, class, or race might permit a greater flexibility than female respectability generally permitted. In Boston, a lady could, as did the young Mrs. Charles Lyman, enjoy the shock she created by appearing at a party in skirts "so short, that she was afraid to stoop for her fan when she dropt it"; or could, as did the wife of Harrison Gray Otis, Jr., sport "very short petticoats" to call attention not just to her "slate colored stockings wrought with black" but to the ankles they covered.[1] Nor did anyone shun wealthy Mary Mason Parkman, who had divorced her errant husband, while Mme D'Hauteville was invited to all the parties despite her public defiance of her husband's legal actions to force her return to his bed.[2]

Yet in most ways ladies were even more tied to convention than were other decent women, for it was they who guarded the gates of social propriety, passing judgment on women whose own or whose husbands' ambitions could be fulfilled only when they were received by ladies as ladies. Making and receiving calls was thus a critical ritual, whose substance was often considerably more than an exchange of visits. Charleston's Floride Colhoun Calhoun, wife of the vice president of the United States, created a political crisis when she refused to call on a former barmaid, unredeemed in her eyes, at least, by marriage to a cabinet officer. And less dramatic, Harriott Horry Rutledge would not return a series of intrusive calls from her new Charleston neighbor, a Mrs. Shubrick, who had "moved into Legare St & filled up the old Ben Elliott rat trap in a style to astonish the old elms." So heavy was the obligation inherent in receiving and returning calls that the wife of Boston congressman Edward Everett could only beg off from so tiresome a chore on the grounds of its being "quite beyond my strength."[3]

Nonetheless, many women eyed ladies' lives with admiration and imitated their life-style as far as their resources permitted. Some, like Cordelia Jenks, daughter of a poor but Harvard-educated Congregational minister, yearned in vain for a single invitation to the Boston aristocracy's "balls and parties." Others, totally unfamiliar with the mansions in which such parties were held, were more easily satisfied with small family parties or public dances. But the latter were hazardous and might plummet a woman into disgrace if she mingled with the wrong sort. Thus a Boston hackman and his wife boycotted Artemus Frost's dancing school when Frances Ely, a young tailoress suspected of having lived an immoral life in New York, began to frequent it.[4] Similar criteria of propriety had to be met if those whose purses precluded summer vacations at Nahant, Newport, or Flat Rock were to enjoy the ladies' bathing facilities at Charleston's White Point Garden or, in Boston, at the ladies' swimming bath at the foot of Chestnut Street. Lacking the carriages in which their betters rode, they sought civil control of the rowdies who marred their strolls down Boston's Beacon and Tremont streets or on the equally stylish promenade along Charleston's Battery. Without entrée to soirées, they amused themselves at elevating lectures and concerts of sacred music. Yet, though imitating ladies by escaping the confines of domesticity, they were even more restrained by the rigid limits of pure womanhood. They lacked the powerful fathers and brothers to protect them when their marriages went sour. They could rely less on family resources to provide economic security in misfortune. They were more exposed to slurs should they depart from a strict appearance of virtue. Therefore, their claim to respect lay in endorsing a popular prescription for woman's proper place that, by chance or circumstance outside their control, might elude them.

That the proper prescription was known and clear to all was assumed—though perhaps unjustly. In Charleston the Episcopal press condemned the unhealthy excitement that dancing bred in women, while the secular press lambasted the Academy of Fine Arts for its "demoralizing influence" in displaying paintings of Adam and Eve without fig leaves. And in Boston, pewholders of the Hollis Street Unitarian Church urged their minister's dismissal because, among other indecencies, John Pierpont had discussed the courtesans of Pauline Corinth with his female parishioners, while a Massachusetts court imprisoned Abner Kneeland for advocating artificial limitations on fertility to his freethinking followers.[5] In short, keepers of the public conscience found open display or discussion of sexuality offensive, especially when it implied a potential loss of self-control—or declaration of independence—that could dash women from their pedestals.

For many, however, all of that implied only sanctimonious preaching of an inapplicable standard. What happened to those to whom reality offered little access to the ideal? What alternatives in either city were there for a woman with neither property nor spouse, whose work garnered wages insufficient for an adequate diet let alone decent shelter or attractive clothing? What of those whose race or poverty or status as slaves excluded them from the cult of domesticity? Women they were; wenches they were perceived to be. Joseph Tuckerman, Boston's famed Unitarian city missionary, addressed the central issue head-on. His 1829 prize essay on the wages paid females examined the intersection of low wages, cultural deprivation, youthful ambition, and vice. Looking particularly at the minimally educated daughters of the urban poor, he traced them as they sought legitimate employment only to find that the wages paid them for long hours at demanding work condemned them to "wants and suffering" beyond endurance. Falling into debt, they moved from place to place, "dunned, and threatened, and harassed" by creditors demanding repayment. Removed from family and friends—or even living with them in neighborhoods where they were subject to "the gaze, and to the address, of the lowest and basest"—their "situation [was] too perilous for human virtue." "They are offered the wages of guilt," Tuckerman lamented, "and they accept them."[6]

Often, however, the impetus to illicit sex, as Tuckerman was well aware, was the importunity of suitors unwilling to wait until marriage bonds sanctified sensuality. In fact, as early-nineteenth-century restraints on premarital intercourse increased, so too did successful breach of promise suits brought by females whose lovers promised marriage, had their fun, and then reneged. Indeed, the courts, except where evidence showed that the women had sought or enjoyed their seduction, generally awarded them damages. Yet that very practice pointed to a chain of overlapping ambiguities. Even in an era when many asserted that women were asexual, wives had no protection from their husbands' demands. As reformer and reluctant mother Caroline Dall put it, "In the eyes of the law, female chastity is only valuable for the work it can do" in forcing a man into marriage.[7] Breach of promise suits were, in fact, testament to the double standard imposed by gender.

"Sad are the accounts," Tuckerman observed, " . . . of conjugal infidelity and profligacy even among some men, who stand well in the world."[8] Men could continue to stand well in the world despite others' knowledge of that profligacy. And if this was true of mature respectability, it was even more blatantly the case among young bloods. One circle of privileged young Boston men teased each other about "all the conquests" they made, "the lips [they] kissed," and the "c———ts [they] felt."[9] They jested about their bachelor friend who, late one night, had found a young infant he presumably had sired abandoned on his doorstep. Yet there was public indignation when a Miss Sampson was revealed to have been made pregnant by a church organist and when a Boston school master was sentenced for adultery. And worst of all were the transgressions of a Congregational minister who was condemned by an ecclesiastical council and fired by his church after an initial revelation that he had seduced a young servant in his own household led to evidence that he had been fornicating with his mature parishioners for years.[10] The distinctions were clear. Men—especially the young and unattached—who sowed their wild oats among women nobody knew were tolerated. But when presumably respectable men who had access to women of their own class and standing violated the trust accorded them, their sins were vigorously condemned. Thus was female virtue guarded. True women and well-placed ladies were by definition chaste unless they flagrantly violated prevailing mores. They were to be protected. But for the boys who would be boys—or men, men—there were the lusty wenches so tarnished by Eve's heritage that they fell outside the bounds of both chastity and marital fidelity.

Records of southern life produce a similar complexity. Most familiar was the sexual exploitation of slave women by their owners or other white men. Indeed, it would be hard to account for so sizable a mulatto population without acknowledging that pattern. But Charleston men, like their Boston equivalents, also seduced white women. One can only guess Diana Clark's standing that left a hung jury after an "amusing altho' vulgar" bastardy trial in the court of general sessions. Similar was the "no bill" finding when William Smith, an unemployed man boarding at the French Coffee House, seduced a fifteen-year-old girl apprenticed to the establishment. But if these men escaped scot-free after being charged, that was not the fate of previously respectable women whose behavior defied propriety. Thus the Congregational church excommunicated Mrs. Sarah Hart for her "grossly immoral conduct" and voted to exclude from the church altogether a Miss Sarah Naser whose "gross sin" had resulted in her bearing a child out of wedlock.[11] For their fall from virtue, these women were ostracized. But however one responds to their fate, it was individual and distinctive, quite different in nature from the presumption that made all black women wenches. And it was that presumption that shaped the nightlife of many young bloods in Charleston. "I have not indulged with a white woman since I came [to town]," wrote one recent arrival. "I have thus far stuck to Carolina 'dark or bright'. You know it is beneath the Dignity of any true Carolinian to '*run over*' a woman of his own color as long as he is a single man—or any other than his wife after marriage."[12]

Even the response to forcible rape varied according to the victim's status. In 1840 the Boston police responded swiftly to the plight of a recently arrived Maine girl strolling through the Common on a summer evening with a respectable man, who ran for help after he had been jumped by three young toughs for whom he was no match. Help arrived to save Miss Bryant from the proverbial fate worse than death—but only barely, for the partially undressed Jeremiah Donovan already had her on the ground. She was, all things considered, lucky. She had been properly escorted, her intentions were not suspect, her respectability was recognized by the press that reported the case, and her reputation was saved. The less respectable were less fortunate, for women of "evil fame" could expect no sympathy. Both in South Carolina and in Massachusetts, the courts assumed that because the testimony of such women must be suspect, they could seek no legal redress against sexual violence. Thus when the mulatto Boston prostitute Maria Griffin charged Joseph Calash, a black man, with rape, the court only chastised her "manners and morals." And because "the evidence against her character [was] conclusive," a police court judge similarly set Patrick Currow free even though he had raped Maryann Mullenn in the presence of witnesses.[13]

Because rapes were neither rare nor unreported, they heightened the fears of sexual violence that women of all classes shared even though the highest incidence of such violence seems to have occurred among the ranks of the poor and of those with little hope of redress. So, if Sarah Grimké spoke for the majority of the abused when she addressed the intense sufferings of slave women who were "at the mercy of irresponsible tyrants" out to gratify their "brutal lust," other privileged Charleston women worried about their own danger. Anna Johnson, eighteen-year-old daughter of a Supreme Court justice, trembled in the aftershock of the abortive slave revolt plotted by Denmark Vesey. Noting that her father, along with Governor Thomas Bennett and Intendant/Mayor James Hamilton, had been slated for murder, she believed that she and her friends had been destined for rape while her cousin had been "set apart for the wife or more properly the 'light of the Haram' [sic] of one of their chiefs."[14]

If Anna Johnson's fears were triggered by unique circumstances, they nonetheless resembled those of many women made uneasy by the gangs of rowdies who roamed the streets of both cities. Carousing late at night, they shouted vulgarities and screamed obscenities. Occasionally they broke down doors and entered houses. And in daylight hours, some exposed themselves to ladies sitting at their windows, while others, with apparent impunity, assaulted women who were doing their shopping.[15]

Least secure were those who found no safety even at home. Sarah Grimké addressed their plight in her *Letters on the Equality of the Sexes* . . . , in which she assumed that domestic violence was largely confined to the poor. Accordingly she explained it in terms of a contracted "sphere of duty" resulting from lower-class men's deprivation "of the means of intellectual culture, and of the opportunity of exercising their judgment."[16] Despite the class bias in Grimké's analysis, it does reflect a public awareness formed by court proceedings and the press. Fairly typical were the events noted in a single year by the *Boston Daily Advertiser*. An otherwise unidentified man living in a rookery on the backside of Beacon Hill assaulted his wife with a knife with clear intent to kill her. In nearby Fayette Street, another such husband did murder his wife. Up in the North End, a young printer who had long ill-treated his wife, finally gave her so severe a beating with a fire iron that she died. And in a tenement crowded with immigrant families, a John Egan tried to strangle his wife in the flat— and bed—they shared with another Irish couple.[17]

Such events were not, of course, exclusive to the poor or the shiftless. Boston's municipal court, in 1834, tried the former editor of the *Castigator*—ironically a journal dedicated to exposing vice—for having assaulted and beaten his wife on at least five occasions in the preceding six months. In 1842 the press reported divorce proceedings in which rising businessman Thomas Dunham was sued by his wife for "neglect and ill-treatment." And such cases were both sufficiently frequent and shocking to create the single exception to the legal doctrine that because husband and wife were one, neither might testify against the other in a court of law. Even ultra-conservative Peter Oxenbridge Thacher, judge of Boston's municipal court for over twenty years, made it a special point to instruct the jury in a suit brought by a much-battered Mrs. Brobston that a wife might testify against her spouse for violence committed against her in her own home.[18]

Although the parallel Charleston court of general sessions seemingly heard no such cases for the entire decade of the 1830s, South Carolina state courts did grant separations with alimony to white women abused by their husbands. In addition, the fragmentary reports of the magistrates and freeholders courts, which tried all cases involving blacks, suggest that cases of domestic violence were not uncommon.

If, in both cities, some women were victimized by men, some also suffered self-inflicted abuse. Living in a country where, in 1830, adult Americans consumed an average of seven gallons of alcohol per year,[19] many women like many men became alcoholics. One may speculate about how many women drank on the sly and went undetected in the privacy of their homes. But at least in Boston they were almost as likely as men to be public drunkards. Almost one half of those appearing before the police court for common drunkenness were women.[20] And this was so great a problem that, in a city where few women engaged in any reform activity, female Charlestonians were highly visible in Washingtonian societies formed in the early 1840s to aid confessed drunkards to achieve sobriety.

Far more extensive in confirming that alcoholism was a major problem for Boston women was the frequency and extent of their signatures on temperance petitions. Doubtless part of their very visible role in fighting demon rum was, as it probably was also in Charleston, their desire to rescue husbands and fathers from the drunkenness often associated with domestic violence. But Boston's Female Total Abstinence Society made no secret of the fact that women were alcohol's direct as well as indirect victims. "Many of our own sex in this goodly city, in the different relations of life, have become subjects of the loathsome vice of intemperance." And just as alarming was the fact that these were not Irish immigrants but rather the mothers, daughters, wives, and sisters of "our own people and kindred." They polluted their own homes, left themselves and their families morally desolate, traduced their role as mothers, and induced a self-image "from which the soul turns away in loathing and despair." What failure of self-control could exceed that which made "the very song that rocks the cradle of infancy . . . the song of the debauch"? What clearer downward slide from true woman to wench than the "hopeless ruin" of alcoholism?[21]

By contrast, women retained their social position when they took solace in drugs rather than alcohol. Often introduced to opium or its derivatives as medicine to relieve menstrual pain or the agonies induced by too frequent childbearing, women became dependent on its psychological numbing. Miss Mary Hort, the Charleston schoolteacher, recorded in her diary her unsuccessful battle with the temptations of "Le D."—probably laudanum. "Resolutions broken—time wasted—Le D. indulged too prevalently—excuse—to keep off worldly cares." Dean of the Charleston bar, James L. Petigru, exulted that, when his wife was diverted by fashionable New York life, she took less morphine and stayed in bed less than she did in Charleston. The eighty-two-year-old mother of Boston's renowned merchant banker William Appleton, who had begun using opium some twenty years earlier as a medicine to treat diarrhea, still consumed a full four pounds of it a year. Yet whatever their underlying problems, these women made drugs a tool of survival and were neither destroyed nor declassed by them. They were safe from the public condemnation of Mary Lane, a prostitute in Charleston's notorious Elliott Street, who "destroyed herself" in 1843 "by taking Laudanum, in a fit of jealousy."[22]

Commonly shared fears and anxieties did not obliterate the role that society defined for reputable women as guardians of personal—and especially sexual—self-control; few reformers, therefore, emphasized universal bonds of sisterhood unqualified by behavioral, class, and race distinctions. Sometimes ladies and other respectable women did assist those who had succumbed to drink or sex. Generally, however, ladies shunned those they deemed their inferiors. Less privileged women frequently envied the life-styles of ladies and scorned those whose failed self-control signaled the dire results that economic misfortune or behavioral misstep might bring. Wenches seldom had much faith in the women from whom their poverty, their deviance, or their exclusion from the cult of true womanhood isolated them. Thus did the ideal of a single female role fall before the fact of complex social realities in both Charleston and Boston.

8

The World of Wenches

No group of women so violated the prescriptions for self-control and domesticity—let alone purity and respectability—as did prostitutes. Some doubtless were driven to the trade by victimization; others deliberately chose it as a means to support themselves or to gain freedom from social and familial restraints. In South Carolina that choice was not illegal because prostitution was not a crime. Unthreatened by police or courts, prostitutes were also largely free from individual public condemnation in a state whose laws made "imputing . . . a want of chastity" to any woman legitimate grounds for civil suit.[1] So with courts and press largely mute on the subject, we can only glimpse the lives of those who walked Charleston's streets or worked in its brothels.

Yet their general outline is clear. Active, overt, and available female sexuality was explicitly identified with black wenches, in whom it was tolerated, expected, even encouraged. When men sought prostitutes, the choice of black over white tailored personal desire to a value structure in which race separated wenches from women deserving respect. William Gilmore Simms, in his defense of *Slavery in America*, connected sexual exploitation directly with involuntary servitude. "The negro and the colored woman in the south, supply the place, which at the north is usually filled with factory and serving girls."[2]

Moreover the public complaints of Charlestonians whose lives were disrupted by their noise and violence map the city's brothels. Residents of the fourth ward denounced the mulattoes and prostitutes who turned Clifford Alley, a scant block from two major churches,

into a "constant scene of nightly brawls and riots." They protested to
the mayor that Dietrick Olandt's tavern was "an improper and disorderly house." And mayoral investigation elicited evidence that Olandt
maintained several females in "the upper portion of his house." Yet
Clifford Alley remained unchanged, as did Elliott Street and Bedon's
Alley, where Cornel June's brothel was only one of several that served
the waterfront trade. And if June's house was denounced in the press
for keeping between six and fifteen white women in service against
their will, there was not even that much sympathy for black women
similarly used. Thus when a favorite young mulatto servant was
beaten to death by two young bloods whose propositions she had
scorned, her owner's only legal recourse was to sue the white assail-
ants for her dead slave's market value.[3]

Despite such knowledge, respectable Charleston women were
less concerned with their men's philandering abroad than with their
sexual indulgence with servants at home. Mary Boykin Chesnut addressed that fact in her famous observation that every southern matron "is ready to tell you who is the father of all the mulatto children in
everybody's household but her own." Sarah Grimké was equally direct
about the white woman made wretched from "seeing the virtue of her
enslaved sister sacrificed . . . [to] the crimes of seduction and illicit
intercourse," the "licentiousness . . . in her own domestic circle."
Open indignation at paid prostitution, therefore, was largely masculine. The Reverend Thomas Smyth of the Second Presbyterian Church
roundly denounced the "gids [sic] and goddesses" who rendezvoused
in the theater's third tier, expressly set apart for their convenience.
Factors and master mariners tried to keep seamen out of the brothels
near the wharves lest ships lack a crew when the tide and wind were
right. Irate householders complained when "disorderly houses" patronized by "wicked and depraved persons of every class" disturbed
their sleep. Judges and juries intervened, though only when a patron
was robbed of a wallet carelessly left in trousers temporarily dis-
carded.[4]

Paradoxically the situation was not that much different in Boston
although prostitution was explicitly illegal and therefore the object of

repeated public attack. There, despite private reform action and governmental cleanup efforts, the city's red light district scarcely changed in the years between 1820 and 1850—except to grow in size. The estimated two thousand prostitutes—both full- and part-time—who in 1820 plied their trade in "numerous, disorderly, and lewd houses" where "vice of almost any kind" was practiced, were not uprooted. Neither raids ordered by Mayor Josiah Quincy in 1823 nor a grand jury investigation launched by Judge Peter Thacher's municipal court in 1831 nor the new police department's sweeps through the city's disorderly houses in the early 1840s had more than a temporary effect.[5]

Perhaps this was so because public officials—like many private reformers—were less concerned with prostitution itself than with its effect on respectable Boston. The grand jury of 1831 focused attention on the way in which the "young and unwary" were "decoyed" into pernicious brothels. Antivice crusader H. K. Stockton laid bare the real danger in the theaters' upper balconies where "Harlots" met their "paramours." He had seen there "the Merchants clerk, the Mechanics apprentice and the Physicians and Lawyers students, all joining hand in hand with the most worthless of the female sex." Or to put the case in dollars and cents, $300,000 a year was diverted from the legitimate economy by such goings-on.[6]

Fathers, like the employers and teachers of young clerks, apprentices, and students, thus found good reason to press their sons—as they did their daughters—into early courtship and marriage because it promised to control male as well as female behavior. Nor was this male response limited to middle- and upper-class men. It was laborers, truckmen, and mechanics who in 1833 rioted against the rookeries of the South End and who in 1834 burned the Ursuline Convent in neighboring Charlestown after Protestant ministers alleged that young Boston ladies were there subjected to sexual irregularities. When humble folk resort to rioting and ministers who begin sermons by condemning prostitution end them by damning wife swapping,[7] we have a strong clue that prostitution was a lightning rod for all sorts of fantasies and anxieties. And in a city where state law barred miscegenation and where abolitionist women made that law a special target, we find that race was clearly one such anxiety. Indeed, the brothels were almost the only places in the city on a hill that were truly interracial. Both court and newspaper reports never failed to stress that point. Maria Williams, a "very black" madam, was convicted for "entertain[ing] white gentry" in her establishment. Rebecca Newcomb, a white "drab," was sentenced to six months for speaking to "any man in the street, without any distinction of rank, character . . . or color." But it took a report on a black male proprietor who employed white prostitutes to expose the most explicit concerns. His was an "unlicensed African Theatre, where white-teethed Othello's could woo and win their Desdemonas."[8]

Responding to this richly symbolic medley, the press abounded with exposés intended either to titillate or shock staid readers. Its reports of cases tried before a police court magistrate or a municipal court judge and jury portrayed the lives of the "lesser sort." Here appeared the women who plied their trade on the congested waterfront where sailors swarmed, on the rough back slope of Beacon Hill were the city's black residents congregated, and in the tangled courts and alleys of the densely populated North End. They had solicited working-class men in dance halls and dram shops or entertained them in bordellos that attracted "idle vagabonds" and "worthless and profligate" individuals "of the most abandoned character." Between Buttolph and Ann streets, in Salem and Hanover streets, along Southac and Gouch streets were such scenes of "sporting life" that in only one month of an 1844 antivice campaign, the police raided sixty-three different brothels.[9]

The madams or proprietors of brothels, when they were arrested, were given jury trials in municipal court while prostitutes generally passed swiftly before a single magistrate sitting on the police court bench. The difference in trial forms, whatever its jurisdictional cause, doubtless also reflected unspoken social attitudes. It may have been that propertied entrepreneurs who engaged in the selling of sex were considered more socially disruptive than were women with few other alternatives. But more demonstrably evident was that the city, despite sizable antivice drives that occurred roughly once each decade, used its police and courts to tax rather than to eradicate prostitution.

Almost uniformly, a prostitute brought before a police court magistrate was fined four or five dollars or, if she could not pay the fine, was sentenced to three months in the house of correction. Normally she either paid the fine herself or was assisted by a patron or pimp. In any case, she customarily returned promptly to her work. Madams, however, were more heavily fined and, if unable to pay a fifty-dollar levy, were sentenced to twice as long a period of correction. On those infrequent occasions when johns were arrested, they were fined but not incarcerated.

Several overlapping factors that help explain this structure were evident in a press report detailing a raid on an Ann Street house. Arrested were Nancy Decker, who kept a "house of illicit intercourse," and her four "girls." The Boston Morning Post reported that "the men, being sailors, were allowed to depart, a little scared. The women were led captive to jail." There, Decker was held for trial because she lacked $300 bail money. But the "young ladies who helped pay her rent" were freed at once after paying their fines. The city watchmen who had made the raid were consoled, the Post observed, with the likelihood that the women so released "might be soon brought up again, and another round of witness fees be earned thereby." One final factor in this and so many other cases that the press chose to report was that Nancy Decker was a Negro and her girls "brown beauties."[10]

The familiar pattern provokes a series of explanatory hypotheses. Men caught in the act might be ridiculed for engaging in illicit sex but were unlikely to be punished. Brothel operators were punished more severely than their employees for reasons other than the protection of public morals. Despite the overt condemnation of interracial sex in newspaper reports, the same reports publicized sexual contacts between black and white. And, despite public demand for police action, professional prostitutes not only were tolerated but also were punished far less severely than women who fell visibly from respectability. Thus, at the same time that a madam might expect punishment of a fifty-dollar fine or six months in jail, a Boston court sentenced an adulteress to two years of hard labor and her paramour to eighteen months. Moreover, the most rigorously punished of Boston's brothel keepers, a Dr. Hollis Churchill, whose alleged hospital employed male and female prostitutes to serve customers of both sexes, was sentenced to a single year of hard labor, half the term given the adulteress.[11] Indeed, one might argue that, though their laws differed fundamentally, Boston and Charleston were much alike in tolerating the sale of sex by women of the lower orders and in laying low women who, swept by passion, lost their self-control. Even Boston's Female Moral Reform Society directed its early efforts not at attempting "to reform the vicious" but at "fortifying the citadel of virtue in our midst" by bolstering woman "with a greater respect for her own character, and a contempt towards those who would beguile her from the path of virtue."[12]

Not surprisingly, neither Boston's official efforts nor the voluntary activity of the Penitent Female's Refuge Society or the Female Moral Reform Society eliminated prostitution. And so, lacking either the ability to support themselves otherwise or the determination to be chaste—or both—wenches continued to pass through city institutions. In the house of correction, to which those convicted by the municipal and police courts were sentenced, women were expected to sew, cook, clean, and nurse but were taught no new trades by which to support themselves. The house of reformation for juvenile offenders, to which wayward and stubborn girls were admitted, taught them only sewing and domestic work—never the mechanical skills in which boys were instructed. A bare 10 to 15 percent of the inmates, girls had no exercise yard or gym of the sort provided males. Their schooling was less systematic. And on Sundays they were at first closeted off in a veiled recess of the chapel and later allowed to worship only in a room directly above the chapel where they heard the word of God through a hole cut in the floor. In 1834, the house's director appealed to city authorities to exclude girls from the house altogether, because boys who might otherwise be reformed were led astray by the girls' unrestrained sexual appetites. And when, six years later, the city did provide them a separate facility, it excluded female delinquents driven by "passions untimely developed" and given over to "frightful activity" by denying entry to all girls over twelve as well as to those younger girls the superintendent found unfit.[13]

Less punitive—at least in theory—was the house of industry in which paupers were confined to learn the value of work. Yet because it was in truth Boston's almshouse and public hospital, the last resort for those deemed the unworthy and disreputable poor, it was a catch-all for the very old, the very young, and the very sick. Its female inmates of an age to be industrious were likely to be "pregnant with bastard children" or nursing the same or suffering either from venereal disease or delirium tremens. Admitted "from the abodes of prostitution and intemperance," their destitution was understood to be the wages of moral failure, the inevitable result of flamboyant sexuality or self-destroying alcoholism.[14] And so, according to the values of their time and place, they were by definition as much wenches as their associates in the houses of correction and reformation. Indeed, residence in any city institution—except perhaps among very old or very young females—testified to a lapse in the self-control that respectable women were expected to exert. To be in a city institution was, by definition, to be a wench—because one was deviant, because one was poor, because one lacked a family connection to give one status, security, and shelter.

Yet many of those in the house of correction had, with whatever results, at least attempted to be independent. They were active women—victims perhaps of social circumstances but defiant, too, in a manner rather different from incarcerated men. In one six-month period, in addition to 64 of the 140 female inmates who had been sentenced for drunkenness, there were 32 convicted of nightwalking or other "wanton and lascivious behavior," and 15 for some form of theft.[15] The distribution of the misdemeanors for which women were committed changed little during the 1830s and 1840s. But the difference that does stand out is that distinguishing female from male prisoners. The specific illegal techniques for dealing with poverty

*The stark architecture and barren landscape of Boston's House of Industry and House of Correction when they opened in 1825 reflect the social as well as physical isolation captured in this illustration from Caleb H. Snow's 1828 His-*tory of Boston. (*Courtesy of the Massachusetts Historical Society*)

were gender related. Though there was little difference between the sexes in age distribution, rates of recidivism, or addiction to drink, the distribution of crimes against property and of sex-related crimes was overwhelmingly determined by the gender of the offender. From December 1842 through June 1843, for instance, there were six men sent up for theft for each woman so sentenced. But in that same period, only 6 men were jailed for lewd and lascivious behavior while 118 women were convicted for prostitution or related activities.[16]

A second characteristic becomes clear as one examines those Boston women sentenced for misbehavior that was neither alcohol nor sex related. Like their male counterparts, they were decidedly more likely to have committed crimes against property than against persons. For one eight-month period in 1835, for example, thirteen women were sentenced by police and municipal courts for larceny and only three were sentenced for assault. And the increase in shoplifting that storekeepers reported during the depression that came on the heels of the 1837 panic also comports with Joseph Tuckerman's observation that in Boston women's crimes—whether prostitution or theft—were rooted in poverty.[17]

Yet the forms that women's criminality took were also a function of their differing urban environments. Although extant Charleston court records reveal comparatively little about women's criminality because very few cases involving them ever reached the court of general sessions, the record that does exist suggests that white women's entanglement with the law, like southern white men's, differed from the Boston pattern. The crimes tried in the southern city were twice as likely to be assaults on persons as theft of property. And even when white Charleston women were charged with offenses against property, the nature of the offense was likely to differ from that of their northern sisters. Most notably they were brought to justice for sheltering fugitive slaves. In addition, perhaps because they were more engaged in retail trade than northern women, they were also more visibly trafficking in stolen goods than stealing them. There may be a connection between the two, for anecdotal evidence sustains the common belief that slaves pilfered the homes and businesses of their owners and fenced the goods in the city. Yet here, too, the case is inferential because thefts of this sort, when discovered, were generally punished by the slave's master rather than by a public institution. Still, the city did maintain a workhouse in which—either at the order of a private owner or the magistrates and freeholders court that tried blacks charged with serious crimes—slaves were punished by being whipped or by being forced to walk the treadmill. When the 1830 census was taken, twenty of the fifty-seven slave inmates in the workhouse were women.[18]

Regional differences shaped other city institutions as well. Poor, native-born white Charleston women, especially those with children, were more likely to be provided outdoor relief and thus less likely to experience the institutionalization that characterized those of similar circumstances in the North. And because Charleston's almshouse was also the city's only hospital—except the marine hospital, which catered exclusively to sailors—its care of the sick, even women in childbirth, less readily identified them as irredeemable wenches. Yet because alcoholism and venereal disease were seemingly as prevalent there as in Boston's house of industry, it is probable that factors other than either illness or poverty alone set its female inmates apart from acceptable respectability. And, as in Boston, they were interconnected. Women patients were overwhelmingly seamstresses—that most notoriously overcrowded and underpaid of female occupations. In a single year, forty-one of the forty-five women admitted to the hospital, or over 90 percent of the total, were seamstresses. And of them, nearly half suffered from intemperance or mania (probably mania a potu or delirium tremens).[19] These white women were made wenches by a combination of poverty and loss of self-control that blurred the distinctions southerners preferred to make between black and white females.

In sum, the majority of women hospital patients were little different from those who simply inhabited the poorhouse. The distinction between them lay rather in the longer periods of the latter's residence and their more frequent returns. But collectively these women did differ notably from the men who comprised the majority of the poorhouse residents. Of the men receiving almshouse shelter, 45 percent were over forty, but only 14 percent of the women were that old.[20] Whether it was this age difference or the different reasons for men's and women's being refused outdoor relief in the first place— and thus for their institutionalization—the women more readily than the men "eloped" through the frequently unlocked gates or over the low walls surrounding the house. Generally, too, after a binge of longer or shorter duration, these escapees returned voluntarily. No one illustrates the hopeless pattern better than Louisa Uttes, who not only eloped regularly but as regularly smuggled liquor onto the premises where she was repeatedly found drunk. In December 1840 the Charleston Poor House rolls recorded her fiftieth admission to the institution.[21] Though no other contemporary compiled so voluminous a record, her behavior was not atypical. Elizabeth Buckley was readmitted in June of the same year racked by mania a potu; Ann

The benign image of the Charleston Orphan House that heads the printed program for its sixty-first anniversary testifies to the nurturing atmosphere associated with this institution. (Courtesy of the South Caroliniana Library)

Peterson and Maria Swords were put into the cells for hiding liquor in the house; and Catherine Lowry lost her rations for the same offense.[22]

In Boston, such behavior would have landed these women in the house of correction. But in Charleston there was no house of correction. Nor was there a house of reformation for juveniles. Indeed, Charleston's single municipal orphan house was reserved not for delinquents but for those of clear promise. Its male inmates, who outnumbered females two to one, were given an academic and practical education sufficient to prepare them to earn their livings as artisans—occasionally even as professionals. But the vocational training it offered girls prepared them only to be domestic servants or seamstresses—or wives.[23] And to that extent even this model institution resembled those that Boston reserved for the deficient.

That which most distinguished Charleston's world of wenches from that of Boston's was slavery. Boston's free black women were little more secure than Charleston's, and the few who were part of the southern city's brown aristocracy probably fared better than any Boston Negroes. The overwhelming fact, therefore, was that within a slave society it was bondage based on race that made black women wenches by definition. They were advertised, bought, and sold as such. No law protected their marriages, their families, or their homes.

Conversely, the cultural imperative to preserve the racial justifications for slavery partially sheltered deviant white women from the treatment many of them would have encountered had they lived in the North.

Nonetheless, institutionalization in either city stigmatized women. It was a public token less that these women lacked the families to shelter them or the financial resources to provide for their own care than it was that these women were flawed. Whether wittingly or not, they had defied prevailing behavioral norms. They might be tolerated in either city for the services they rendered even when those services were illegal. But they would also be harassed when their activity threatened those who prescribed the norms, when they performed no marketable service, when their defiance was too flamboyant, or when they burdened society with their care. Then they were physically set apart from the decent, the respectable, the better sort. They might be isolated in institutions for their own punishment—even perhaps reformation. They might also merely be ostracized. In either case, they were expelled from a mainstream society whose value system demanded that a woman, to be respected as a woman, should behave as these females did not.

9
Choice and
Constraint
Revisited

Recent historians have analyzed the experience of nineteenth-century women from many vantage points. Some have concentrated primarily on categories: the domesticated gentlewoman, the servant to her husband, the teacher of her children, the maiden aunt, the pious evangelical, the radical reformer, the isolated maid, the exploited but resilient slave, the assertive shopgirl, the rebellious mill worker, the belle, the lady bountiful. Others have emphasized process: the feminization of religion, the impact of industrialization on domestic manufacture, the demographic implications of factory towns, the restructuring of property rights demanded by economic modernization, the institutionalization of charity. And, relating the one to the other, some have analyzed the interaction among categories—the slave and her mistress, the social reformer and her working-class clients; others, the dynamics within a single category—intimate friendships, mother-daughter relationships.

Because historians customarily locate their studies in place as well as time, they have scrutinized these nineteenth-century categories and processes in the North and in the South, on farms and in cities. But while there have so far been more studies of urban and northern women—and of literate, middle-class women—than of their opposites, Suzanne Lebsock's *The Free Women of Petersburg* (Virginia) is to date the principal study exploring how women of all classes and both races—except, alas, slaves—acted within their own categories, interacted with other groups, and reacted to the dynamics of their city.[1] Comparing the female worlds of Boston and Charleston adds to our understanding of the ways in which regional variations in public prescriptions, categorical attributes, and urban processes shaped the existence of ladies, women, and wenches and thereby clarifies how gender as a force in itself either imposed constraints or gave latitude for choice.

There is, to be sure, nothing new in the observation that living in a city differed from country living not only by depriving most women of the participation in family work that farming demanded but also by opening options and providing the potential for autonomy. The availability of schooling; the possibility of earning a living through commerce, stage performance, and teaching; the potential for active participation in philanthropy and reform increased with the size and density of population. Towns promised more than farms or villages; cities, more than towns. On the other hand, urban life reduced the security that marriage and wifely dependence implied. Urban mortality rates for mature adults, like those for small children, far exceeded the death rates of most rural areas. And, when hard times or personal failure stripped a man of his earning power, his wife and children lacked the rural homestead's provision of food, fuel, and shelter.

But, if urban life created visible—often startling—differences from traditional rural life, that impact was further shaped by a city's location. The cultural differences imposed by region—and especially that of slavery's existence in Charleston but not Boston—created distinctive textures of female life. Slave women largely lacked even the few occupational alternatives available to poor workingwomen in Boston; slaves' mistresses either enjoyed more leisure or assumed more managerial responsibilities than did their northern equivalents. And, although Bostonians might share the southern assumption that black women were inherently voluptuous, their more limited belief in every white woman's chastity increased the likelihood that errant behavior would topple a previously decent woman from her pedestal.

Harder to pin down but no less central to individual lives were the conflicting messages and possibilities among which women charted a course that often veered in response to their own life-clock as well as to the changing times of society as a whole. In so doing, women—and especially urban women—not only defined themselves but attempted, with varying degrees of success, to control their own lives. Often the results were unanticipated, for an assertion or denial in a particular sphere of their lives necessarily affected all others.

Fundamental to this process was shaping an image of self: the ideal that each woman would choose if she had the power to do so. In the early nineteenth century, girls grew up and adults lived their lives in a culture that gave them conflicting signals. Rooted in the American War of Independence, their society demanded that all citizens be responsible for their own lives and that of their country. While much of this imperative was political, a realm from which women were largely excluded, that republican mandate nonetheless dominated their lives, demanding that they rear children in the beliefs, habits, and knowledge necessary to the new nation's survival. Yet hand in hand with republican self-reliance came ever more restrictive definitions of femininity, creating thereby gender-determined roles inconsonant with "manly independence." And so girls, who attended the same patriotic festivities and received the same lessons in republican virtues as their brothers, were confronted with irreconcilable alternatives. Their patriotic exertion as adults must be largely vicarious as women taught sons to be responsible citizens and exercise the rights and privileges denied their mothers and their sisters. And, although dependence was a servile posture, and dependence on charity, a disgrace, for them to depend on a father or a husband was called the highest virtue.

With humankind's amazing ability to reconcile opposites, it is probable that few women spent as much time and effort coping with the intellectual inconsistencies of such a world as did Frances Appleton. Yet her thoughts, provoked by watching a baby girl stretch out her arms to the world, must have encompassed the inchoate response of many women to being a nineteenth-century female American. "Poor child, you resemble us older children—we are ever stretching out our soul's arms for we know not what, with a vague longing; you

Daughter of a Boston merchant, manufacturer, banker, and congressman, Frances Appleton's troubled youth is reflected in this 1834 portrait by George P. A. Healy, painted well before her happy marriage to poet-professor Henry Wadsworth Longfellow. (Courtesy of the Longfellow National Historic Site, National Park Service)

have yet to learn, like your older sisters, that your arm is short & your hand is small, not even able to retain the few baubles it succeeds in grasping. Slowly, slowly may that experience dawn on you—grasp on, hope on."[2]

Grasping and holding on, however, inevitably produced ambivalence. Caroline Gilman recalled at sixty her anguish at seeing her first poem in print when she was only sixteen. She was ashamed, as if she "had been detected in man's apparel."[3] Moreover, she fretted about her gender image for the rest of her life. After she had chosen a literary career, she asked her sister to keep a letter private because it was "too womanish, & wifelike & mother-ish."[4] She enjoyed riding because being on horseback gave her a sense of independence. Yet, ironically, in what was undoubtedly her most striking fictional description of a woman on horseback, she portrayed Mrs. Alwyn as a person "masculine in her proportions," domineering, and loud.[5] Similar ambivalence haunted the Charleston-reared bluestocking, Louisa Cheves McCord, whose articles critical of protective tariffs and protective of slavery's economic benefits were published in *De Bow's Review* and the *Southern Quarterly Review*. Yet, when she submitted a piece to the latter, she accompanied it with a note of feminine self-deprecation. "I hope you will not for one instant hesitate to reject it as I *expect you to do*, but return it as soon as you please."[6]

The emotional and familial pressures on young women to guard their chastity while simultaneously seeking a mate reflected similarly confusing public prescriptions and personal dilemmas. Indeed, the question whether to marry at all and enjoy a matron's life-style and status only complicated their struggle to shape their lives. In part, the dilemma was sexual. It was somewhat less a problem for slave women, whose own culture accepted youthful pregnancies unsanctioned by marriage although white culture arbitrarily cast them in the mold of a mammy—mothering children, supervising a household, and withal deferential—or a Jezebel, a sexual object unsuited to all of the above. But for free white women, emotional and physical desires had to be juggled with pedestal propriety as they sought husbands or scorned marriage altogether. These choices were even tougher for those whose self-image comported ill with the run-of-the-mill prescription that no woman should marry "unless she is willing to devote herself heart and soul to promote the good of her husband."[7] Rich and talented, Julia Ward nonetheless gave up secure freedom to marry Boston reformer Samuel Gridley Howe only to confront her mistaken concession to social expectations. After her first year of marriage she recorded her "Darkest Moment":

> Hope died as I was led
> Unto my marriage bed;
> Nay, do not weep, 'twas I
> Not thou, that slew my happiest destiny.[8]

On the other hand, few young women had the options from which Julia Ward chose. Not yet twenty, Hannah Jackson felt trapped in her parents' home. She believed they deserved help "from a daughter for whom *they* have suffered so much," and she told herself that it was downright "ungrateful . . . for a daughter to leave her parents as soon as she is old enough to share their cares." Nonetheless, she wished she had money enough to free herself to marry as she chose.[9] Elizabeth Dorr, who chose not to marry at all but rather to support herself by teaching, was called upon to assume similar duties just because she was the single daughter. Responding to her married sister, she chafed at giving up "all desirable society" to live at home. "Does duty to my parents require the sacrifice & the trial?"[10] And even transcendental-ist Elizabeth Peabody, who readily manipulated the lives of all her siblings, was thirty-four before she concluded "that to be true to one's self is the first thing—that to sacrifice the perfect culture of my mind to social duties is not the thing," in this case deciding that she need not give up a room of her own in her family's Boston home just to set younger brothers a good example.[11] Such rebelliousness, as well as a shifting urban gender balance, contributed to ever greater numbers of lifelong spinsters, even among those who had been taught as girls that to be married was "the sine qua non of human happiness and human existence."[12] Conversely, those lessons and the cultural assumptions underlying them account for the vast majority of women who married despite all personal doubts and hesitations.

Intimately connected with such decisions was yet another factor: an individual woman's ability to achieve and maintain independence. An education offering the means of self-knowledge as well as the tools of self-support was critical in this respect. Moreover, those girls who went away to boarding school might use the institutional experience itself and the semi-independence it brought as a bridge from parental guidance to self-reliance, though most, in fact, did not. Similarly, those with property and the ability to manage it might better delay marriage until a suitor who offered more than simple financial support appeared or opt for singlehood if one did not. And though only a few considered autonomy—if not full independence—so personally essential that all else was secondary, public culture and personal experience nonetheless led women to value it.

Creation of ways for married women to retain and even control their property was but one example. Widows' determination to support their children and save them from dependence or private charity or disgrace in a public institution was another. As Lydia Crafts explained when she asked the commissioners of the Charleston Orphan House to release the daughter she had earlier placed there, "I wish above all things in this world . . . to have her finish her education and to learn her to be useful to herself that she may[,] if left as I was with her[,] know how to do as well as I have done for her and [am] still doing."[13] For the much better educated Maria Child, intellectual and financial independence was key to her existence whether married or single. At eighteen she summed up her economic goal: "If I am industrious and prudent, I shall be *independent*."[14] Yet it was also freedom of action she sought—to be an abolitionist when writing for the cause wrecked profitable sales of her other books, to scorn antislavery orthodoxy when doing so threatened the editorial post on which she relied for her income. It is scarcely surprising that Child, like social critic Margaret Fuller and reformer Maria Chapman, was well educated, had supported herself by teaching, and had rejected authoritarian religion for the individual discovery allowed Unitarians.

Related to, yet separate from, personal autonomy was access to power. Indeed, domestic politics might give greater dominance to women ostensibly dependent on the men of their families than to autonomous single women. Interestingly enough, although contemporaries generally discussed the issue in terms of influence rather than power, they gave it hearty endorsement. Sarah Josepha Hale, warning that "authority over the men must . . . never be usurped," still encouraged women to "exert their talents" to obtain "an influence in society that will be paramount to authority."[15] Catharine Beecher asserted that, in the education of children, the selection of a pastor, the operation of benevolence, and the enforcement of manners and morals, women not only should have a "superior influence" but generally did—albeit only through the influence they wielded over their husbands.[16] That this was not only preaching but also practice is borne out by letters among the much-interrelated Lees and Jacksons of Boston. When Hannah Jackson wrote cousin Henry Lee about her brother's impending marriage, she assured him that Patrick's fiancée was gentle, believed that the man should rule the roost, and heartily approved of Petruchio's taming of the shrew. But Hannah was just as sure that Susan "has so much character & such a winning way withal that he will never rule her with despotic sway as he would a weaker character." And surely her meaning was clear to Henry, who had long watched his mother manage his father. Indeed, Mary Jackson Lee even offered suggestions about her husband's business "because I think that much of your anxiety on this point is on my account." But then she would go on to soothe potentially ruffled feathers with reassurances of her faith in him. "I have a great opinion of your willingness to work."[17]

Some women went so far as openly to seek power in spheres customarily confined to men. Certainly their participation in antislavery and women's rights campaigns was seen and condemned as such. Yet, when she voiced a more popular cause, a woman might safely venture into the public—even political—sphere. The Pinckney sisters of Charleston so embodied their city's support for state sovereignty and nullification that political parades and rallies often ended under their balcony. And Maria Pinckney's would-be simplification of complex political argument, *Quintessence of Long Speeches Arranged as a Political Catechism*, became a standard nullifier text.[18] If no Boston woman equaled Miss Pinckney's prominence in the mainstream of public life, it must be conceded that she was also unique in Charleston. Generally the wives, daughters, and sisters of politicians in both cities were content with domestic influence and consulted their menfolk when they received occasional requests for their active endorsement of a social cause with political implications. Generally too those women who acted to address public needs acted in single-gender groups and organizations and under the umbrella of the benevolence deemed a peculiarly female sphere. When "the cup of human misery [was] full," it was "the peculiar duty of females" to address that which only they could—or would—understand.[19]

Finally, there was the catch-22 of women's mobility within an open society where economic success and social rewards were deemed to be the fruits of individual effort. Young women were urged to prepare themselves either to be "rapidly elevated to wealthy independence" or to fall to "the bitterness of poverty."[20] Their rise, however, would not come from their own endeavor, except as they served the man whose coattails they rode. It is true that on their own they might achieve financial independence and a modicum of property. But the roads that men took to the top were closed to women— whether higher education's route to the professions or the aggressive use of land, capital, and entrepreneurial skill. Yet, if significant upward mobility by their own action was unlikely, downward mobility was not. Sexual indiscretion or a fondness for too much alcohol could produce poverty, disgrace, and destitution.

One may, of course, argue convincingly that belief in upward mobility by individual effort is ill based in statistical fact. One may note that it was of little concern to slaves and immigrants of either sex, whose prime concern beyond survival was preserving family stability. But one cannot deny that a belief in individual success was as much part of the American myth as the belief in progress. That women were so largely excluded from achieving upward mobility on their own, that their personal effort had to be directed primarily against falling, may explain why they so often were and were expected to be guardians of old values and social stasis. On the other hand, their benevolence to the less fortunate and their defiance of propriety on behalf of prostitutes and slaves reflect some women's determination to resolve the tensions of living in a society that celebrated both republican self-reliance and gentle domesticity. All knew that their choices were more limited than men's. All knew that the constraints surrounding them were not completely rigid. Most realized inherent contradictions in the rules governing womanly propriety. Some barely tested the possible alternatives. Others pressed the outer limits. None was altogether victim. None was altogether free.

Notes

Abbreviations Used in the Notes

BL	Baker Library, Harvard School of Business Administration, Cambridge, Mass.
BPL	Boston Public Library, Boston, Mass.
CC	College of Charleston, Charleston, S.C.
DU	Duke University, Durham, N.C.
GS	Genealogical Society of Utah, Salt Lake City, Utah
LC	Library of Congress, Washington, D.C.
LS	Longfellow National Historic Site, National Park Service, Cambridge, Mass.
MHS	Massachusetts Historical Society, Boston, Mass.
SCA	South Carolina Archives, Columbia, S.C.
SCHS	South Carolina Historical Society, Charleston, S.C.
SL	Arthur and Elizabeth Schlesinger Library, Radcliffe College, Cambridge, Mass.
UNC	Southern Historical Collection, University of North Carolina, Chapel Hill, N.C.
USC	South Caroliniana Library, University of South Carolina, Columbia, S.C.

Chapter 1

1. Linda K. Kerber, "Separate Spheres, Female Worlds, Women's Place: The Rhetoric of Women's History," *Journal of American History* 75 (June 1988): 9–39, is a useful interpretive essay on conceptualizations in recent women's history. See also the bibliographical essay for a selective survey of recent women's history.

2. Anne Firor Scott, "The Ever Widening Circle: The Diffusion of Femi-

nist Values from the Troy Female Seminary, 1822–1872," *History of Education Quarterly* 19 (Spring 1979): 3–4, is a clear exception in defining the feminism of 1825–60 in terms of a continuum. Suzanne Lebsock, *The Free Women of Petersburg: Status and Culture in a Southern Town, 1784–1860* (New York: W. W. Norton, 1985), implies a continuous social spectrum rather than sharp duality.

3. Elizabeth Fox-Genovese, *Within the Plantation Household: Black and White Women of the Old South* (Chapel Hill: University of North Carolina Press, 1988), 196–97, 202–3, 230, explores the lady, woman, and wench typology within southern cultural patterns. Christine Stansell, *City of Women: Sex and Class in New York, 1789–1860* (New York: Alfred A. Knopf, 1986), probes a distinctly female working-class behavior.

4. For a more complete comparison of these two cities, see William H. Pease and Jane H. Pease, *The Web of Progress: Private Values and Public Styles in Boston and Charleston, 1828–1843* (New York: Oxford University Press, 1985). Susan J. Kleinberg, "The Systematic Study of Urban Women," *Historical Methods Newsletter*, 9 (December 1975): 14–25, poses an agenda for comparative studies of urban women though largely in the late nineteenth and early twentieth centuries and in the heavily statistical framework of the "new" urban history.

5. Peter Knights, *The Plain People of Boston, 1830–1860: A Study in City Growth* (New York: Oxford University Press, 1971), 121.

6. Reprinted from the *North American Review* in *Charleston Mercury*, October 10, 1837.

Chapter 2

1. Lemuel Shattuck, *Report to the Committee of the City Council Appointed to Obtain the Census of Boston for the Year 1845 . . .* (Boston: John H. Eastburn, 1846), 61. Of 33,916 women over twenty, 18,324 were married, 11,879 were single, and 3,804 were widows.

2. J. L. Dawson and H. W. DeSaussure, *Census of the City of Charleston, South Carolina, for the Year 1848 . . .* (Charleston: J. B. Nixon, 1849), 26–27. Of 4,108 white women over twenty, 2,058 were married, 1,173 were single, and 877 were widows.

3. Ibid., 7; U.S., Fifth Census of the United States, 1830, Population Schedule, [Charleston District], South Carolina, vol. 2, microfilm, roll 170, National Archives, Washington, D.C.

4. Dawson and DeSaussure, *City of Charleston*, 26–27; Shattuck, *Census of Boston*, 47.

5. Shattuck, *Census of Boston*, 160; Dawson and DeSaussure, *City of Charleston*, 222–24.

6. Shattuck reports that in the years 1841–45, 47 percent of Boston deaths were children under five (*Census of Boston*, 153); Dawson and De-Saussure report that in 1841–48, 33 percent of all deaths, 26 percent of white deaths, and 38 percent of black deaths were children under five (*City of Charleston*, 216–17).

7. William Capers et al., *Exposition of the Causes and Character of the Difficulties in the Church in Charleston in the Year 1833* . . . (n.p., [1833]), 3–17; *A Rejoinder to "An Exposition of the Late Schism in the Methodist Episcopal Church in Charleston"* (Charleston: W. Riley, 1834), 6–7; Christine Stansell, *City of Women: Sex and Class in New York, 1789–1860* (New York: Alfred A. Knopf, 1986), elaborates a pattern for the social lives of working-class women that doubtless existed in other cities as well.

8. *Charleston Mercury*, February 9, 1838, carried S. Babcock's advertisement for party games. For partying generally, see, for example, Harriott H. Rutledge to Mrs. Edward C. Rutledge, June 7, 1841, Harriott Horry Rutledge Papers, DU; Marie Esther Huger Huger, Personal Recollections, 1820–40, Habersham Elliott Papers, UNC; and Thomas Wright Bacot to Dewar Bacot, April 7, 1837, Bacot Huger Papers, Bacot Correspondence, SCHS. Differing perceptions of the gala race-week balls can be found in Susan Petigru King's novel *Lily* (New York: Harper and Brothers, 1855), 270, and Caroline Gilman, *Recollections of a Southern Matron and a New England Bride* (1838, 1836; reprint, 2 vols. in 1, Philadelphia: John E. Potter and Co., 1867), 134–36, and a negative view of the Jockey Club ball in Elizabeth F. McCall to B. F. Perry, March 7, 1837, Benjamin Franklin Perry Papers, USC.

9. See Lois W. Banner, *American Beauty* (New York: Alfred A. Knopf, 1983), 61, for descriptions of 1820 and 1830 styles. A Carolina gentleman describing New York styles to his wife in 1823 did, however, criticize their skimpy skirts as well as tight bodices. Christopher C. Jenkins to Mrs. Jenkins, September 25, 1823, Mrs. Christopher Jenkins Papers, DU, quoted in John Hope Franklin, *A Southern Odyssey* (Baton Rouge: Louisiana State University Press, 1976), 95.

10. Hannah Jackson to Sarah J. Russell, December 22, 1838, typescript, Almy Family Papers, SL, observes that at Papanti assemblies in Boston the Sears, Parker, and Appleton women waltzed while the Dwights, Gardners, and, alas, Jacksons did not. Harriott Kinloch Middleton did not permit her daughters to waltz even at a private ball at William Aiken's home in Charleston. H. K. Middleton to Francis Kinloch, February 24, 1839, Cheves-Middleton Papers, SCHS. The Swedish traveler, Carl Arfwedson, in his *The United*

States and Canada, in 1832, 1833, and 1834, 2 vols. ([1834]; reprint, New York: Johnson Reprint, 1969), 1:220, commented on the distance between dancing partners. Charles Francis Adams to Louisa C. Adams, August 2, 1828, Adams Papers, microfilm, reel 487, MHS.

11. Francis L. Lee to Henry Lee, Jr., January 20, 1843, and Anna C. L. Dwight to Henry Lee, Jr., January 11, 1839, Lee Family Papers, MHS.

12. For Caroline Gilman's description of Sullivan's Island, see *Southern Matron*, 186–87. Quotation from "Eugene to Caroline," in *Charleston Courier*, August 5, 1841. Descriptions of the varied activities of Boston's upper-class young ladies abound, inter alia, in Frances E. Appleton, Diary, March–December 1832, LS, and several of Hannah L. Jackson's letters to Sarah Jackson Russell, 1837–38, Almy Family Papers, SL. See also Calista Billings, Diary, September 1848, 57–61, SL, for the account of a seventeen-year-old Boston girl.

13. Eliza [?] to Laura Covert, April 27, 1840, and [Bond of Agreement among Several Students], March 14, 1855, South Carolina Collegiate Institute (Barhamville Academy) Papers, USC; *Charleston Mercury*, January 6, 1837.

14. R. G. Dun and Co., Credit Ledgers, 1845–51, Dun and Bradstreet Collection, BL; *Hints to a Young Tradesman, and Maxims for Merchants* (Boston: Perkins and Marvin, 1838); Joseph T. Buckingham, *An Address Delivered Before the Massachusetts Charitable Mechanics Association . . . October 7, 1830* (Boston: John Cotton, 1830), 18; Amos Lawrence to A. A. Lawrence, July 28, August 9, 1833, A. A. Lawrence Papers, MHS.

15. Shattuck, *Census of Boston*, 45; Dawson and DeSaussure, *City of Charleston*, 12.

16. Sarah M. Grimké, *Letters on the Equality of the Sexes, and the Condition of Woman* . . . (Boston: Isaac Knapp, 1838; reprint, New York: Source Book Press, 1970), 47; Anna H. Johnson to Elizabeth Haywood, September 16, 1822, Ernest Haywood Collection, UNC; Georgina Amory to John Lowell, Jr., April 16, December 5, 1824, John Lowell, Jr., Papers, MHS, quoted in Ellen Rothman, *Hands and Hearts: A History of Courtship in America* (New York: Basic Books, 1984), 72–73.

17. Lydia Maria Francis Child, *The Mother's Book*, 2d ed. (Boston: Carter and Hendee, 1831), 162–64; Harrison Gray Otis to George Harrison, January 15, 1838, Harrison Gray Otis Papers, MHS.

18. Frederick A. Porcher, "Memoirs of Frederick Adolphus Porcher," ed. Samuel Gaillard Stoney, *South Carolina Historical and Genealogical Magazine* 47 (1946): 51; William Middleton to Mrs. J. G. Elliott, September 14, 1829, Miscellaneous Manuscripts, Charleston Library Society, Charleston, S.C.

19. Anna Johnson's story is told in a series of letters from her to Elizabeth

Haywood, April–October 1822, Ernest Haywood Collection, UNC.

20. Charlotte Everett to Edward Everett, January 24, 1834, Edward Everett Papers, MHS; Harrison Gray Otis to George Harrison, December 7, 1838, Harrison Gray Otis Papers, MHS; John Henry Jenks to William Joseph Jenks, February 3, 1831, William Jenks Papers, MHS.

21. On the binding nature of an engagement, see Horace Mann to Elizabeth Peabody, [1830s], Horace Mann Papers, MHS. Hannah L. Jackson to Sarah J. Russell, March 15, 1839, Almy Family Papers, SL. See *Boston Morning Post,* July 10, February 19, 1833, for the Davis and Bradlee affairs.

22. James L. Petigru to Adele P. Allston, October 18, 1836, Robert F. W. Allston Papers, SCHS; A. H. Stock to Bowen Cooke, October 19, 1847, Bowen Cooke Papers, SCHS. Charleston author Susan Petigru King warned of the disastrous consequences when a family failed to inquire into the "habits, the principles, the morals, the antecedents of the man to whom [their daughter] becomes the veritable slave" (*Lily*, 260). Some parents, however, did make such inquiries.

23. Harriott Kinloch Middleton to Francis Kinloch, February 24, 1839, Cheves-Middleton Papers, SCHS; Harrison Gray Otis to George Harrison, August 20, 1838, Harrison Gray Otis Papers, MHS.

24. Ann Reid to William Moultrie Reid, 1830s, Reid Family Papers, DU; Anna Lesesne, Diary, 1836, SCHS; Lydia Maria Francis to Mary Preston, June 11, 1826, in Lydia Maria Child, *Selected Letters, 1817–1880*, ed. Milton Meltzer and Patricia G. Holland (Amherst: University of Massachusetts Press, 1982), 7; Child, *Mother's Book*, 165; M. T. Torrey to Samuel T. Morse, May 26, 1839, Samuel Torrey Morse Papers, MHS; Daniel F. Child and Mary D. (Guild) Child, Diary, September 26, 1841, MHS.

25. Edward Brooks, *An Answer to the Pamphlet of Mr. John A. Lowell Entitled Reply to a Pamphlet Recently Circulated by Mr. Edward Brooks with New Facts and Further Proofs* (Boston: Eastburn's, 1851), 174; Hannah Burgess, Diary, August–September, 1852, SL.

26. William H. Bullard to Henry Lee, Jr., December 23, 1842, Lee Family Papers, MHS.

27. Caroline Gilman, *Recollections of a Southern Matron and a New England Bride* (1838, 1836; reprint, 2 vols. in 1, Philadelphia: John E. Potter and Co., 1867). Quotations from *New England Bride*, 384, and *Southern Matron*, 291, 297–98.

28. Susan Petigru King, "Old Maidism Versus Marriage," in *Busy Moments of an Idle Woman* (New York: D. Appleton and Co., 1854), 252; William A. Alcott, *The Young Wife, or Duties of Woman in the Marriage Relation* (Boston: George W. Light, 1837), 76.

29. Gilman, *Southern Matron*, 305–6; Lydia Maria Francis to Mary Pres-

ton, January 6, 1827, in Child, *Selected Letters*, 9.

30. Maris A. Vinovskis, *Fertility in Massachusetts from the Revolution to the Civil War* (New York: Academic Press, 1981), especially 49, 51, 56, 97, 105; Joseph Kett, *Rites of Passage* (New York: Basic Books, 1977), 115.

31. These data have been derived from the *Charleston Mercury* and *Courier*, 1838–43. Robert Fogel and Stanley Engerman, *Time on the Cross* (Boston: Little, Brown, 1974), 137, gives the average age of slave women giving birth as 22.5 and the median age as 20.5. Herbert Gutman, *The Black Family in Slavery and Freedom, 1750–1925* (New York: Pantheon, 1976), 50, 171, gives median ages from different plantations ranging from 17.7 to 19.6.

32. Henry C. Wright, Journal, February 1, 1835, BPL; Simeon L. Crockett, *A Voice from Leverett Street Prison, on His Life, Trial, and Confession of Arson*, 10th ed. (Boston: The Proprietors, [1836]), 4–8.

33. Caroline H. Gilman to Mrs. A. M. White, August 7, 1820, and Caroline H. Gilman to Harriet Fay, December 17, 1827, Caroline H. Gilman Papers, SCHS; Mary Crowninshield Mifflin, Diary, 1842, 1844, 1845, BPL; Caroline Laurens, Diary, [December] 1824, June 1, October [?], 1826, photocopy, UNC. More generally, see Judith Waltzer Leavitt, "Under the Shadow of Maternity: American Women's Responses to Death and Debility Fears in Nineteenth-Century Childbirth," *Feminist Studies* 12 (1986): 129–54.

34. Shattuck, *Census of Boston*, Appendix, 86; Dawson and DeSaussure, *City of Charleston*, 251.

35. Thomas Young Simons, *Introductory Lecture Delivered at the Opening of the Session of the Medical College of S. Carolina . . . 1837* (Charleston: E. C. Councell, 1838), 16–17; Boston Medical Association, *Boston Medical Police: Rules and Regulations of the Boston Medical Association* (Boston: Dutton and Wentworth, 1843), 17–18; James Moultrie, *Introductory Address Delivered at the Opening of the Medical College of the State of South-Carolina . . . 1834* (Charleston: J. S. Burges, 1834), 14.

36. Boston Lying-In Hospital, *Act of Incorporation, By-Laws, Trustees, Regulations, and Officers . . .* (Boston: J. E. Hinckley and Co., 1832); [Circular Letter], April 5, 1836, broadside, MHS; Charleston, Records of the Poor House, 1834–40, 34, SCHS; Richard Henry Dana, *The Journal of Richard Henry Dana, Jr.*, 4 vols., ed. Robert F. Lucid (Cambridge: Harvard University Press, 1968), 1:68–69; Daniel F. Child and Mary D. (Guild) Child, Diary, May 26, 27, 1841, MHS; Meta Grimball, Diary, July 11, 1861, quoted in Russell Lindley Blake, "Ties of Intimacy: Social Values and Personal Relationships of Antebellum Slaveholders" (Ph.D. diss., University of Michigan, 1978), 18.

37. Daniel F. Child and Mary D. (Guild) Child, Diaries, 1841–43, MHS; William G. Brooks, Diary, December 1838–January 1839, MHS; and Marga-

ret Adger Smyth to Thomas Smyth, June 9, 1844, Smyth-Stoney-Adger Papers, SCHS, all chronicle the postpartum schedule. The Child diaries and Mary A. Appleton to William G. Appleton, August 16, 1833, William Appleton and Company Collection, BL, illustrate delays in naming a baby. Anne Firor Scott, *The Southern Lady: From Pedestal to Politics, 1830–1930* (Chicago: University of Chicago Press, 1970), 37–40, explores southern women's absence from home. See also Daniel Scott Smith, "Family Limitation, Sexual Control, and Domestic Feminism in Victorian America," *Feminist Studies* 1 (Winter–Spring 1973): 40–58. Many diaries and almanacs of Boston women in both BPL and MHS note monthly, "not feeling well," and when such notations cease, they are often followed nine months later with a memo that a new child has been born.

38. Quotations from *Boston Morning Post*, March 3, 8, 1837.

39. *Boston Morning Post*, March 17, 1837. For the list of women who publicly supported the lectures, see *Morning Post*, March 8, 1837.

40. For Mary Gove, see *Boston Morning Post*, November 19, 1838, December 14, 1839. For Abner Kneeland's imprisonment, see *Morning Post*, June 19, 1838. Quotation from Alexander H. Everett, Journal/Diary, April 16, 1832, Everett-Noble Collection, MHS. B. C. Pressley, *The Law of Magistrates and Constables in the State of South Carolina* . . . (Charleston: Walker and Burke, 1848), 73–75. For an example of abortifacients, see advertisement for Dr. T. Stillman's Medical and Surgical Infirmary, *Charleston Mercury*, December 8, 1838. James Mohr, *Abortion in America: The Origins and Evolution of National Policy, 1800–1900* (New York: Oxford University Press, 1978), 46–85, notes an upsurge in abortion in the years 1840–80.

41. Linda K. Kerber, *Women of the Republic: Intellect and Ideology in Revolutionary America* (Chapel Hill: University of North Carolina Press, 1980), 284–87; Caroline Laurens, Diary, May 1, 19, 1827, UNC; Margaret A. Smyth to Thomas Smyth, July 9, 1844, Smyth-Stoney-Adger Papers, SCHS; *Southern Rose Bud*, 2 (January 11, 1834); Annie Middleton to Nathaniel R. Middleton, June 9, 1845, Nathaniel R. Middleton Papers, UNC; Daniel F. Child and Mary D. (Guild) Child, Diary, February–April 1843, March–April 1844, MHS.

42. Child, *Mother's Book*, 15–16, 25; Mary Lee to Henry Lee, Jr., January 30, 1843, September 2, 1835, Lee Family Papers, MHS; Maria Weston Chapman, writing in *Non-Resistant*, September 21, 1839; Caroline Weston to Deborah Weston, June 28, [1839 or 1840], Weston Papers, BPL.

43. Gilman, *New England Bride*, 358, and *Southern Matron*, 236; *Rose Bud*, 1 (September 29, 1832).

44. For mother-son relations, see, for example, Alicia Middleton to Na-

thaniel R. Middleton, July 13, 1827, Nathaniel R. Middleton Papers, UNC; Ann Vanderhorst to Elias Vanderhorst, December 13, 1838, Arnoldus Vanderhorst Collection, SCHS; and Jonathan Amory to Thomas C. Amory, September 4, 1826, Amory Family Papers, MHS. For mother-daughter relations, see Child, *Mother's Book*, 92, 117–18, 151, 153; King, *Lily*, 24; Harriott Kinloch Middleton to Francis Middleton, February 24, 28, 1839, Cheves-Middleton Papers, SCHS; Eliza [?] to Laura Nelson Covert, April 4, 1836, South Carolina Collegiate Institute (Barhamville Academy) Papers, USC; Gilman, *Southern Matron*, 32; and Hannah Lowell Jackson to Sarah (Jackson) Russell, February 8, 1836, typescript, Almy Family Papers, SL. On guilt, see Gilman, *Southern Matron*, 28, and Frances E. Appleton, Diary, February–May 1833, April 22, 1841, LS. Lucy Larcom, *A New England Girlhood*, quoted in Nancy F. Cott, ed., *Root of Bitterness* (New York: E. P. Dutton, 1972), 128.

45. Eliza Ravenel to John Ravenel, December 9, 1830, and John Ravenel to Eliza Ravenel, January 3, 13, 1831, John Ravenel Papers, USC; [Robert F. W. Allston] to Adele Allston, May 7, 1854, Allston Family Papers, USC.

46. William R. Lawrence to Amos A. Lawrence, March 17, 1840, and C. H. Parker to Amos A. Lawrence, June 19, 1840, A. A. Lawrence Papers, MHS; State v. Mrs. Bradley, April 16, 1838, Charleston County, S.C., Court of General Sessions, Records of Indictments and Subpoenas, SCA.

47. Child, *Mother's Book*, 51; Alcott, *Young Wife*, 51; Marylynn Salmon, *Women and the Law of Property in Early America* (Chapel Hill: University of North Carolina Press, 1986), 63. Given state law, it is notable that Charleston's Beth Elohim congregation granted Rabbi Poznanski the right, in well-founded cases, to grant a religious divorce (Kaal Kadosh Beth Elohim, Board of Trustees Minutes, November 29, 1840, Beth Elohim Archives, Charleston, S.C.); and Professor John Hagy of the College of Charleston has identified such divorces even prior to 1800 (Lecture before the Institute of Southern Studies, March 24, 1988, USC).

48. Frederic Tudor, Diaries, 1834–36, Tudor Family–Ice Company Collection, BL, see especially entries for January 1834 (marginal notation by Euphemia Tudor), July 13, 1834, Summer 1836 (marginal notation, dated November 2, 1864), and July 13, 1834 (marginal notation); Charlotte Everett to Edward Everett, April 10, 1834, Edward Everett Papers, MHS.

49. The Childs' story is from their diaries, 1839–45, MHS. The quotation is from the March 26, 1841 entry.

50. Ibid., September 9, 1841, MHS.

51. Gilman, *New England Bride*, 355. This was but part of the family cycle analyzed in Tamara Hareven, "The Family as Process: The Historical Study of the Family Cycle," *Journal of Social History* 7 (Spring 1974): 322–29.

52. Gilman, *Southern Matron*, 271–72; *Charleston Mercury*, January 16, 1838; N. S. Dodge, "A Charleston Venue in 1842," *Galaxy Magazine* January 1869, 119–23.

53. *Charleston Mercury*, 1838–40; *Charleston Courier*, 1841–43.

54. Charleston Independent Congregational Church and Circular Church, Records, April 27, 1829, SCHS.

55. Ibid., December 19, 1836, August 8, 1837, February 20, August 20, 1838; Case of Isaac, slave of Edward Carew, 1834, Slave Trials, SCA.

56. James Hamilton, Jr., to Martin Van Buren, August 25, 1829, Martin Van Buren Papers, microfilm, ser. 2, reel 8, LC; Ann Amory McLean Lee, Will, October 13, 1834, Suffolk County, Mass., Probate Records, vol. 132, pt. 2, 225–44, microfilm, GS.

57. *Charleston Mercury*, July 19, 1836; German Friendly Society, Minutes, 1829–33, typescript, CC; J. Calhoun Levy, *An Address Delivered in Charleston, South-Carolina, 5th November, 1834. Before the Hebrew Orphan Society* . . . (Charleston: J. S. Burges, 1834); "Rules and Regulations of the Brown Fellowship Society, . . ." [1830s], Brown Fellowship Society Manuscripts, USC; South Carolina Society, Minutes, January 30, February 3, 1827, typescript, CC; Society for the Relief of Orphans and Widows of the Clergy of the Protestant Episcopal Church in South Carolina, Minutes, 1829–43, and Cash Account Book, 1824–91, in the society's records, SCHS; Fellowship Society, Minutes, September 16, 1829, in the society's records, USC. See also the records of Charleston's St. John's German Lutheran Church (typescript, CC) and the Second Presbyterian Church (microfilm, GS).

58. Society of the Cincinnati, Records, 1825–26, MHS; Widows' Society, *Twentieth Annual Report* (Boston: Tuttle, Weeks and Dennett, 1837); Fatherless and Widows' Society, *Constitution and Report for 1827* (Boston: W. L. Lewis, 1827), 2; *Boston Morning Post*, January 22, 1840; Charleston, Journals of the Commissioners of Free Schools, 1812–34, December 24, 1832, SCHS; *Charleston Courier*, March 10, 1832.

59. M. Amory to Miss Odiorne, November 31 [*sic*], 1834, Sullivan Family Papers, MHS.

60. Ann Weston to Carolyn and Deborah Weston, [1841], Weston Papers, BPL; Maria Weston Chapman to E. P. Nichols, December 10, June 26, 1860, Garrison Papers, BPL.

Chapter 3

1. J. L. Dawson and H. W. DeSaussure, *Census of the City of Charleston, South Carolina, for the Year 1848* . . . (Charleston: J. B. Nixon, 1849), 33–35;

Lemuel Shattuck, *Report to the Committee of the City Council Appointed to Obtain the Census of Boston for the Year 1845* . . . (Boston: John H. Eastburn, 1846), 89–90.

2. For a discussion of the general nature of household tasks and equipment, see Faye E. Dudden, *Serving Women: Household Service in Nineteenth-Century America* (Middletown: Wesleyan University Press, 1983), 104–7, 128–32, 142; and Lydia Maria Francis Child, *The American Frugal Housewife* . . . (Boston: Carter, Hendee, and Co., 1832).

3. Caroline Gilman, *Recollections of a Southern Matron and a New England Bride* (1838, 1836; reprint, 2 vols. in 1, Philadelphia: John E. Potter and Co., 1867), 141–45, 317–23, 375–81.

4. William H. Pease and Jane H. Pease, *The Web of Progress: Private Values and Public Styles in Boston and Charleston, 1828–1843* (New York: Oxford University Press, 1985), 94–95, 196–97; Charlotte Everett to Edward Everett, [February] 23, 1834, Edward Everett Papers, MHS; William Hume to Henry L. Pinckney, December 18, [1838], in Henry Laurens Pinckney, *Remarks . . . on the Subject of Interments and the Policy of Establishing a Public Cemetery, Beyond the Precincts of the City* (Charleston: W. Riley, 1839), 1–2; Dawson and DeSaussure, *City of Charleston*, 22–24.

5. Mary Esther Huger Huger, Personal Recollections, 1820–40, Habersham Elliott Papers, UNC; M. W. Bowen to Susan Cook, April 20, 1825, Bowen Cooke Papers, SCHS; Margaret A. Smyth to Thomas Smyth, July 16, 1844, Smyth-Stoney-Adger Papers, SCHS.

6. Nathaniel I. Bowditch to Henry Bowditch, July 25, 1832, Forbes Family Papers, microfilm, reel 38, pt. 5, MHS; Sarah Josepha Hale, ed., *Keeping House and House Keeping: A Story of Domestic Life* (New York: Harper and Brothers, 1845), 38–39; Louisa Lee Waterhouse, Diary, [1840], MHS. Studies of women's work at home abound. See, for example, Catharine E. Beecher, *A Treatise on Domestic Economy, for the Use of Young Ladies at Home, and at School* (Boston: Marsh, Capen, Lyon, and Webb, 1841; reprint, New York: Source Book Press, 1970); and [Sarah Rutledge], *The Carolina Housewife, or House and Home* (Charleston: W. R. Babcock, 1847), in addition to titles cited elsewhere.

7. Shattuck, *Census of Boston*, 83–84, 86, Appendix, 39–40. Shattuck does not report at all on the numbers of seamstresses in the city, probably because they usually worked in their own homes, but all anecdotal references agree that they comprised the greatest number of laboring women.

8. *Boston Morning Post*, September 23, 1833; Joseph Tuckerman, *Prize Essay: On the Wages Paid to Females for their Labour* (Philadelphia: Carey and Hart, 1830), 14–15; William Hague, *True Charity a Check to Pauperism* . . .

(Boston: Gould, Kendall, and Lincoln, 1841), 47; Seaman's Aid Society of the City of Boston, *Third Annual Report* (Boston: James B. Dow, 1836), 8.

9. Thomas Thwing, *An Address Delivered before the Association of Delegates from the Benevolent Societies of Boston* . . . *1843* ([Boston]: The Association, 1843), 5; Robert G. Waterston, *An Address on Pauperism: Its Extent, Causes, and the Best Means of Prevention* . . . (Boston: Charles C. Little and James Brown, 1844), 16–24.

10. Mary Crowninshield Mifflin, Diary, 1841–45, BPL; Julia Webster Appleton, Journal, October–December 1843, MHS; Louisa Lee Waterhouse, Diaries, 1836–40, MHS, quotation from 1839, 102.

11. Hale, *Keeping House*, 1–12; Seaman's Aid Society of the City of Boston, *First Annual Report* (Boston: David H. Ela, 1834), 8–9; Society for the Mutual Benefit of Female Domestics and Their Employers, *Constitution* . . . (Boston: Munroe and Francis, 1827); Charlotte Everett to Edward Everett, March 19, 1828, Edward Everett Papers, MHS.

12. "Sketches of American Character, No. 8: The Springs," *Ladies Magazine* 1 (August 1828): 348–49. On wages, see Mary Aldret, Receipt Book, 1829–76, entries for 1829–35, SCHS; and see *Charleston Mercury*, May 22, 31, November 9, 1838, for typical classified advertisements for help.

13. *Charleston Mercury*, January 19, 1841; *Charleston Courier*, October 31, 1842; Duke Goodman to Richard Singleton, March 26, 1825, Singleton Papers, UNC.

14. George B. Eckhard, comp., *A Digest of the Ordinances of the City Council of Charleston, from the Year 1783 to October 1844* . . . (Charleston: Walker and Burke, 1844), 169–77, 376–82.

15. State v. A. and P. A. Montgomery, September 2, 1834, Charleston County, S.C., Court of General Sessions, Records of Indictments and Subpoenas, SCA.

16. Ann Smith, Will, March 12, 1830 (vol. 38, bk. B), and Elizabeth King, Will, August 8, 1831 (vol. 39, bk. C), Charleston County, S.C., Probate Court, Record of Wills, 1826–34, typescript, Charleston County Library, Charleston, S.C.; microfilm, GS.

17. Dawson and DeSaussure, *City of Charleston*, 30–35; Sarah M. Grimké, *Letters on the Equality of the Sexes, and the Condition of Woman* . . . (Boston: Isaac Knapp, 1838; reprint, New York: Source Book Press, 1970), 50–51.

18. Dawson and DeSaussure, *City of Charleston*, 30–35; Samuel Henry Dickson, *Address Delivered at the Opening of the New Edifice of the Charleston Apprentices' Library Society* . . . (Charleston: W. Riley, 1841), 29–30. For various Charleston businesses operated by women, see State v. Wilson and Kirk,

December 7, 1839, Charleston County, S.C., Court of General Sessions, Records of Indictments and Subpoenas, SCA; *Charleston Mercury*, June 22, October 13, December 14, 1836, April 16, 1838, April 2, 13, 26, 1841; and James Smith, *The Charleston Directory and Register for 1835–6* (Charleston: Daniel J. Dowling, 1835). For women planters, see T. C. Foy, *Charleston Directory and Stranger's Guide for 1840 and 1841* . . . (Charleston, 1840).

19. R. G. Dun and Co., Credit Ledgers, 1845–51, 27, 67, Dun and Bradstreet Collection, BL; Shattuck, *Census of Boston*, Appendix, 40; *Boston Daily Advertiser*, August 22, 1829.

20. Catharine M. Sedgwick, *Means and Ends, of Self-Training* (Boston: Marsh, Capen, Lyon, and Webb, 1839), 123. For Charleston nurses' wages, see Charleston, Records of the Poor House, 1832–43, SCHS, especially Minutes of the Commissioners' Meeting, August 11, 1831; *Charleston Mercury*, August 27, 1840; and John Berkley Grimball, Diary, October 10, 1832, August 14, 1833, UNC. On aspects of the medical profession, see *Charleston Mercury*, March 10, 1837, February 9, 1838; *Boston Morning Post*, April 24, July 23, 1840, January 23, 1839, February 13, 1841; and Medical Society of South Carolina, Minute Books, Minutes, 1825–26, USC.

21. Louisa May Alcott, *Work: A Story of Experience* (Boston: Roberts Brothers, 1873); *Charleston Courier*, March 23, 1829; Alexander H. Everett, Journal, April 16–17, 1833, Everett-Noble Collection, MHS.

22. Lois W. Banner, *American Beauty* (New York: Alfred A. Knopf, 1983), 64; *Boston Morning Post*, October 14, 19, 1841; *Charleston Courier*, January 5, 1841; *Charleston Mercury*, December 18, 1840; *Morning Post*, September 8, 1840.

23. St. John's German Lutheran Church, Minutes, July 11, 1837, and Mary Strobel to President and Vestry, March 4, 1841, Minutes, 1830–45, typescript, CC.

24. References to women as writers and editors are readily observed in the public press of the day as well as in a variety of other sources. See, for example, Sarah Josepha Hale to H. A. S. Dearborn, February 13, 1830, Manuscript Collection, BPL; Catherine Heriot to Maria Doane, August 10, 1844, James B. Campbell Papers, SCHS; Sarah Jenks Merritt to Joseph William Jenks, November 7, 1840, William Jenks Papers, MHS; and Lydia Maria Francis Child, *The Mother's Book*, 2d ed. (Boston: Carter and Hendee, 1831), 19–21.

25. Tuckerman, *Prize Essay*, 14–19; Thomas Cooper, *Lectures on the Elements of Political Economy* (Columbia: D. E. Sweeny, 1826), 110–11.

26. Quotations from Lydia Maria Child to George Ticknor, 1829, in Lydia Maria Child, *Selected Letters, 1817–1880*, ed. Milton Meltzer and Patricia

G. Holland (Amherst: University of Massachusetts Press, 1982), 15; Charlotte Everett to Edward Everett, January 10, 1830, Edward Everett Papers, MHS; Lydia Maria Child to David L. Child, July 28, 1836, in Child, *Selected Letters*, 50.

27. Lydia Maria Child to Ellis G. Loring, June 12, [1843], Lydia Maria Child Papers, New York Public Library, New York, N.Y.

28. [Lydia Maria Child to Francis G. Shaw], June 3, 1854, Child Papers, Houghton Library, Harvard University, Cambridge, Mass.

Chapter 4

1. *Boston Daily Advertiser*, November 11, January 26, 1829; *Ladies Magazine* 1 (January 1829): 44; John Pierce, Memoirs, 5:384–90, MHS.

2. Boston Lyceum, *Sixth Annual Report* . . . (Boston: Perkins and Marvin, 1835), 4; Ann Douglas, *The Feminization of American Culture* (New York: Alfred A. Knopf, 1979), 270; Susan Phinney Conrad, *Perish the Thought: Intellectual Women in Romantic America, 1830–1860* (New York: Oxford University Press, 1976), 63–64; Richard H. Dana, printed circular letters, September 15, 1835, 1837, Dana Family Papers, MHS.

3. Frances E. Appleton, Diary, 1840, quotation from June 16, 1840, LS; Mary [Peabody] to Miss Rawlins Pickman, September 25, 1829, Horace Mann Papers, MHS.

4. Amos Lawrence to A. A. Lawrence, April 28, 1833, A. A. Lawrence Papers, MHS; Lydia Maria Child to Ellis Gray Loring, December 5, 1838, quoting a letter from George Bancroft to Mrs. Jonathan Dwight, n.d., Lydia Maria Child Papers, New York Public Library, New York, N.Y.; Hannah Lowell Jackson Cabot, Diary, September 4, 1839, typescript, SL; Lydia Maria Francis Child, *The Mother's Book*, 2d ed. (Boston: Carter and Hendee, 1831), 86.

5. Carl Kaestle, *Pillars of the Republic: Common Schools and American Society, 1780–1860* (New York: Hill and Wang, 1983), 9, 27–28; James Savage to George Ticknor, February 12, 1841, in "Ten Documents in Regard to Primary Schools in Boston," Manuscript Collection, BPL; Lemuel Shattuck, *Report to the Committee of the City Council Appointed to Obtain the Census of Boston for the Year 1845* . . . (Boston: John H. Eastburn, 1846), 65–66.

6. Shattuck, *Census of Boston*, 68; Boston School Committee, *Public Schools of the City of Boston September 1838* (Boston: J. H. Eastburn, 1838), 7, 15; *Boston Morning Post*, October 19, 1838, October 29, 1835.

7. Mary Ann Connolly, "The Boston Schools in the New Republic, 1776–1840" (Ed.D. diss., Harvard University, 1963), 141–43.

8. Josiah Quincy, *A Municipal History of the Town and City of Boston* . . .

(Boston: C. C. Little and J. Brown, 1852), 217–24; Quotation from Josiah Quincy, "An Address to the Board of Aldermen . . . January 1, 1828," in *The Inaugural Addresses of the Mayors of Boston* (Boston: Rockwell and Churchill, 1894), 10–11.

9. Boston School Committee, *Report of a Sub-Committee . . . Recommending Various Improvements in the System of Instruction in the Grammar and Writing Schools of This City* (Boston: Nathan Hale, 1828), 33–35. The report was signed by the chairman, Josiah Quincy.

10. Ebenezer Bailey, *Review of the Mayor's Report on the Subject of Schools, So Far as it Relates to the High School for Girls* (Boston: Bowles and Dearborn, 1828), 5–20; Josiah Quincy, *Address, January 3, 1829, on Taking Leave of the Office of Mayor* (Boston: Crocker and Brewster, 1829), 17; Boston Common Council, *Report of Standing Committee on Public Instruction of Petition of Samuel Prince . . . [Relating to the] High School for Girls* (Boston: Common Council Document No. 1, 1836), 6–10.

11. Richard P. DuFour, "The Exclusion of Female Students from the Public Secondary Schools of Boston, 1820–1920" (Ed.D. diss., Northern Illinois University, 1981), 82; Boston School Committee, *[Report of a Sub-Committee of the School Committee] to Take into Consideration the Present System of Instruction Prescribed for the English Grammar and Writing Schools . . .* ([Boston, 1830]), 6–19; Boston School Committee, *Regulations* (Boston: John H. Eastburn, 1830), 12–16; *Boston Morning Post*, December 23, 1837, January 2, 1838; Boston School Committee, *Report on the Distribution of Scholars* (Boston: City Document. No. 3, 1838), 2–15; Boston School Committee, *Regulations Adopted . . . May 1838* (Boston: John H. Eastburn, 1838), 12; Shattuck, *Census of Boston*, Appendix, 28.

12. *Boston Daily Advertiser*, November 4, 1830; Boston Common Council, *High School for Girls*, 9–10.

13. *Boston Daily Advertiser*, March 11, 1834; Boston School Committee, *[Sub-Committee] Report on Removing the High School to the Adams School House . . .* ([Boston: City Document, unnumbered, 1837]), 9, 8.

14. Monitorial School, *[Instructors'] Report to the Proprietors* ([Boston, 1830]), 8 and passim; Paul H. Mattingly, *The Classless Profession: American Schoolmen in the Nineteenth Century* (New York: New York University Press, 1975), 87.

15. *Boston Daily Advertiser*, November 6, 1828; "Young Ladies' Seminaries," *Ladies Magazine* 2 (March 1829): 191–94; Young Ladies High School, *Catalogues of the Teachers and Scholars 1829–1837* (various titles and imprints, 1830–37); "Mrs. Inglis's Establishment for Young Ladies," June 1843, broadside, MHS; *Daily Advertiser*, August 18, 19, 1834; Boston Citizens Committee

to Investigate the Destruction of the Ursuline Convent, *Report . . . August 11, 1834* (Boston: J. H. Eastburn, 1834), 5–8.

16. Catharine E. Beecher, *A Treatise on Domestic Economy, for the Use of Young Ladies at Home, and at School* (Boston: Marsh, Capen, Lyon, and Webb, 1841; reprint, New York: Source Book Press, 1970), 37; Hannah Lowell Jackson to Sarah Jackson Russell, August 29, 1835, typescript, Almy Family Papers, SL.

17. On primary and secondary education in both Charleston and Boston, see William H. Pease and Jane H. Pease, *The Web of Progress: Private Values and Public Styles in Boston and Charleston, 1828–1843* (New York: Oxford University Press, 1985), 108–14. Charleston, Journals of the Commissioners of Free Schools, 1812–34, especially 1829–34, SCHS; John F. Thomason, *The Foundations of the Public Schools of South Carolina* (Columbia: State Company, 1925), 162; Maris A. Vinovskis, *Fertility in Massachusetts from the Revolution to the Civil War* (New York: Academic Press, 1981), 128; Catherine Clinton, *The Plantation Mistress: Woman's World in the Old South* (New York: Pantheon, 1982), 137.

18. *Charleston Courier*, August 11, 19, 1841.

19. James L. Petigru to Jane Petigru North, August 4, 1835, photocopy, James L. Petigru Papers, LC.

20. *Charleston Courier*, January 18, 1830, March 7, 20, 1834; Literary and Philosophical Society of South Carolina, *Address to the People of the State, on the Classification, Character, and Exercises, of the Objects and Advantages of the Lyceum System . . .* (Charleston: Observer Office, 1834), 30, 35–36; Henry Bruns to Joseph Milligan, April 24, 1835, Milligan Papers, UNC; *Charleston Courier*, September 19, 1832, April 23, 1833; German Friendly Society, Minutes, May 1, 1833, typescript, CC.

21. *Charleston Courier*, March 3, 1835; Mary Kelley, *Private Woman, Public Stage: Literary Domesticity in Nineteenth-Century America* (New York: Oxford University Press, 1984), 72–73, quoting Caroline Gilman in *Southern Rose*.

22. Gerda Lerner, *The Grimké Sisters from South Carolina: Rebels against Slavery* (Boston: Houghton Mifflin, 1967), 17, 19; Sarah M. Grimké, *Letters on the Equality of the Sexes, and the Condition of Woman . . .* (Boston: Isaac Knapp, 1838; reprint, New York: Source Book Press, 1970), 46–49.

23. Anna Hayes Johnson to Elizabeth Haywood, August 17, 1822, Ernest Haywood Collection, UNC; *Gospel Messenger* 14 (May 1837): 84; Charles Fraser, *Reminiscences of Charleston* (Charleston: Russell, 1854), 111–13. Louisa Petigru Porcher to Adele Petigru Allston, January 17, 24, 1851, Robert F. W. Allston Papers, SCHS, elaborates Porcher's preference for home educa-

tion over sending her daughters to a school only a few blocks from home and her firm opposition to all thoughts of a boarding school.

24. Harriott Horry Rutledge to Mrs. Edward C. Rutledge, September 17, [1841], and Harriott Horry Rutledge [aunt] to Mrs. Edward C. Rutledge, June 18, 1841, Harriott Horry Rutledge Papers, DU; Susan Petigru King, *Lily* (New York: Harper and Brothers, 1855), 119–20; Caroline Gilman, *Recollections of a Southern Matron and a New England Bride* (1838, 1836; reprint, 2 vols. in 1, Philadelphia: John E. Potter and Co., 1867), 60.

25. Thomason, *Foundations*, 163–64; J. L. Dawson and H. W. DeSaussure, *Census of the City of Charleston, South Carolina, for the Year 1848* (Charleston: J. B. Nixon, 1849), 54–55; Charleston, Journals of the Commissioners of Free Schools, 1812–34, February 18, 1833, SCHS; *Charleston Courier*, August 4, 1841.

26. Shattuck, *Census of Boston*, 68–71; Edward R. Laurens, *Address Delivered in Charleston Before the Agricultural Society of South-Carolina . . . 1832* (Charleston: A. E. Miller, 1832), 8–9.

27. For the South Carolina Society, see South Carolina Society, *Rules . . . ,* 8th ed. (Charleston: A. E. Miller, 1827), 1–29; and *Charleston Courier*, December 8, 1829, December 23, 1833, January 15, 1835. For the Fellowship Society, see Fellowship Society, Minutes, 1827–40, microfilm, USC.

28. For the German Friendly Society, see German Friendly Society, Minutes, 1828–33, typescript, CC, quotation from November 5, 1828.

29. "Historical Extracts," 3, quoting John England's *History of the Diocese of Charleston*, 261, Sisters of Charity of Our Lady of Mercy, Collections, Mother House, May Forest, Charleston, S.C.; *Charleston Courier*, January 4, 1843.

30. *Charleston Courier*, January 2, 1829; *Charleston Mercury*, April 12, 1841; Kaal Kadosh Beth Elohim, Board of Trustees Minutes, March 11, 1839, Beth Elohim Archives, Charleston, S.C.

31. Samuel Gilman to M. L. Hurlbut, January 26, 1832, Unitarian Church, Records, Charleston, S.C.; *Charleston Mercury*, April 4, October 31, July 9, 1836, May 2, 1838; *Charleston Courier*, March 1, 1843.

32. References to numerous proprietary schools appear in both the *Charleston Courier* and *Mercury*, 1825–45. See especially, for the schools noted, the *Courier*, October 5–December 3, 1841, and March 19–October 4, 1842.

33. James [B. Campbell] to Mary B. Campbell, September 7, 1833, James B. Campbell Papers, SCHS.

34. Receipt bill, A. W. Talvande to William Kincaid, May 1831, Kincaid-Anderson Family Papers, USC; Alexander Robertson to Robert F. W. Allston, January 16, 1838, in J. H. Easterby, ed., *The South Carolina Rice Plantation as*

Revealed in the Papers of Robert F. W. Allston (Chicago: University of Chicago Press, 1945), 405–6.

35. Edwina Chamberlain, Recollections, in Henry Campbell Davis, "Notes on South Carolina Female Institute at Barhamville," especially Report Card for Mary A. Cantey, August 1832, Bill to Laura Gaillard for Schooling, [June 1839], and Monthly Statement of Costs for E. Nelson McFaddin, October 4, 1858, South Carolina Collegiate Institute (Barhamville Academy) Papers, USC, which can be compared to Bill to H. A. Middleton from Miss Binsee's Academy, [June 17, 1837], Cheves-Middleton Papers, SCHS, advertisements in the *Charleston Courier*, January 1843; *Barhamville Register*, 1847, 5, 10; and M. H. McAliley to [father], October 11, 1852, Eliza [?] to Laura Nelson Covert, April 1, 4, 1836, South Carolina Collegiate Institute (Barhamville Academy) Papers, USC.

36. [Mary Bates], "Female Education," *The Magnolia*, n.s., 2 (January 1843): 65–66.

37. Commissioners of the Poor House, Minutes, December 30, 1830, Charleston, Records of the Poor House, SCHS; Report, June 30–November 16, 1832, Weekly Reports of the Steward, 1830–39, Charleston, Records of the Orphan House, SCHS; Boston Female Asylum, *Annual Reports . . . 1841 and 1842* (Boston: T. R. Marvin, 1842), 9–10; Harriet Martineau, *Retrospect of Western Travel*, 2 vols. (London: Saunders and Otley, 1838), 1:234; *Boston Morning Post*, March 25, 1835; Benevolent Fraternity of Churches, *Third Annual Report* (Boston: Isaac R. Butts, 1837), 3–7; Seaman's Aid Society of the City of Boston, *Third Annual Report* (Boston: James B. Dow, 1836), 17–18; Warren Street Chapel, *Proceedings of the Sixth Annual Meeting . . .* (Boston: John Putnam, 1843), 4–20; Hannah Lowell Jackson to Sarah Jackson Russell, February 8, 1836, Almy Family Papers, SL.

38. Louisa Lee Waterhouse, Diary, June 22, 1839, MHS; Catharine M. Sedgwick, *Means and Ends, of Self-Training* (Boston: Marsh, Capen, Lyon, and Webb, 1839), 28–31.

39. Boston Primary School Committee, *Rules and Regulations; Revised November 1838* (Boston: John H. Eastburn, 1838), 14–16; Boston City Council, *Rules and Orders of the Common Council . . . with a List of City Officers* (Boston: J. H. Eastburn, 1838), 54–55; Vinovskis, *Fertility in Massachusetts*, 63–64; Boston School Committee, *Report . . . [on] Establishing a Model School* (Boston: City Document No. 22, 1838); Horace Mann, Journal, February 3, 1838, Horace Mann Papers, MHS; Joseph Miller Wightman, comp., *Annals of the Boston Primary School Committee . . .* (Boston: G. C. Rand, 1860), 170–71; Boston Academy of Music, *Sixth Annual Report* (Boston: Perkins, Marvin, and Co., 1838), 7.

40. Richard M. Bernard and Maris A. Vinovskis, "The Female School

Teacher in Antebellum Massachusetts," *Journal of Social History* 10 (March 1977): 332–45; Patrick T. Jackson to Henry Lee, Jr., July 21, 1843, Lee Family Papers, MHS; Sallie Holley to Caroline Putnam, January 9, 1853, in John White Chadwick, ed., *A Life for Liberty: Anti-Slavery and other Letters of Sallie Holley* (New York: G. P. Putnam's Sons, 1899), 114.

41. Dawson and DeSaussure, *City of Charleston*, 54–55.

42. For Mary Hort's story, see excerpts from her diary, 1842–44, in Mary Hort Papers, USC.

43. James L. Petigru to Jane Petigru North, January 29, 1838, in James Petigru Carson, ed., *Life, Letters, and Speeches of James Louis Petigru . . .* (Washington: W. H. Lowdermilk, 1920), 195.

44. Sedgwick, *Means and Ends*, 17–19.

45. Minnie (Mary Hooper) to A. M. Hooper, September 9, 1836, John DeBerniere Hooper Papers, UNC.

Chapter 5

1. The literature on both the legal and cultural aspects of women, property, and marriage is extensive. See, for example, Norma Basch, *In the Eyes of the Law: Women, Marriage, and Property in Nineteenth-Century New York* (Ithaca: Cornell University Press, 1982); Michael Grossberg, *Governing the Hearth: Law and the Family in Nineteenth-Century America* (Chapel Hill: University of North Carolina Press, 1985); and Marylynn Salmon, *Women and the Law of Property in Early America* (Chapel Hill: University of North Carolina Press, 1986).

2. Lawrence T. McDonnell, "Desertion, Divorce, and Class Struggle: Contradictions of Patriarchy in Antebellum South Carolina" (typescript, 1985, in authors' possession), 10, quoting John C. Calhoun, in R. W. Meriwether, ed., *Papers of John C. Calhoun* (Columbus, 1859), 54–55; Salmon, *Women and the Law*, 13.

3. For material specifically dealing with marriage and divorce in Massachusetts and South Carolina, see Marylynn Salmon, "Women and Property in South Carolina: The Evidence from Marriage Settlements, 1730–1830," *William and Mary Quarterly*, 3d ser., 39 (October 1982), 655–85; Suzanne D. Lebsock, "The Married Women's Property Acts of the South" (typescript, 1975, in authors' possession); Joshua Prescott, *A Digest of the Probate Laws of Massachusetts, Relative to the Power and Duty of Executors, Administrators, Guardians, Heirs, Legatees, and Creditors . . .* (Boston: John Weston, 1824); and Benjamin James, *A Digest of the Laws of South Carolina Containing the Public Statute Laws of the State Down to the Year 1822 . . .* (Columbia: Telescope Press,

1822; microfiche, Woodbridge, Conn.: Research Publications, 1984).

4. James, *Laws of South Carolina*, 521; on John Belton O'Neall, see Boyce v. Owens (1833) and McCarty v. McCarty (1847) in McDonnell, "Desertion, Divorce, and Class Struggle," 4–5.

5. *Report of the D'Hauteville Case: The Commonwealth of Pennsylvania . . . versus David Sears [et al.] . . .* (Philadelphia: William S. Martin, 1840), 66. The general outline of the story that follows is contained in this report.

6. Ibid., 19–20.

7. Ibid., 68.

8. Ibid., 25, 105, 42.

9. Ibid., 25.

10. Ibid., 15–17.

11. Ibid., 47 52, 9.

12. *The Petition of Henry C. DeRham to the General Assembly of Rhode Island, to Exempt Paul Daniel Gonsalve Grand D'Hauteville from the Operation of the Law . . .* (Providence: Knowles and Vose, 1841), 11.

13. Ibid., 30, 107, 53.

14. For South Carolina, see Salmon, "Women and Property," quotation at 674. For Massachusetts, see Salmon, *Women and the Law*, 90, 133, 140.

15. South Carolina, Secretary of State, Marriage Settlements, 1824–45, SCA.

16. *Charleston Courier*, March 4, 21, 1843.

17. South Carolina, Secretary of State, Marriage Settlements, 1824–45, SCA.

18. For Maria Chapman (1827) and Eliza Schnierle (1838), see ibid., bk. 9:392–94; 14:90–92.

19. Ibid., bk. 14:406–7. The Somers contract is dated December 2, 1840.

20. Ibid., bk. 13:63–64, 279–80, 431–32, for traditional Jewish contracts. The French contract is March 8, 1827, in bk. 9:354–58.

21. Ibid., August 9, 1830, and October 18, 1827, bk. 11:43–48 and 9:420–22.

22. Richard H. Chused, "Married Women's Property Law: 1800–1850," *Georgetown Law Journal* 71 (1983): 1359–1425.

23. Unless otherwise specified, the property data that follow are drawn from Charleston County, S.C., Probate Court, Wills and Inventories, 1825–43, and Suffolk County, Mass., Probate Records, 1825–43, microfilm, GS. The samples were drawn by noting all wills and inventories probated in a given month (i.e., January in 1825, February in 1826, etc., unless there were fewer than ten wills probated in a month, in which case enough to make ten

were drawn from the next month) and the related inventories for each will and will for each inventory regardless of when probated. The Charleston probate records contain almost no inventories after 1835. There are 198 wills and 190 inventories in the Boston sample and 225 wills and 126 inventories in the Charleston sample. Of these, 62 of the Boston wills and 44 of the inventories and 101 of the Charleston wills and 45 of the inventories were those of women.

24. For the Merrimack shareholders, see Paul F. McGouldrick, *New England Textiles in the Nineteenth Century: Profits and Investments* (Cambridge: Harvard University Press, 1968), 81. Jackson Company shareholders list, June 23, 1838, A. A. Lawrence Papers, MHS.

25. Because most Charleston inventories are either vague or silent about dollar values, the values of Charleston testators' estates are drawn from Charleston County, S.C., Probate Court, Letters of Administration, 1828–43, microfilm, GS.

26. The public records on which this observation is based comprise the Boston Assessor's *Lists of Persons, Copartnerships, and Corporations who were Taxed Twenty-five Dollars and Upwards in the City of Boston* (Boston: various publishers, 1829, 1836, and 1841). In Charleston a wealth index was built on slave ownership derived from the manuscript censuses of 1830 and 1840, on real property recorded in the Charleston County Registry of Mesne Conveyance records of deed, 1820–43, and on scattered lists of corporate stock owners. In Boston ownership of $30,000 or more in property was thought to make the owner rich, and possession of $80,000 in total property or $50,000 in assessed personalty (generally understood to be substantially underassessed) marked a person as having great wealth. In Charleston an indexing system approximating the Boston stratification but not based on dollar values was used to make similar categories. See William H. Pease and Jane H. Pease, *The Web of Progress: Private Values and Public Styles in Boston and Charleston, 1828–1843* (New York: Oxford University Press, 1985), 225–58.

27. Thomas L. V. Wilson [Abner Forbes], *The Aristocracy of Boston; Who They Are and What They Were . . .* (Boston: published by the author, 1848); Richard Hildreth, *"Our First Men:" A Calendar of Wealth, Fashion and Gentility . . . in the City of Boston . . .* (Boston: All Booksellers, 1846).

28. Alicia Hopton Middleton, *Life in Carolina and New England during the Nineteenth Century* (Bristol, R.I.: privately printed, 1929), 63; William R. Lawrence to A. A. Lawrence, March 17, 1840, A. A. Lawrence Papers, MHS; Deborah Pickman Clifford, *Mine Eyes Have Seen the Glory: A Biography of Julia Ward Howe* (Boston: Little, Brown, 1979).

29. John Jacob Schnell, Will, September 2, 1830, and Robert Ling, Will,

September 21, 1832, Charleston County, S.C., Probate Court, Record of Wills, 1826–34, microfilm, GS; *Boston Morning Post*, December 31, 1832.

30. Thomas Hanscome, Will, January 3, 1832, John Weston, Will, August 17, 1830, and Joe Rogers, Will, August 2, 1833, Charleston County, S.C., Probate Court, Record of Wills, 1826–34, microfilm, GS.

31. Chused, "Married Women's Property Law," 1366–67 nn. 27–28; Mary M. Prioleau Ford, Will, March 20, 1832, Charleston County, S.C., Probate Court, Record of Wills, 1826–34, microfilm, GS

32. Eliza Pinckney to Dear Sir, June 13, 1859, Eliza Izard Pinckney Letters, USC; Esther Palmer, Will, June 25, 1832, Ann Drayton Perry, Will, November 23, 1830, and Harriet Hockley Bampfield, Will, September 24, 1830, Charleston County, S.C., Probate Court, Record of Wills, 1826–34, microfilm, GS. That this may have been a characteristic pattern for antebellum American women is suggested by the similar pattern that Suzanne Lebsock reveals in *The Free Women of Petersburg: Status and Culture in a Southern Town, 1784–1860* (New York: W. W. Norton, 1985), 134–35.

33. Joel Poinsett to James B. Campbell, June 16, 1836, and James B. Campbell to Mary Campbell, January 19, 1837, James B. Campbell Papers, SCHS.

34. Edward McCrady to Joel R. Poinsett, October 6, 1838, and Thomas Bennett to Joel R. Poinsett, October 12, 1838, Joel R. Poinsett Papers, Historical Society of Pennsylvania, Philadelphia, Pa.

35. Thomas Bennett to Joel R. Poinsett, October 12, 1838, ibid.

36. Thomas Bennett to Joel R. Poinsett, October 20, 1838, ibid.

37. Margaret Adger Smyth to Thomas Smyth, May 27, June 5, 1844, Smyth-Stoney-Adger Papers, SCHS.

38. Margaret Adger Smyth to Thomas Smyth, September 11, 1844, ibid.

39. Ibid.

40. Tenah Glen, Will, June 4, 1830, Charleston County, S.C., Probate Court, Record of Wills, 1826–34, microfilm, GS; Thomas Gates, Will, 1852, SCA; *Charleston Courier*, August 6, 18, 1832; Jacob Schirmer, Diary, August 4, 1832, SCHS; Basil Manly, Diary, August 4, 1832, Manly Family Papers, microfilm, USC, original at University of Alabama, University, Ala.; Petition of Mary Douglas, December 19, 1837, Slavery Petitions, SCA.

Chapter 6

1. Cotton Mather, *A Family Well-Ordered* (Boston, 1699), 59, quoted in Barbara L. Epstein, *The Politics of Domesticity: Women, Evangelism, and Temperance in Nineteenth-Century America* (Middletown: Wesleyan University Press,

1981), 34; Ann Douglas, *The Feminization of American Culture* (New York: Alfred A. Knopf, 1979). Mary P. Ryan, *Cradle of the Middle Class: The Family in Oneida County, New York, 1790–1865* (Cambridge: Cambridge University Press, 1981), 60–104, is the most important empirical study to elaborate the phenomenon.

2. Catharine M. Sedgwick, *Means and Ends, of Self-Training* (Boston: Marsh, Capen, Lyon, and Webb, 1839), 21–24; William G. Brooks, Diary, October 21, 1839, MHS; Mary Amory to Thomas C. Amory, April 12, 1829, Amory Family Papers, MHS; Mary Hort, Diary, January 1846, Mary Hort Papers, USC; Frances E. Appleton, [Commonplace Book and Yearly Reflections], June 9, [1834], LS.

3. Paul Trapier, "Notices of Ancestors and Relatives . . . ," 90, SCHS; Albert S. Thomas, *An Historical Account of the Protestant Episcopal Church in South Carolina, 1820–1957* (Columbia: R. L. Bryon Co., 1957), 255; Charleston Independent Congregational Church and Circular Church, Records, 1829–41, SCHS; St. John's German Lutheran Church, "List of Members and Families of Deceased Members also Members without Charge, 1829–1844," typescript, CC.

4. For Boston Congregational Churches, see Boston City Missionary Society, *Fourth Annual Report . . . 1844* (Boston: The Society, 1845); St. Paul's Episcopal Church, "A Catalogue of the Proprietors and Parishioners of St. Paul's Church, Boston, 1820–1840," Episcopal Diocesan Library and Archives, Boston, Mass.; and Second Universalist Church, Baldwin Place Baptist Church, and Hanover Street Methodist Episcopal Church, Boston, Records and Index, 1828–43, microfilm, GS.

5. Pauline Holmes, *One Hundred Years of Mount Vernon Church, 1842–1942* (Boston: The Church, 1942), 2 n. 3; *Boston Morning Post,* July 4, December 31, 1840, January 28, 18, 1842; *Southern Evangelist* 3 (August 27, October 1, 1836).

6. Second Presbyterian Church, Records of Session, January 11, April 11, 1833, typescript, USC; Presbyterian Church of the City of Charleston, *By-Laws, 1838* (Philadelphia: Adam Waldie, 1838), 7–10; Trinity Church, Pew Records, vol. 16, 1831–43, New England Historical and Genealogical Society, Boston, Mass.; Henry Wilder Foote, *Annals of King's Chapel from the Puritan Age of New England to the Present,* 3 vols. (Boston: Little, Brown, 1882–1940), 2:588ff.

7. Christ Protestant Episcopal Church, Proprietors and Vestry Minutes, May 4, 8, 1840, Episcopal Diocesan Library and Archives, Boston, Mass.; Jane H. Pease and William H. Pease, "Whose Right Hand of Fellowship? Pew and Pulpit in Shaping Church Practice," in Conrad E. Wright, ed., *American*

Unitarianism, 1805–1865 (Boston: Northeastern University Press, 1989), 194–98; Lewis Glover Pray, *Historical Sketch of the Twelfth Congregational Society in Boston* (Boston: John Wilson and Son, 1863), 15–16.

8. Mary Clark to Francis Jackson, August 14, 1837, Manuscript Collections, BPL.

9. Hannah Lowell Jackson to Sarah Jackson Russell, March 13, 1836, typescript, Almy Family Papers, SL; Charleston Independent Congregational Church and Circular Church, Records, 12:119, SCHS; Protestant Episcopal Sunday School Society, *Twelfth Annual Report* (Charleston: A. E. Miller, 1831), 3.

10. Hollis Street Church, Church School, Records, 1832–45, and Howard Sunday School, Records, 1827–45, especially October 22, 1833, November 10, December 8, 1834, January 12, February 9, April 13, 1834, Bulfinch Place Church Records, Harvard Divinity School, Cambridge, Mass.

11. Sisters of Charity of Our Lady of Mercy, Historical Extracts and Membership Rolls, Mother House, May Forest, Charleston, S.C.; Sister Anne Francis Campbell, "Bishop England's Sisterhood, 1829–1929" (Ph.D. diss., St. Louis University, 1968), 1–66, quotation at 34.

12. Henry Laurens Pinckney, *Address Delivered before the Methodist Benevolent Society . . . July 1835* (Charleston: E. J. Van Brunt, 1835), 17; [Daniel Cobia], reported in the *Gospel Messenger* 12 (September 1835): 258.

13. Ladies Benevolent Society, Journal 2, 1824–43, typescript, USC. The statistical compilation is drawn from those women who, between 1828 and 1843, held office in the Female Seamen's Friend Society, the Fuel Society, the Ladies Benevolent Society, the Neck Female Charitable Association, the Epidemic Hospital, the Charleston Infant School, and the Methodist Benevolent Society.

14. The philanthropic statistical compilation is drawn from those women who, between 1828 and 1843, held office in the Children's Aid Society, the Children's Friend Society, the Boston Female Asylum, the Fatherless and Widows' Society, the Female Philanthropic Society, the Fragment Society, the Ladies Benevolent Society of the Twelfth Congregational Church, the Ladies Shoe Society, the Seaman's Aid Society, the Unitarian Female Charitable Society, and the Widows' Society. The reform leaders were women who, between 1828 and 1843, held office in the Female Improvement Society, the Female Moral Reform Society, the Female Total Abstinence Society, the Golden Rule Society, and the Penitent Female and Refuge Ladies Auxiliary. Nancy A. Hewitt, *Women's Activism and Social Change: Rochester, New York, 1822–1872* (Ithaca: Cornell University Press, 1984), found similar patterns among urban women's charitable and reform organizations in western New

York. Anne M. Boylan, "Timid Girls, Venerable Widows and Dignified Matrons: Life Cycle Patterns among Organized Women in New York and Boston, 1797–1840," *American Quarterly* 38 (Winter 1986), 782, 787, found that in nine Boston organizations the proportion of officers who were married ranged from 47 to 100 percent, but she makes no distinction between married women and widows. She also argues that reform organizations, of which none had existed for more than seven years in 1840, attracted more young and single women than did the benevolent societies, the earliest of which was founded in 1800.

15. William H. Pease and Jane H. Pease, *The Web of Progress: Private Values and Public Styles in Boston and Charleston, 1828–1843* (New York: Oxford University Press, 1985), 90–103, 142–52, provides more of the context.

16. Boston Female Asylum, *An Account . . . with the Act of Incorporation . . .* (Boston: J. R. Hinckley and Co., 1833), 10; Amos Lawrence to Robert Lawrence, August 24, 1841, A. A. Lawrence Papers, MHS.

17. Fragment Society, *Constitution and By-Laws . . .* (Boston: Munroe and Francis, 1825), 34; Dorcas Society, *Constitution . . .* (Boston, 1829); Female Philanthropic Society, *Constitution . . .* (Boston, 1823); *Boston Morning Post*, November 4, 1841; Fatherless and Widows' Society, *Nineteenth Annual Report* (Boston: Cassady and March, 1836), 9–10. Fatherless and Widows' Society, *The Twenty-Sixth Annual Report* (Boston: Crocker and Brewster, 1843), 15, lists all members. All annual reports give officers. See, for example, Widows' Society, *Twentieth Annual Report* (Boston: Tuttle, Weeks and Dennett, 1837), 3. Directresses and committees are listed, ibid., 12, and Widows' Society, *Twenty-Second Annual Report* (Boston: William A. Hall, 1839), 8.

18. Boston Children's Friend Society, *Ninth Annual Report* (Boston: Samuel Harris, 1842); Boston Children's Aid Society, *Constitution as Amended with Reports . . .* (Boston: Marden and Kimball, 1837); Samaritan Asylum for Indigent Children, *Constitution . . .* (Boston: Isaac Knapp, 1836).

19. Boston Seaman's Friend Society, *Thirteenth Annual Report* (Boston: T. Marvin, [1828]), 4; Seaman's Aid Society of the City of Boston, *First–Twelfth Annual Reports* (Boston: various imprints, 1834–45).

20. Seaman's Aid Society of the City of Boston, *Third Annual Report* (Boston: James B. Dow, 1836), 15, and *Fourth Annual Report* (Boston: Marsh, Capen, and Lyon, 1837), 17–18, quoted in Barbara J. Berg, *The Remembered Gate: Origins of American Feminism—The Woman and the City, 1800–1860* (New York: Oxford University Press, 1978), 230–31.

21. Penitent Female's Refuge Society, *Constitution of the Auxiliary Society* (Boston: Lincoln and Edmands, 1825), 4–6; Boston Female Moral Reform Society, *Second Annual Report* (Boston: Isaac Knapp, 1837), 13.

22. Odd Ladies Mutual Aid Society, *Constitution . . . adopted March 1844* (Boston: J. B. Chisholm, 1847), 3.

23. *Liberator*, November 17, 1832, January 25, 1856; *Boston Morning Post*, October 21, 22, 1835.

24. American Anti-Slavery Society, *Third Annual Report . . .* (New York: William S. Dorr, 1836), 91; Boston Female Anti-Slavery Society, *Fourth Annual Report, 1837* (Boston: Isaac Knapp, 1838), 25, and *Fifth Annual Report, 1838* (Boston: Isaac Knapp, 1839).

25. [Maria Weston Chapman], *Right and Wrong in Massachusetts* (Boston: Dow and Jackson Anti-Slavery Press, 1839), 52.

26. Gerda Lerner, *The Grimké Sisters from South Carolina: Rebels against Slavery* (Boston: Houghton Mifflin, 1967).

27. Sarah and Angelina Grimké to Henry C. Wright, August 12, 1837, in Gilbert H. Barnes and Dwight L. Dumond, eds., *Letters of Theodore Dwight Weld, Angelina Grimké Weld, and Sarah Grimké, 1822–1844* (2 vols., 1934; reprint, 2 vols., Gloucester, Mass.: Peter Smith, 1965), 1:420.

28. Amos A. Phelps to Charlotte Phelps, July 14, 1837, Amos A. Phelps Papers, BPL.

29. Sarah M. Grimké, *Letters on the Equality of the Sexes, and the Condition of Woman . . .* (Boston: Isaac Knapp, 1838; reprint, New York: Source Book Press, 1970), 98.

30. Robert H. Abzug, *Passionate Liberator: Theodore Dwight Weld and the Dilemma of Reform* (New York: Oxford University Press, 1980), 201–43.

31. Jane H. Pease and William H. Pease, "The Boston Bluestocking: Maria Weston Chapman," in *Bound with Them in Chains: A Biographical History of the Antislavery Movement* (Westport, Conn.: Greenwood Press, 1972), 28–59.

32. Edmund Quincy to Richard D. Webb, January 29, 1843, Edmund Quincy Papers, MHS.

33. Boston Female Anti-Slavery Society, *[Second] Annual Report . . . 1835* (Boston: The Society, 1836), 52.

34. Harriet Martineau, *Autobiography with Memorials by Maria Weston Chapman*, 2 vols. (London: Smith, Elder and Co., 1877), 2:28.

Chapter 7

1. Charlotte B. Everett to Edward Everett, January 4, 1830, Edward Everett Papers, MHS.

2. Richard Hildreth, *"Our First Men:" A Calendar of Wealth, Fashion and Gentility . . . in the City of Boston . . .* (Boston: All Booksellers, 1846), 35, 40.

3. Harriott Horry Rutledge to Mrs. Edward C. Rutledge, June 18, 1841, Harriott Horry Rutledge Papers, DU; Charlotte B. Everett to Edward Everett, December 10, 1833, Edward Everett Papers, MHS.

4. Cordelia Jenks to Lemuel Pope Jenks, January 20, 1839, William Jenks Papers, MHS; *Boston Morning Post*, April 20, 21, 1840.

5. *Gospel Messenger* 14 (May 1837): 72–73; *Charleston Courier*, February 7, 1834; [Emory Washburn], *Argument Before an Ecclesiastical Council . . . July, 1841, With the Charges Preferred against the Rev. John Pierpont . . .* (Boston: S. N. Dickinson, 1841), 16–17; *Boston Daily Advertiser*, February 13, 1834.

6. Joseph Tuckerman, *Prize Essay: On the Wages Paid to Females for their Labour* (Philadelphia: Carey and Hart, 1830), 25–27.

7. Michael Grossberg, *Governing the Hearth: Law and the Family in Nineteenth-Century America* (Chapel Hill: University of North Carolina Press, 1985), 38 49.

8. John Pierce, Memoirs, reporting a conversation with Tuckerman, 7:423, MHS.

9. John S[ullivan] to Thomas C. Amory, July 8, 1833, Amory Family Papers, MHS; Gardiner H. Shaw to Henry Lee, Jr., February 5, 1843, Lee Family Papers, MHS. Steven M. Stowe, *Intimacy and Power in the Old South: Ritual in the Lives of Planters* (Baltimore: Johns Hopkins University Press, 1987), 81–82, reports similar comments among young male Charlestonians.

10. Diary of an Unidentified Bostonian, March 30, April 1, 1842, H. H. Edes Collection, MHS; *Boston Daily Advertiser*, June 18, 1834; William G. Brooks, Diary, August 31, 1839, MHS.

11. Jacob Schirmer, Diary, May 16, 1833, SCHS; State v. William Smith, September 9, 1833, Charleston County, S.C., Court of General Sessions, Records of Indictments and Subpoenas, SCA; Charleston Independent Congregational Church and Circular Church, Records, vol. 14, June 1836, August 22, 1836, SCHS.

12. J. N. B[arrillon] to John T. Seibels, April 16, 1831, Seibels Family Papers, USC.

13. *Boston Morning Post*, September 25, 1840; Benjamin James, *A Digest of the Laws of South Carolina Containing the Public Statute Laws of the State Down to the Year 1822 . . .* (Columbia: Telescope Press, 1822), 540; *Morning Post*, April 16, 1839, May 2, 1833.

14. Sarah M. Grimké, *Letters on the Equality of the Sexes, and the Condition of Woman . . .* (Boston: Isaac Knapp, 1838; reprint, New York: Source Book Press, 1970), 51; Anna Hayes Johnson to Elizabeth Haywood, June 23, 1822, Ernest Haywood Collection, UNC.

15. *Charleston Courier*, June 29, 1832; *Boston Daily Advertiser*, May 21,

1830, June 14, 1834; *Boston Morning Post*, April 24, 1833.

16. Grimké, *Equality of the Sexes*, 88.

17. *Boston Daily Advertiser*, March 4, 1828, August 28, 1830, January 29, 1831; *Boston Morning Post*, June 12, 1833.

18. *Boston Daily Advertiser*, May 12, 1834; *Boston Morning Post*, November 26, 1842, December 18, 1840.

19. Barbara L. Epstein, *The Politics of Domesticity: Women, Evangelism, and Temperance in Nineteenth-Century America* (Middletown: Wesleyan University Press, 1981), 91.

20. John Augustus, *A Report of the Labors . . . for the Last Ten Years in Aid of the Unfortunate* (Boston: Wright and Hasty, 1852), 46, cites 2,238 males and 1,962 females convicted in police court for drunkenness in a six-year period. Women thus comprised 47 percent of those convicted. The *Boston Morning Post*, May 14, 1840, observed that "the number of masculine common drunkards is on the decrease, while that of feminine drunkards is on the increase." Female Total Abstinence Society, *First Annual Report . . . 1842* (Boston: J. N. Bang, 1842), 7.

21. Female Total Abstinence Society, *First Annual Report*, 4, 7.

22. Mary Hort, Diary, January 1846, Mary Hort Papers, USC. David T. Courtwright to Jane H. Pease, September 10, 1987, suggested that "Le D." might well be a "coded reference to Laudanum." James L. Petigru to Jane Petigru North, August 4, 1835, photocopy, James L. Petigru Papers, LC; William Appleton, Diary, June 13, 1837, William Appleton and Company Collection, BL; *Charleston Courier*, November 23, 1843.

Chapter 8

1. B. C. Pressley, *The Law of Magistrates and Constables in the State of South Carolina . . .* (Charleston: Walker and Burke, 1848), 77–78, specifies that "a woman cannot be indicted for being a bawd generally, for that the bare solicitation of chastity is not indictable"; but that she can be indicted for keeping a bawdy house because it is a "common nuisance." South Carolina, *The Statutes at Large*, 10 vols., ed. David J. McCord (Columbia: A. S. Johnston, 1839), 6:236.

2. William Gilmore Simms, *Slavery in America: Being a Brief Review of Miss Martineau on That Subject* (Richmond: Thomas H. White, 1838), 38.

3. *Charleston Mercury*, September 16, 21, 1837, June 20, 1839; *Boston Morning Post*, November 7, 1835, carried the story on June's brothel; James M. Walker to Mitchell King, September 19, 1839, Mitchell King Papers, UNC.

4. Mary Boykin Chesnut, *A Diary from Dixie*, ed. Ben Ames Williams

(Boston: Houghton Mifflin, © 1905, 1949), 21–22; Sarah M. Grimké, *Letters on the Equality of the Sexes, and the Condition of Woman* ... (Boston: Isaac Knapp, 1838; reprint, New York: Source Book Press, 1970), 53–54; Otway (pseud.), *The Theatre Defended: A Reply to Two Discourses of the Rev. Thomas Smyth* (Charleston: Thomas J. Eccles, 1838); *Charleston Mercury*, September 16, 20, 1837, June 20, 1839, November 12, 1840; State v. Margaret Davis, April 17, 1830, Charleston County, S.C., Court of General Sessions, Records of Indictments and Subpoenas, SCA.

5. "Report of a Sub-Committee Appointed to Make Enquiry, Respecting the Necessity & Practicability of Establishing a Penitentiary in This Town," [1820], Manuscript Collections, BPL; Robert A. McCaughey, *Josiah Quincy, 1772–1864: The Last Federalist* (Cambridge: Harvard University Press, 1974), 118–19. Boston Society for the Religious and Moral Instruction of the Poor, *Twelfth Annual Report, Dec. 4, 1828*, William Jenks Papers, MHS; *Boston Daily Advertiser*, February 25, 1830; and *Boston Morning Post*, May 6, 1840, all list the same areas mentioned in the 1820 report as the locations of brothels and disorderly houses. For the grand jury proceedings, see *Daily Advertiser*, November 17, 1831; for the police raids, see *Morning Post*, May 6, 1840, April 28, May 1, 1841, July 25, August 23, 1842.

6. *Boston Daily Advertiser*, November 17, 1831; H. K. Stockton to Moses Grant, [Report on Obscene Pictures], August 30, 1834, 7–9, and "Establishing a Penitentiary," [1820], Manuscript Collections, BPL.

7. *Boston Morning Post*, May 13, 22, 1833, describes riots against brothels. *Boston Daily Advertiser*, August 12, 1834, and Boston Citizens Committee to Investigate the Destruction of the Ursuline Convent, *Report ... August 11, 1834* (Boston: J. H. Eastburn, 1834), 4, link the arson to rumors of "corruption." Lyman Beecher commented on the wife-swapping proclivities of Bostonians who resisted his 1826 revivals, in his *Autobiography and Correspondence ...*, 2 vols., ed. Charles Beecher (New York: Harper and Brothers, 1865), 1:76.

8. *Boston Morning Post*, July 18, January 31, 1839, July 13, 1835.

9. *Boston Daily Advertiser*, February 25, 1830, June 1, November 17, 1831; Boston Society for the Religious and Moral Instruction of the Poor, *Twelfth Annual Report, December 4, 1828*, William Jenks Papers, MHS; William J. Snelling, *Exposé of the Vice of Gaming, as it lately Existed in Massachusetts [Boston]* ... (Boston: W. J. Snelling, 1833); Robert C. Waterston, *An Address on Pauperism: Its Extent, Causes, and the Best Means of Prevention* ... (Boston: Charles C. Little and James Brown, 1844), 15.

10. The *Boston Morning Post* established this pattern in the years 1840–42 in many reports of police and municipal court proceedings

against prostitutes and brothel keepers; see May 5, 6, 1840, April 28, May 1, 1841, and July 25, August 23, 1842. The Decker case is reported on August 14, September 10, 1840.

11. *Boston Morning Post*, May 13, 1840, November 26, December 16, 1839.

12. Boston Female Moral Reform Society, *The Second Annual Report . . . 1837* (Boston: Isaac Knapp, 1837), 7, 10–11, 13.

13. Boston City Council, *Report of the Standing Committee . . . on the Subject of the House of Reformation for Juvenile Offenders* (Boston: J. H. Eastburn, 1832), 15, 21–26, and *Report . . . on a Memorial of the Directors of the House of Reformation, 1834* (Boston City Document No. 8, 1834, microfilm, BPL); House of Reformation, Directors, *Report on Confining Children of Both Sexes in the Same Building, February 3, 1840* (Boston City Document No. 6, 1840, microfilm, BPL), 2–11.

14. Board of Guardians of the Poor of the City and Districts of Philadelphia, *Report of the Committee to Visit the Cities of Baltimore, New York, Providence, Boston, and Salem* (Philadelphia: Samuel Parker, 1827), 15–16; House of Industry, Directors, *Annual Report 1832* (Boston City Document No. 5, 1832, microfilm, BPL), 2.

15. Suffolk County, Inspectors of Prisons, *Report . . . as to the Gaol, House of Correction, House of Reformation and House of Industry, December 1837* (Boston: J. H. Eastburn, 1837), 18–19.

16. Suffolk County, Inspectors of Prisons, *Reports . . . June 1843* (Boston: J. H. Eastburn, 1843), 27–36.

17. Report of the Grand Jury, November 1835, Municipal Court Records, Suffolk County, Office of the Clerk of Superior Court, Boston, Mass.; *Boston Morning Post*, February 3, 1840; Joseph Tuckerman, *Prize Essay: On the Wages Paid to Females for their Labour* (Philadelphia: Carey and Hart, 1830), 17–19.

18. Charleston County, S.C., Court of General Sessions, Records of Indictments and Subpoenas, 1830–40, SCA. On sheltering fugitives, see especially State v. Bize, July 26–30, 1839, ibid., and *Charleston Mercury*, June 12, 1840. On receiving stolen goods, see State v. Elizabeth Mills, May 9, 1835, Charleston County, S.C., Court of General Sessions, Records of Indictments and Subpoenas, SCA, and Jacob Schirmer, Diary, October 2, 1839, SCHS. U.S., Fifth Census of the United States, 1830, Population Schedule, [Charleston District], South Carolina, vol. 2, microfilm, roll 170, National Archives, Washington, D.C.

19. Charleston, Records of the Poor House, November 20, 1829–November 20, 1830, SCHS.

20. Ibid., 1830, 1840.

21. Ibid., December 23, 1840.

22. Ibid., June 20, November 11, August 29, 1840, February 25, 1830.

23. Charleston, Records of the Orphan House, Weekly Reports of the Steward, 1830–48, SCHS; Charleston Orphan House, *The Proceedings on the Sixty-Sixth Anniversary* . . . (Charleston: A. E. Miller, 1855); J. L. Dawson and H. W. DeSaussure, *Census of the City of Charleston, South Carolina, for the Year 1848* . . . (Charleston: J. B. Nixon, 1849), 43–45.

Chapter 9

1. Suzanne Lebsock, *The Free Women of Petersburg: Status and Culture in a Southern Town, 1784–1860* (New York: W. W. Norton, 1985).

2. Frances E. Appleton, Diary, September 2, 1839, LS.

3. Quoted in Mary Kelley, *Private Woman, Public Stage: Literary Domesticity in Nineteenth-Century America* (New York: Oxford University Press, 1984), 180.

4. Caroline Gilman to Harriet Fay, December 17, 1827, Caroline H. Gilman Papers, SCHS.

5. Caroline Gilman, *Recollections of a Southern Matron and a New England Bride* (1838, 1836; reprint, 2 vols. in 1, Philadelphia: John E. Potter and Co., 1867), 216.

6. Louisa S. McCord to James H. Thornwell, [July 1856], James Henly Thornwell Papers, USC.

7. Deborah Gray White, *"Ar'n't I a Woman": Female Slaves in the Plantation South* (New York: W. W. Norton, 1985), 56–58; [James L. Petigru] to Jane [Petigru North], August 31, 1827, photocopy, James L. Petigru Papers, LC.

8. Quoted in Deborah Pickman Clifford, *Mine Eyes Have Seen the Glory: A Biography of Julia Ward Howe* (Boston: Little, Brown, 1979), 83.

9. Hannah Lowell Cabot, Diary, February 21, 1840, typescript, Almy Family Papers, SL.

10. Elizabeth Dorr, Journal, October 24, 1835, MHS.

11. Elizabeth Peabody to Sophia Peabody, July 31, 1838, in Bruce A. Ronda, ed., *Letters of Elizabeth Palmer Peabody, American Renaissance Woman* (Middletown: Wesleyan University Press, 1984), 206.

12. Sarah M. Grimké, *Letters on the Equality of the Sexes, and the Condition of Woman* . . . (Boston: Isaac Knapp, 1838; reprint, New York: Source Book Press, 1970), 48.

13. Lydia Crafts to the Commissioners of the Orphan House, June 14, 1833, quoted in Barbara L. Bellows, "'My Children, Gentlemen, Are My Own':

Poor Women, the Urban Elite, and the Bonds of Obligation in Antebellum Charleston," in Walter J. Fraser et al., eds., *The Web of Southern Social Relations: Women, Family, and Education* (Athens: University of Georgia Press, 1985), 58.

14. [Lydia Maria Francis to Convers Francis, 1820], quoted in Milton Meltzer, *Tongue of Flame: The Life of Lydia Maria Child* (New York: Thomas Y. Crowell Co., 1965), 11.

15. Sarah Josepha Hale, writing in the *Ladies Magazine* (1828), quoted in Ann Douglas, *The Feminization of American Culture* (New York: Alfred A. Knopf, 1979), 73.

16. Catharine E. Beecher, *A Treatise on Domestic Economy, for the Use of Young Ladies at Home, and at School* (Boston: Marsh, Capen, Lyon, and Webb, 1841), 9

17. H. L. Jackson to Henry Lee, Jr., February 11, 1843, Lee Family Papers, MHS; Mary Lee to Henry Lee, May 23, 1820, quoted in Frank Rollins Morse, ed., *Henry and Mary Lee: Letters and Journals, with Other Family Letters, 1802–1860* (Boston: privately printed, 1926), 228–29.

18. Maria Henrietta Pinckney, *Quintessence of Long Speeches Arranged as a Political Catechism* (Charleston: A. E. Miller, 1830).

19. [Charleston] Female Charitable Association Papers, Minutes, July 21, 1824, SCHS.

20. Mrs. Cornelius, *The Young Housekeeper's Friend; or, A Guide to Domestic Economy and Comfort* (Boston: John M. Whittemore, 1848), 18.

Bibliographical Essay

As recently as 1970 one sought in vain for a solid reading list to assign in an undergraduate course on the history of American women. Now, amid a plethora of books and articles, both topically diverse and excellent in quality, it is equally difficult to winnow a manageable selection. This bibliographical essay, therefore, attempts to note only those secondary studies that have formed the intellectual context or provided the general background within which this book was written. Central to our thinking, though often peripheral to our immediate topic, they have as often as not posed questions rather than provided answers. Thus to acknowledge them in individual notes would be repetitious on the one hand and often abstruse on the other. Yet not to acknowledge them at all would be to overlook the debt we owe to those whose work has been essential to ours—even when, as we often did, we disagreed with it.

Provocative of much that we now call the new women's history were Barbara Welter, "The Cult of True Womanhood, 1820–1860," *American Quarterly* 17 (Summer 1966): 151–74; Gerda Lerner, "The Lady and the Mill Girl: Changes in the Status of Women in the Age of Jackson," (1969) in her *The Majority Finds Its Past: Placing Women in History* (New York: Oxford University Press, 1979), 15–30; and Anne Firor Scott, *The Southern Lady: From Pedestal to Politics, 1830–1930* (Chicago: University of Chicago Press, 1970). Challenges to these seminal works include Ronald W. Hogeland, "The Female Appendage: Feminine Life-Styles in America, 1820–1860," *Civil War History* 17 (June 1971): 104–14; Regina Markell Morantz, "The Perils of Feminist History," *Journal of Interdisciplinary History* 4 (Spring 1974): 650–

60; and Jean Matthews, "Race, Sex, and the Dimensions of Liberty in Antebellum America," *Journal of the Early Republic* 6 (Fall 1986): 275–91. Daniel Scott Smith, "Family Limitation, Sexual Control, and Domestic Feminism in Victorian America," *Feminist Studies* 1 (Winter–Spring 1973): 40–58, turns the tables on domesticity, arguing that it comprised the dominant feminism. Two recent synthetic overviews are Carl N. Degler, *At Odds: Women and the Family in America from the Revolution to the Present* (New York: Oxford University Press, 1980), and Catherine Clinton, *The Other Civil War: American Women in the Nineteenth Century* (New York: Hill and Wang, 1984).

Works that treat specifically how the city affected women's lives include Barbara J. Berg, *The Remembered Gate: Origins of American Feminism—The Woman and the City, 1800–1860* (New York: Oxford University Press, 1978); Suzanne Lebsock, *The Free Women of Petersburg: Status and Culture in a Southern Town, 1784–1860* (New York: W. W. Norton, 1985); and, more immediately relevant to our own work, Steven M. Stowe, "City, Country, and the Feminine Voice," in Michael O'Brien and David Moltke-Hansen, eds., *Intellectual Life in Antebellum Charleston* (Knoxville: University of Tennessee Press, 1986), 295–324. Christine Stansell, *City of Women: Sex and Class in New York, 1789–1860* (New York: Alfred A. Knopf, 1986), probes the life-styles of urban working-class women.

Women's emotions and intimate ties are the focus of Carroll Smith-Rosenberg, "The Female World of Love and Ritual: Relations between Women in Nineteenth Century America," *Signs: A Journal of Women in Culture and Society* 1 (1975): 1–29; Nancy F. Cott, "Passionlessness: An Interpretation of Victorian Sexual Ideology, 1790–1850," *Signs: A Journal of Women in Culture and Society* 4 (Winter 1978): 219–36; and Steven M. Stowe, *Intimacy and Power in the Old South: Ritual in the Lives of Planters* (Baltimore: Johns Hopkins University Press, 1987). Ellen Rothman, *Hands and Hearts: A History of Courtship in America* (New York: Basic Books, 1984), deals with the preliminaries to marriage; and Edward Pessen, "Marital Theory and Practice of the Antebellum Elite," *New York History* 53 (October 1972): 388–410, discusses the social and economic imperatives in upper-class urban marriages.

James C. Mohr, *Abortion in America: The Origins and Evolution of National Policy, 1800–1900* (New York: Oxford University Press, 1978), addresses the limits of birth control, while Judith Waltzer Leavitt, "Under the Shadow of Maternity: American Women's Responses to Death and Debility Fears in Nineteenth-Century Childbirth," *Feminist Studies* 12 (1986): 129–54, and Nancy Schrom Dye and Daniel Blake Smith, "Mother Love and Infant Death, 1750–1850," *Journal of American History* 73 (September 1986): 329–53, both examine the circumstances creating the psychological toll inherent in bearing children. Linda Gordon, *Woman's Body, Woman's Right: A Social History of Birth Control in America* (New York: Grossman, 1976), though somewhat polemical, is a useful overview. Edward Shorter, "Female Emancipation, Birth Control, and Fertility in European History," *American Historical Review* 88 (June 1973): 605–40, suggests a more complex interaction of class, ideology, and technology.

Those who did not marry are the subjects of Lee Virginia Chambers-Schiller's *Liberty, A Better Husband—Single Women in America: The Generations of 1780–1840* (New Haven: Yale University Press, 1985) and Carol Lasser's "'The World's Dread Laugh': Singlehood and Service in Nineteenth-Century Boston," in Herbert G. Gutman and Donald H. Bell, eds., *The New England Working Class and the New Labor History* (Urbana: University of Illinois Press, 1987), 72–88. Susan Cotts Watkins utilized cultural comparisons to probe the meaning of differential rates of spinsterhood by geographical region in her "Spinsters," *Journal of Family History* 9 (Winter 1984): 310–25.

Changing patterns of fertility are traced by Robert V. Wells in his "Demographic Change and the Life Cycle of American Families," *Journal of Interdisciplinary History* 2 (Autumn 1971): 273–82, and *Revolutions in Americans' Lives: A Demographic Perspective on the History of Americans, Their Families, and Their Society* (Westport: Greenwood, 1982), and by Maris A. Vinovskis in *Fertility in Massachusetts from the Revolution to the Civil War* (New York: Academic Press, 1981). Howard P. Chudacoff, "The Life Course of Women: Age and Age Consciousness, 1865–1915," *Journal of Family History* 5 (Fall 1980): 274–92, is suggestive, even though it addresses a later period.

Herbert G. Gutman studied slave women and slave families, albeit mostly in rural settings, in *The Black Family in Slavery and Freedom, 1750–1925* (New York: Pantheon, 1976), and Cheryll Ann Cody, "Slave Demography and Family Formation: A Community Study of the Ball Family Plantations, 1720–1896" (Ph.D. diss., University of Minnesota, 1982), has followed his pioneering lead. Deborah Gray White, *"Ar'n't I a Woman": Female Slaves in the Plantation South* (New York: W. W. Norton, 1985), addresses slave women's diverse work roles and life patterns as well.

Regional patterns shaping the lives of privileged white women are treated by Catherine Clinton, *The Plantation Mistress: Woman's World in the Old South* (New York: Pantheon, 1982), as well as by Anne Firor Scott in *The Southern Lady*. And assessing the interaction of southern lady and slave is Elizabeth Fox-Genovese, *Within the Plantation Household: Black and White Women of the Old South* (Chapel Hill: University of North Carolina Press, 1988). Barbara L. Bellows, "'My Children, Gentlemen, Are My Own': Poor Women, the Urban Elite, and the Bonds of Obligation in Antebellum Charleston," in Walter J. Fraser, Jr., et al., eds., *The Web of Southern Social Relations: Women, Family, and Education* (Athens: University of Georgia Press, 1985), 52–71, begins work on poor white southern urban women. Nancy F. Cott in her *The Bonds of Womanhood: "Women's Sphere" in New England, 1780–1835* (New Haven: Yale University Press, 1977) is unusually aware that New England sources do produce a regional and not necessarily a national pattern.

On women's work in their own homes, Ruth Schwartz Cowan, *More Work for Mother: The Ironies of Household Technology from the Open Hearth to the Microwave* (New York: Basic Books, 1983), and Jeanne Boydston, "To Earn Her Daily Bread: Housework and Antebellum Working-Class Subsistence," *Radical History Review*, no. 35 (1986): 7–25, are most useful. In addition, aspects of domestic service are developed in Faye E. Dudden, *Serving Women: Household Service in Nineteenth-Century America* (Middletown: Wesleyan University Press, 1983); Hasia R. Diner, *Erin's Daughters in America: Irish Immigrant Women in the Nineteenth Century* (Baltimore: Johns Hopkins University Press, 1983); and Carol Lasser, "The Domestic Balance of Power: Relations between Mistress and Maid in Nineteenth-Century New England," *Labor History* 28 (Winter 1987): 5–22.

The modern starting point on women's work is Alice Kessler-Harris, *Out to Work: A History of Wage-Earning Women in the United States* (New York: Oxford University Press, 1982). More specific in time is Claudia Goldin, "The Economic Status of Women in the Early Republic: Quantitative Evidence," *Journal of Interdisciplinary History* 16 (Winter 1986): 375–404. On the kinds of obstacles barring women from the professions, Mary Roth Walsh, *"Doctors Wanted: No Women Need Apply": Sexual Barriers in the Medical Profession, 1835–1975* (New Haven: Yale University Press, 1977), is a good example.

Women's own intellectual lives and how they shaped national culture are the principal concerns of several studies: Susan Phinney Conrad, *Perish the Thought: Intellectual Women in Romantic America, 1830–1860* (New York: Oxford University Press, 1976); Ann Douglas, *The Feminization of American Culture* (New York: Alfred A. Knopf, 1979); Linda K. Kerber, *Women of the Republic: Intellect and Ideology in Revolutionary America* (Chapel Hill: University of North Carolina Press, 1980); and Mary Kelley, *Private Woman, Public Stage: Literary Domesticity in Nineteenth-Century America* (New York: Oxford University Press, 1984). Kirk Jeffrey, "Marriage, Career, and Feminine Ideology in Nineteenth-Century America: Reconstructing the Marital Experience of Lydia Maria Child, 1828–1874," *Feminist Studies* 2 (1975): 113–30, elaborates the interaction of one intellectual's work and marriage with an eye to explaining nineteenth-century career choices as well as Victorian marriages.

Why and how education was so central a part of the lives of women, whether they were learners or teachers, are the main questions in Anne L. Kuhn, *The Mother's Role in Childhood Education: New England Concepts, 1830–1860* (New Haven: Yale University Press,

1947); Phillida Bunkle, "Sentimental Womanhood and Domestic Education, 1830–1870," *History of Education Quarterly* 14 (Spring 1974): 13–30; Richard M. Bernard and Maris A. Vinovskis, "The Female School Teacher in Antebellum Massachusetts," *Journal of Social History* 10 (March 1977): 332–45; Anne Firor Scott, "The Ever Widening Circle: The Diffusion of Feminist Values from the Troy Female Seminary, 1822–1872," *History of Education Quarterly* 19 (Spring 1979): 3–25; and Catherine Clinton, "Equally Their Due: The Education of the Planter Daughter in the Early Republic," *Journal of the Early Republic* 1 (Spring 1982): 39–60.

It is hard to imagine a more central concern in the study of the history of women than the law. The legal dynamics of marriage, divorce, child custody, and property rights of antebellum women have, indeed, stimulated much investigation. At the national level are surveys by Richard H. Chused, "Married Women's Property Law: 1800–1850," *Georgetown Law Journal* 71 (1983): 1359–1425, and Michael Grossberg, *Governing the Hearth: Law and the Family in Nineteenth-Century America* (Chapel Hill: University of North Carolina Press, 1985). For our work, Marylynn Salmon, *Women and the Law of Property in Early America* (Chapel Hill: University of North Carolina Press, 1986), has been extraordinarily useful because it deals specifically and meticulously, inter alia, with both Massachusetts and South Carolina. Likewise, Salmon covers unique South Carolina practices in "Women and Property in South Carolina: The Evidence from Marriage Settlements, 1730–1830," *William and Mary Quarterly*, 3d ser., 39 (October 1982): 655–85, as does John E. Crowley in "Family Relations and Inheritance in Early South Carolina," *Histoire Sociale–Social History* 17 (May 1984): 35–57. Jane Turner Censer, "'Smiling through Her Tears': Ante-Bellum Southern Women and Divorce," *American Journal of Legal History* 25 (January 1986): 24–47, covers a broader but still-regional pattern. And a landmark study that was provocative though not immediately relevant for us is Norma Basch, *In the Eyes of the Law: Women, Marriage, and Property in Nineteenth-Century New York* (Ithaca: Cornell University Press, 1982).

Central to examining factors determining religion, philanthropy, and reform activity are Mary P. Ryan, *Cradle of the Middle Class: The Family in Oneida County, New York, 1790–1865* (Cambridge: Cambridge University Press, 1981), and Nancy A. Hewitt, *Women's Activism and Social Change: Rochester, New York, 1822–1872* (Ithaca: Cornell University Press, 1984). Useful also are Barbara L. Epstein, *The Politics of Domesticity: Women, Evangelism, and Temperance in Nineteenth-Century America* (Middletown: Wesleyan University Press, 1981), and Estelle B. Freedman, *Their Sisters' Keepers: Women's Prison Reform in America, 1830–1930* (Ann Arbor: University of Michigan Press, 1981).

Three very different ways of looking at prostitution are presented in Judith R. Walkowitz and Daniel J. Walkowitz, "'We Are Not Beasts of the Field': Prostitution and the Poor in Plymouth and Southampton under the Contagious Diseases Acts," *Feminist Studies* 1 (1973): 73–105, portraying it as one form of work open to working-class women not much different from other alternatives; in Ruth Rosen, *The Lost Sisterhood: Prostitution in America, 1900–1918* (Baltimore: Johns Hopkins University Press, 1982), as a subculture developed as a matter of life-style as well as work preference; and in Anne M. Butler, *Daughters of Joy, Sisters of Misery: Prostitutes in the American West, 1865–1890* (Urbana: University of Illinois Press, 1985), as a desperate way of life leading to inevitable degradation. Different ways of perceiving women in institutions have been less sharply controversial. In addition to Lasser, "'The World's Dread Laugh,'" Amy Gilman, "From Widowhood to Wickedness: The Politics of Class and Gender in New York City Private Charity, 1799–1860," *History of Education Quarterly* 24 (Spring 1984): 59–74, and Steven Ruggles, "Fallen Women: The Inmates of the Magdalen Society Asylum of Philadelphia, 1836–1908," *Journal of Social History* 16 (Summer 1983): 65–82, deal with important aspects of the problem.

From such a full harvest over the past two decades, we have profited enormously.

Index

Naser, Sarah, 142
Nurses, 25, 27, 55–56

Obstetrics, 25
Occupations, 45–46, 52–58
Odd Ladies Mutual Aid Society
(Boston), 127
Olandt, Dietrick, 149
O'Neall, John Belton, 92–93
Orphan house (Charleston), 158,
158 (illus.)
Otis, Harrison Gray, 18, 19, 56
Otis, Mrs. Harrison Gray, Jr., 138

Palmer, Esther, 109
Parkman, Mary Mason, 104–5, 138
Park Street Church (Boston), 117
Peabody, Elizabeth, 165
Peabody, Mary, 65
Penitent Female's Refuge Society
(Boston), 127, 153
Perry, Ann Drayton, 109
Perry, Edward, 109
Petigru, Caroline, 74
Petigru, James Louis, 73–74, 87,
146
Petigru, Jane Postell, 146
Philanthropic societies, 122–27
Physicians, 25–26, 56
Pierpont, John, 118, 140
Pinckney, Eliza, 108–9
Pinckney, Maria, 168
Poinsett, Joel R., 110–11
Poor house (Charleston), 156–58
Porcher, Frederick, 18
Poverty, 38–40, 44, 46–47, 58–61,
140–41, 157
Pregnancy, 22, 24–27, 32–34, 36–
37, 142
Prentiss, Jane, 51

Prescott, Mrs. William, 124
Prioleau, Mrs. Samuel, 44
Property: ownership, 101–5, 108–9,
123; management, 102–3
Prostitution, 127, 140–42, 148–55
Protestant Episcopal Female Domestic Missionary Society (Charleston), 119

Quincy, Josiah, 67–69

Randall, Nancy, 107
Rape, 143–44
Ravenel, Eliza, 30–31
Ravenel, John, 30–31
Reform societies, 128
Rehpenn, John, 99–100
Reid, Ann, 21
Religion, 36, 115–16, 129, 133
Remarriage, 19, 38
Reynolds, Bishop I. A., 121
Rogers, Joe, 107–8
Rutledge, Harriott Horry, 76, 139

St. John's Lutheran Church
(Charleston), 116
St. Mary's Hall, 81
St. Michael's Episcopal Church
(Charleston), 116
St. Patrick's Benevolent Association
(Charleston), 38
St. Paul's Episcopal Church (Boston), 116
St. Philip's Episcopal Church
(Charleston), 116
Salmon, Marylynn, 91, 97–98
Samaritan Society for Indigent Children (Boston), 126
Schnell, Cordelia, 107
Schnell, John Jacob, 107